PHILOSOPHY OF GURU GRANTH SAHIB

PHILOSOPHY OF GURU GRANTH SAHIB

By

Devinder Singh Sekhon

Ph.D. (Chem. & Educational Admin.)

ANMOL PUBLICATIONS PVT. LTD.

NEW DELHI - 110 002 (INDIA)

ANMOL PUBLICATIONS PVT. LTD.
4374/4B, Ansari Road, Daryaganj
New Delhi - 110 002
Ph.: 23261597, 23278000
Visit us at: www.anmolpublications.com

Philosophy of Guru Granth Sahib

First Published, 2005
ISBN 81-261-2357-5

PRINTED IN INDIA

Published by J.L. Kumar for Anmol Publications Pvt. Ltd., New Delhi - 110 002 and Printed at Mehra Offset Press, Delhi.

Dedication

This manuscript is dedicated to all the Sikhs who lead their lives according to the Golden Principles of Guru Granth Sahib, and help others do the same.

CONTENTS

FOREWORD

This is my second book on theology. Even though I had written a number of articles on religious topics which were published in magazines and newspapers, and were very well received by the readers, my first book was on the life of Sri Guru Nanak Dev Ji, and was titled "Select Stories from the life of Sri Guru Nanak Dev Ji". It was published in August, 2001. The book was well received and most readers enjoyed it. I was encouraged by their warm response to write another book. Inspired by many readers, I undertook a much bigger responsibility to write a book on the philosophy of Sri Guru Granth Sahib. The timing to write the book could not be better because this year it is the 400th year of the compilation of Sri Guru Granth Sahib by Sri Guru Arjun Dev Ji, and my humble effort in the form of this book will be an appropriate mark of respect for Sri Guru Granth Sahib on my part. This was a very challenging task, and I wanted to make sure that I did not misinterpret the Divine Knowledge contained in the revered Guru Granth Sahib. It has taken me three full years to complete the job, and I am still not fully satisfied. However, realizing that only Waheguru and His other form, the Perfect Guru, are the only infallible powers, and no man-made thing can ever be perfect, I decided to present this book to readers for their evaluation.

Some people were surprised by my deep interest in religion because I am a scientist by profession. They could not believe that a person like me with a background in science would be so interested in religion. But, I tell you that the more science I studied, the deeper was the respect that I developed for Guru Nanak Sahib and His other spiritual incarnations for Their knowledge about the Supreme Power and His universe, and Their service to mankind. It is my deep reverence for the Great Guru Nanak Dev Ji, that prompted me to write this book.

I realize there are quite a few books in the market on the subject in Punjabi, and may be in English too, but this book will be somewhat different from them in style and also in ideas. For example, some modern scholars believe that Guru Gobind Singh Ji never administered "amrit" to Sikhs, so, administering amrit to Sikhs should be discontinued. I, on the other hand, firmly believe that the "dagger and the bowl" pahul was administered by Guru sahib, and have tried to prove that. Likewise, I have found, and presented strong support for supernatural powers. It is all together a different matter whether such powers were ever used by Guru Sahiban or not. The underlying idea of my effort is to carry the message of Guru Granth Sahib to our youth who cannot read Gurmukhi very well or who do not understand Punjabi for their lack of exposure to the language. The book can be equally beneficial to any other person who has some knowledge of English.

Each concept presented in the book has been supported by a number of holy shabads (hymns) from Guru Granth Sahib, and every effort has been made to ensure that meanings of the holy shabads quoted in the book have not been distorted in any way to support my ideas. On the contrary, I have developed ideas based on the meanings of the holy Gurbani. **Principal Sahib Singh's translation of Guru Granth Sahib has been used as the basis for the interpretation of Gurbani, and I am highly indebted to**

the late Principal Sahib for that. Most of the topics included in the book are in response to the questions posed by my young children on Gurbani during our discussions on the subject. I believe most young children have similar questions when it comes to Gurmat. I was not able to cover all the topics I intended to cover in the present volume. More topics will be covered in the future books.

I can never be thankful enough to Guru Sahiban who brought awareness to mankind about the purpose of life on Earth, and taught us how to live it meaningfully. They have left an invaluable treasure of knowledge for us, and gave us the 'Living Guru" in the form of Sri Guru Granth Sahib. My wish was to expose this Treasure, at least in part, to a section of the society. The success of my efforts will be judged by the readers.

Many people have helped directly or indirectly in writing this manuscript, and I am thankful to all of them. However, my special thanks go to a very special couple, Dr Surjit Singh Malhotra and Mrs Harinder Kaur Malhotra of Edmonton, Alberta. They spent months to proofread and correct the manuscript. They also made some very constructive suggestions to improve the manuscript. I have no words to express my thanks to them.

Suggestions for future improvements are invited from everyone and anyone, and will be gratefully acknowledged.

Devinder Singh Sekhon

PhD (Chem & Ed. Admin.)

Instructor in Sciences

Grande Prairie Regional College

Grande Prairie, Alberta. Canada

1

Purpose of Human Life

"Waheguru Ji ka Khalsa, Waheguru Ji ki Fateh, dear members of the congregation, I extend a hearty welcome to all of you to my humble farmhouse. We are very lucky to have Bhai Dalip Singh Ji among us. Bhai Sahib is a well-known touring Sikh scholar who has dedicated his life to promote Gurmat. He has been spreading the message of Guru Granth Sahib for the last five years in rural areas of Punjab. He has magic in his voice, and explains the Principles of Gurmart with such clarity that even a child can understand. He leads an exemplary personal life in accordance with the Principles of Gurmat and has influenced the lives of thousands of people. His style is very effective because he starts with questions from the audience. You can ask any question related to Gurmat. However, when he starts on a particular topic, he prefers to stay focused on that topic until it has been well covered. He plans to stay in our village for about a month, and the sessions will start at 5:30 p.m. every evening with the recitation of Rahiras Sahib. The lectures will start at 6:30 and will be followed by *lungar* (food) around 8:30. I will not stand between you and Bhai Sahib now. I ask you to join me in welcoming the great scholar and Gurmukh - Bhai Dalip Singh Ji." Bhai Kashmir Singh introduced Bhai Dalip Singh to a gathering of about two hundred people who had arrived from several nearby villages. The recitation of Rahiras Sahib was just over. The evening sky began to echo with slogans of 'Bolle so Nihal, Sat Sri Akal'.

It was a beautiful evening in mid September. Bhai Kashmir

Singh's farmhouse was situated near the intersection of an important road and a big canal. The rice crop was nearing the harvest time. The tall sugarcane fields were enhancing the beauty of the natural surroundings of the farmhouse. The congregation was held in the open yard. Everybody sat on a carpet spread in the yard. Inside the house, a few ladies were cooking food on an open pit fire. The whole environment was magically pleasing. Bhai Dalip Singh rose to address the gathering.

"Dear Khalsa Ji, I am overwhelmed by the very generous introduction by Bhai Kashmir Singh, but, the fact is, I am just one of you. I do have a fervor to share my knowledge of the holy Guru Granth Sahib with you. It's all because of the efforts of Bhai Kashmir Singh that I've the privilege to be amongst you tonight. Guru Granth Sahib is such a vast source of Divine Knowledge that after studying and cultivating understanding about it, you realize that you've wasted many precious years of your life on unimportant and meaningless things. I'm here to share with you the message of Guru Granth Sahib and its importance. Tonight's topic is 'Purpose of human life on earth'. After an introductory statement, I'll invite questions from you, and will try to answer them as best as I can. We will continue to follow this approach if this is okay with you." Bhai Dalip Singh explained his approach. "That will just be perfect." A few voices were heard from the crowd.

"According to Guru Granth Sahib, the human soul is part of the Supreme Soul - Waheguru. Because we have bodies, we look different from Him Who is formless. And because of the unacceptable deeds that we do with our bodies, we stay separated from Him. However, we are a part of Him just as a bubble on the surface of water is a part of the body of water even though it looks different. There is a large number of holy shabads (hymns) in Guru Granth Sahib that allude to this fact. I'll quote only a few by way of example.

- Waheguru is residing in every heart (human body). He is operating invisibly in the sky, on the earth, and in the underworld, but can be realized through Guru's Shabad. **(Sorith M:1,597)**
- We have been separate from You because of our deeds, oh Waheguru! Please, be merciful and connect us with Yourself. **(Bara Maha, M:5, 133)**
- Oh my Lord! The difference between You and me is the same as between gold and a gold bracelet, or between water and a water wave traveling on its surface. **(Siri Raag, Ravidas Ji, 93)**
- Recognize your roots oh my mind (soul)! You are a manifestation of the Supreme Light - Waheguru. **(Assa M:3, Chhant, 441)**
- The Supreme being resides in the human body Who looks after everybody. **(Suhi M:3, Ashatpadian, 754)**
- It is none other than the Supreme Being which is alive in every heart. **(Malli Gaura, Naam Dev Ji, 988)**

From these holy hymns it is very clear that Waheguru resides in every human heart. In fact, Waheguru resides in every living being, but, it is only in the human form that we can realize Waheguru. Once we recognize that we are a part of Waheguru, the objective of human life becomes very clear. Waheguru has given us human bodies as an opportunity for us to unite our souls with Him. As humans, we have the intelligence to recognize the existence of Waheguru, and can use our bodies to do noble deeds, and to worship Him. No other life form is capable of understanding the concept of Waheguru, and is therefore unable to realize Him. Again, there are a large number of holy shabads (hymns) in Guru Granth Sahib emphasizing the objective of human life. And as before, I'll quote only a few. Bhai Dalip Singh continued.

- Now that you have been given the human body, this is an opportunity for you to realize Waheguru, oh man! No worldly task will connect you with Waheguru. Worship Waheguru's Naam in the company of holy men. **(Assa M:5, 378)**
- Worship Waheguru, oh man! Your life time is slipping away day and night by the minute, and you are wasting away your human life by not worshiping Waheguru. You lost your childhood in ignorance and your youth in enjoying sensual pleasures. You are old now, but, you still do not realize the real purpose of life (of realizing Waheguru). What ill advise is guiding you? **(Ramkali M:9, 928)**
- You were given the invaluable human form by Waheguru for some good deeds on your part, oh man! Bur now you are just wasting it by not worshiping Waheguru. Even if you had a palace as big as god Inder's (the ruler of the Paradise and of all gods) and all other luxuries enjoyed by him, they are all useless if you do not worship Waheguru. Because only worshiping Waheguru will connect you with Him. **(Sorith Ravi Das Ji, 658)**
- You got the invaluable human life because of your great luck, oh man! A person who does not worship Waheguru, is a murderer of his soul. Without worshiping Waheguru, life is purposeless. People, who do not worship Waheguru should rather be dead. **(Gauri M:5, 188)**
- A hedonistic man spends his days and nights seeking sensual pleasures. In his conceit, he does not worship Waheguru, and thus gambles away his precious human life. **(Sarang M:5,1205)**

Again, it is clear from these holy hymns that the purpose of human life is to realize Waheguru. If we do not make an effort to realize Waheguru in this life, we miss an opportunity, and are born again and again in lower forms of life. The birth - death cycle continues until we work hard to be one with Waheguru, and that is possible only in the human form. No other life form is capable of realizing Waheguru. Sri Guru Granth Sahib makes it very clear that Waheguru can be realized only in the human form. Bhai Dalip Singh continued with quotes from Sri Guru Granth Sahib.

- It is your opportunity to realize Waheguru now that you have been given the human form, oh man! You are fully occupied in worldly affairs, and are thus wasting away an opportunity to realize Waheguru. Make an effort to swim across this sea of *maya,* and realize Waheguru. **(Assa M:5, 378)**
- You have been through thousands of life forms before you were given the priceless human form, oh man!. You will not get this golden opportunity again. So, wake up and worship Waheguru to break the life-death cycle, and be one with Him. **(Gauri Bawan Akkhari M:5, 258)**
- You have been through eight hundred and forty thousand life forms before you were given the human form, oh man! You were worshiping Waheguru while hanging up side down in the womb of your mother. That is how you survived the high temperature of the womb. But as soon as you saw the outside world, you forgot Waheguru completely. Sing the praise of Waheguru, oh human soul! **(Gauri, Kabir Ji, 337)**
- For many lives you were born as a worm and a bug, oh man! For several other lives you were born as an elephant, a fish and a deer. For some other lives you lived as a bird, and as a snake, and you spent many more lives as a horse and as an ox. After a long journey through many life forms,

your attained the human form. This is your opportunity to realize Waheguru, oh man!. **(Gauri Guareri M:5, 176)**

- After having been through a large number of life forms, you have been unsuccessful in realizing peace of mind and your final destination (of realizing Waheguru), oh man! Now that you have been given the human body, Nanak advises you that you worship Waheguru to find eternal peace. **(Sorith M: 9, 632)**
- After having been through eight hundred and forty thousand life forms, now you have been given the invaluable human form oh man! (in which you could realize Waheguru). But, you are clinging to the cheap sensual pleasures, oh fool! The immortal nectar (Amrit) of *Naam* resides in you, but you are engrossed in the poisonous *maya*. **(Maru M:5, Ashatpadian, 1017)**
- Through service to the Guru, you were successful in your efforts to please Waheguru to the extent that you have been given this human body, oh man! Even gods cherish human bodies so that they could realize Waheguru. Now that you have been given human body, do not forget to worship Waheguru because this is the only opportunity for you to realize Waheguru, oh man! **(Bhairon Kabir Ji, 1159)**

As you can see clearly from the holy shabads just quoted and hundreds more like these, our Gurus advise us to worship Waheguru to realize Him. If we don't do it in this life form, who knows how many life forms we will have to go through before we get human form again! Therefore, it is essential that we worship Waheguru now as best as we can so that we may make best use of this life." Bhai Dalip Singh advised.

About Enjoying Life

"I have a question, if you don't mind, Bhai Sahib." Bhai Karnail Singh said from among the gathering. His dress and his style of conversation revealed that he was an educated person.

"By all means, please. In fact, it is very important that we seek clarification on issues which are not clear to us. Unless the issues are clear, our mind keeps questioning them and we cannot build faith in them, and cannot develop love and respect for Gurbani which is not only essential, but fundamental to worshiping Waheguru. So, I encourage all of you to seek clarification. I cannot guarantee that I will be able to answer all your questions right away, but I can seek some other Gurmukh's advice on them and answer them later. Please go ahead, Bhai Sahib." Bhai Dalip Singh said very politely.

"If we have been given the human body after so many life forms as you say, and we are advised to spend our time worshiping Waheguru, when will we get the opportunity to enjoy life? If this is our only opportunity for human life, why shouldn't we spend our time in enjoying life? Who knows when will we have this opportunity again? Bhai Karnail Singh asked an honest question.

"This is a very valid and important question. I'm glad that you asked. Let's look for the answer from the sacred Gurbani. First, Gurbani doesn't place any restriction on your enjoyment as long as it is moral, and as long as you do not become a slave to a habit. Also your enjoyment should not hurt anybody else, or should not encroach upon the rights of others. Within these parameters, you can enjoy life. I'm sure not only our sacred Gurbani, but, all civilized people will also expect the same limited restrictions placed on the enjoyment of people. Other than that, Gurbani has no problems with us enjoying life even though the concept of enjoyment will vary greatly from person to person. In fact, Gurbani prompts us to enjoy, and not suffer in life. Guru Nanak Dev Ji has strongly disapproved of people who deliberately deny themselves enjoyment in life. In fact, the Bhagats (great souls), on our behalf, have openly begged Waheguru to provide enough for everybody's basic needs. Listen to the following sacred utterings of the Gurus and the Bhagats carefully.

- If we have a perfect guru to guide us, we can lead our lives successfully, and find salvation while enjoying our life laughing, playing, eating and dressing well, oh Nanak! **(Gujri ki Vaar, M:5, 522)**
- A family with too much wealth is worried all the time (for fear of losing it). A family with too little wealth cannot enjoy satisfaction or peace of mind. Only those are comfortable who live between these extreme situations. **(Maru M:5, Ashatpadian, 1019)**
- Eating and drinking are sacred because these gifts are provided by Waheguru to all His creation. **(Assa ki Vaar, Sloak M:1, 472)**
- Waheguru cannot be worshiped empty on an stomach. I cannot afford to be shy with You, oh Waheguru! If You do not provide for my basic needs of life on your own, I have no hesitation in asking for them from You. I ask for two kilograms of flour, a quarter kilo of butter oil, and enough salt. Please also provide half a kilo of beans for me to live through the day. I need a cot to sleep on, a pillow, a mattress, and a comforter. When my basic needs are met, I can dedicate myself to worship You. I have shown no greed in my needs, oh Waheguru! **(Sorith,Kabir Ji, 656)**
- I am a beggar at your door, oh Waheguru! You fulfil the needs of your devotees very kindly. I ask for beans, flour and butter oil to live joyfully

everyday. I also ask for shoes and fancy clothes. I ask for grains produced in well cultivated soil. I need a cow or a buffalo for milk, and a fine horse to ride on. Your devotee Dhanna also asks for a wife for family. **(Dhanasari, Dhanna Ji, 695)**

- I ask Thee for strength, for recognition, for wealth, for a son and for other necessities of life, oh Waheguru! **(Sorith M:5,)**

It is clear from these and many other holy shabads (hymns) in Sri Guru Granth Sahib) that there is no restriction on enjoying life in a moral way that does not hurt other people in any way. Guru Nanak Dev Ji was not against rich people or people in positions of authority. He blessed rulers like Rai Bular, Rajah Shiv Nabh of Sri Lanka and Malik Bhago, and very wealthy people like Bhai Mansukh, Bhai Duni Chand, and Baba Lehna Ji (The Second Guru). Guru Sahiban themselves have set practical examples to earn reasonable amount of wealth, albeit by honest means, to have comfortable life, and pursued activities to enjoy life as well. Guru Nanak Dev Ji did farming with His own hands for about fifteen years. Guru Har Gobind Sahib, and Guru Gobind Singh Ji took some time off from their daily routine and went hunting. They also had assemblies of poets and other scholars and inspired them to write poetry to raise morale and morality among the masses. Gurmat promotes the institution of marriage and family life, which requires reasonable enjoyment in life. So, Bhai Sahib, sure, you can enjoy life as long as your enjoyment is not immoral and does not hurt other human beings in any way. Have I answered your question Bhai Sahib?" Bhai Dalip Singh asked.

"Very clearly Bhai Sahib. Thank you very much." Bhai Karnail Singh replied.

The Ultimate Level of Bliss

"Now people have their own concept of enjoyment. There

are all sorts of people in this world, and each has a different concept of enjoyment. Some people enjoy by taking long vacations and visiting places. Others enjoy wearing fancy clothes and eating good food. Some enjoy being leaders, while some enjoy gathering immense amounts of wealth. In order to save money, some will eat poor quality food and wear poor quality clothes. Some people will enjoy helping others. And for some, just getting three meals a day - no matter how poor the meals are - and having a roof on their heads is a matter of great pleasure. Believe it or not, some people enjoy by working very hard; nothing else appeals to them than working hard. They are workaholics.

There are thousands of ways in which people enjoy their lives. People who enjoy one style of life often ridicule the way some others do. They have no idea of what kind of enjoyment other people get from their own styles. However, Guru Sahiban tell us that there is no enjoyment in life that comes even close to the enjoyment or bliss that we achieve when we are one with Waheguru. That is the ultimate level of bliss in life. All other types of enjoyment are short lived, and have their negative side effects. For example, if drinking alcohol is the way to have enjoyment for someone, he will suffer from a large number of side effects on top of the fact that the effect of the intoxicant will be over in a few hours. During the period he is intoxicated, he may do many foolish things for which he may repent later. He may get into some accident or may do some other foolish things. Once the effect is over, he might get a hangover, or his health may suffer. He will be worse off economically, and so on. But being one with Waheguru is everlasting and has only positive side effects. First, you will always be in a state of bliss and will not do anything immoral. Your own life will be wonderful, and you will be a source of comfort for all others. Second, all those who come in contact with you, will learn something good from you. So, there will be no bad side effect. Listen what Guru Sahiban have to say about this stage.

- A man who has had the taste of Waheguru's *Naam* realizes that he is in a state of supreme bliss. To him all other tastes (enjoyments) in life are of very low quality in comparison to Waheguru's *Naam*. Waheguru's devotee is always intoxicated (in a state of real bliss) with *Naam* while the effect of all other forms of intoxications is short lived. Also, other intoxicants cause many worries whereas the intoxication of Waheguru's *Naam* keeps one in a state of eternal bliss. **(Assa M:5, 377)**
- Drink the nectar of Waheguru's *Naam* (utter the *Naam*), oh my tongue!. You will be fully satisfied for ever. You have tasted very many delicious foods before, but you have never been satisfied. In fact the more you taste, the more you are dissatisfied. But if you taste the nectar of Waheguru's *Naam* once, you will stay satisfied for ever. **(Gauri Guareri, M: 5, 180)**
- Everybody talks about bliss (enjoyment), but the concept of real bliss comes only from the Guru. **(Anand Sahib, M:3, 917)**
- Once you taste the nectar of Waheguru's *Naam*, you will not enjoy any other taste in life. However, you cannot taste the nectar of *Naam* as long as you are engrossed in lower pursuits tastes of life. **(Gauri Bawan Akkhari, Kabir Ji, 342)**
- I have experienced all tastes in life, but the nectar of Waheguru's *Naam* is the sweetest of all. Whoever tastes the nectar of *Naam*, is completely satisfied, and is freed from the cycle of life and death. **(Maajh M:5, 100)**
- The devotees enjoy nothing else but Waheguru's *Naam*. Through personal experience they realize that all other activities in the world are tasteless. Their ailment of ignorance and of dissatisfaction is dispelled by the mediator - Guru. For them

everything in life is Waheguru, and they find the worldly things unattractive because they are short lived. **(Jaitsari ki Vaar, 708)**

So, as you can see, the most enjoyable thing in this universe is the realization of Waheguru. A person who has realized Waheguru achieves the perfect state of contentment, and is left with no desire to seek sensual pleasures or to acquire worldly luxuries. Because everyone is seeking enjoyment in life, realizing Waheguru is the ultimate enjoyment in life. So, why not go for it Also, not realizing Waheguru in this life perpetuates the cycle of life and death, and one is born again and again. As long as you do not forget Waheguru, you can enjoy life as we discussed earlier. In fact, there is a beautiful holy shabad by Guru Ram Das Ji which approves the possession of luxury items by a GurSikh. The Shabad goes like this:

- The use of wealth, enjoyment of rich foods, and wearing of expensive clothes is all sacred for the Sikhs who are imbued in Waheguru's Naam. Their mansion -like houses, palaces, and inns are all pious where the GurSikhs spend some time as guests and, enjoy the comforts. ———**(Sorith ki Vaar, M:4, Pauri, 648)**

As we can see from these holy shabads (and there are many more like these) that Gurbani does not put any restriction on the Sikhs enjoying life as long as they have earned their wealth by honest means and their enjoyment does not hurt others in any way, and of course, as long as we do not become slave to any of the comforts. So, go ahead and enjoy life within limits." Bhai Dalip Singh assured the congregation.

"Any other question." Bhai Sahib asked smilingly.

Nobody had further questions. Bhai Kashmir Singh thanked Bhai Dalip Singh for his very informative lecture, and the audience for being good listeners.

The session ended with a loud traditional slogan:

'Waheguru Ji ka Khalsa Waheguru Ji ki Fateh' and everybody headed for the lungar (food) which had been prepared with love and affection by ladies of Bhai Kashmir Singh's family and friends.

2

Stages in Spiritual Path Laavan and Unhad Shabad

"Dear brothers and sisters, an important question that is asked quite regularly pertains to the progress in spiritual journey. In other words, people want to know how to measure the progress, if they have made any, in the spiritual world. It is a very pertinent question and most of you would like to know the answer which lies in the five spiritual stages as described by Guru Nanak Dev Ji in the holy 'Jap Ji Sahib'. So, we will discuss those five stages in the spiritual path tonight." Bhai Dalip Singh started a new and a very important topic.

"As a Sikh starts his spiritual journey to be one with Waheguru, he traverses different stages or levels of awareness. As we discussed the very first day, the objective of human life is to realize Waheguru. To achieve the objective, a Sikh starts to recite Waheguru's Naam (singing the praise of Waheguru) and starts to lead his life according to the Teachings of the Guru (Guru Granth Sahib). Guru Nanak Sahib has labeled this stage as the stage of Dharma (religious duty). In all, Guru Nanak Sahib has identified **five stages in spiritual journey:** The stage of Dharma, the stage of Divine Knowledge, the stage of Hard Labour, the stage of Benevolence, and the stage of Eternal Truth. (Jap Ji Sahib). Let's discuss -all these stages. I'll simply translate the holy writings of Guru Nanak Sahib, and discuss their implications only if needed.

(a) The stage of Dharma: According to Guru Nanak

Sahib, Waheguru has created this Earth as a dharamsaal (religious school) for human beings to realize Waheguru. It is an opportunity for them to realize Waheguru. So, they are expected to perform this dharma (duty) to worship Waheguru. To make life possible and comfortable on earth, Waheguru has created days, nights, different seasons, dates and different phases of the moon. He has also provided air, water, fire and underworld to sustain life. There are many different forms of life on earth which have countless names. The living beings have a limited life-span, whereas Waheguru is eternal. His court or system of justice is based on pure Truth which means His judgment is completely unbiased . There is no favoritism or no held-over grudges. The deeds of all human beings are weighed impartially in the Court of Waheguru, and the individuals get the treatment they deserve. True saints win respect as kind glance of Waheguru puts the stamp of approval on their deeds. (Guru) Nanak says that you acquire this knowledge (of impartial treatment) only when you arrive in the Court of Waheguru.

(b) The stage of Divine Knowledge: Guru Nanak Sahib says that the stage of Dharma demands that all human being do their duty to worship Waheguru and lead their lives according to the Teachings of the Guru. When an individual has dedicated himself to the praise of Waheguru, he attains the stage of Divine Knowledge where he realizes that instead of just a single god supervising each element of air, water, fire etc. as stated in ancient Hindu books, there are countless such gods, and there are countless Krishanas and Shivas. There are countless Brahamas who are sculpting an infinite variety of appearances and shapes. He will find that there are infinite dharamshals like the earth, and there are countless Mairu mountains (a mythical mountain in heaven replete precious metals and stones). There are countless sermons like that for Bhagat Dhruv. There are countless clouds, moons, suns, and galaxies. There are infinite gurus of Sidh yogis, infinite Budhas, infinite gurus of the Naths (a sect of yogis) and infinite goddesses with different dress codes. There are infinite gods, demons, munis (holy people who never talk), and an infinite number of seas full of jewels. There are infinite ways by which living beings are reproduced, and infinite ways of communication. There are infinite kingdoms of rulers. Likewise, there are infinite individuals who concentrate on Waheguru's Naam, and infinite assistants to Waheguru. There is no limit to His Creation.

In this sacred part of Jap Ji Sahib, Guru Nanak Sahib has challenged the old Hindu and some Muslim beliefs where they have put definite numbers on the creation of Waheguru. For example, the holy Hindu books claim that there is a god for each element - air, water, fire and so on. But by saying that there are infinite, Guru Nanak Sahib implies that there is none. Waheguru Himself controls everything. Likewise, when He says there are infinite Brahamas, Guru Ji is implying again, that there is none. The Muslim holy books say that there are seven skies above our earth and seven below. Guru Sahib says there are infinite. Their books also say that there are 56000 chains of clouds, but Guru Sahib refutes that claim too. Also Guru Nanak Sahib does not believe in the four major ways of reproduction of living beings - birth of live animals, from eggs, vegetation, and life forms that come to life under conducive environment. **Guru Sahib claims that there are infinite ways by which living beings can reproduce. Biological research strongly support this claim.** There are some organisms that multiply themselves by breaking up into two or more segments. Plants multiply by sexual and asexual reproduction in a variety of ways. **(World Book Encyclopedia).**

The Hindu religious books also claim that there are four different sources of producing sound - vocal chords, lips, tongue, and down from the stomach. Guru Sahib does not believe in that either, and maintains that there are infinite ways by which animals produce sounds or communicate.

This is a level of high awareness which an individual attains after he has been worshiping Waheguru with dedication for some time. Guru sahib says that in this stage, knowledge regarding Creation is the predominant attainment, and an individual thus blessed is in a state of bliss where he feels to hear melodious music, and experiences supernatural happenings which lead to a high degree of amazement.

(c) The stage of Hard Labour: Once an individual attains the stage of Divine Knowledge, he begins to feel more and more blissful and starts to work harder which means he devotes more time in the praise of Waheguru. One can only enjoy that stage, but, cannot describe his/her mental state at that level. If someone tries to do that, he simply feels foolish because he realizes that no matter how hard he tries, he is unable to find suitable words to describe that stage. The only thing that can be said to describe this stage is 'wonderful' - everything about the individual is just beautiful. His body becomes beautiful because he does only noble deeds. He dedicates his body to the service of humanity. He is gifted with sacred thinking, sacred mind, sacred intelligence, and the ability to sacred listening. He is further gifted with the level of awareness of gods and of great souls. **(These very gifts are also mentioned in the 13th pauri of Jap Ji Sahib. One can attain this level of spirituality by acting upon the advice of the Guru).**

(d) The stage of Benevolence: At this level of awareness, a Sikh sees nothing but the presence of Waheguru all around him and inside him. His mind becomes very powerful and no immoral thoughts can mislead him. He envisions great souls who have overcome their sensual pleasures with moral strength and who are fully enlightened with Divine Light. They are fully connected with Waheguru and sing His praise all the time. Their mental beauty cannot be described. No worldly attractions can distract them, and they become immortal because Waheguru has enlightened their hearts.

They also envision great souls from many different planets who feel highly blissful because Waheguru now resides in their hearts. In other words, because of His own grace, Waheguru has embraced the individual who had put in high spiritual labour by singing the praise of Waheguru and overcoming his weaknesses for worldly attractions.

(e) The stage of Eternal Truth: After Waheguru has appeared in the heart of the labouring Sikh, he becomes one with Waheguru and attains the stage of Eternal Truth. He sees Waheguru all around, and how He casts His kind glance on His blissful labouring Sikhs. He sees galaxies upon galaxies in this stage, but like the stage of Hard Labour, no one is able to describe this stage. The Sikh in this stage sees living beings from different planets who function in accordance with Waheguru's Laws. Waheguru always remembers, and looks after His creation, and is very pleased to do that. (Guru) Nanak says that to describe all that, is as tough as steel i.e. extremely difficult."

Bhai Dalip Singh kept the audience spell bound. Everybody was listening to him very carefully.

"Are there any questions so far?" Bhai Sahib asked.

"You've done an excellent job of explaining the five stages, Bhai Sahib. But, could you provide a little more detail on the process by which a Sikh passes from one stage to the other. For example, what are the signs that indicate that a Sikh has advanced from the stage of Knowledge to the stage of Hard Labour?. Is it possible to provide more detail on that." Bhai Chanan Singh asked politely.

"Absolutely. But who am I to do that? Guru Nanak Sahib has done a wonderful job in describing the different spiritual stages, but, as you said, the attainment of these stages requires a little more detail. And the Fourth Nanak, Guru Ram Das Ji, has kindly done that for us. "Laavan" - the holy Shabads (Hymns) that we sing during Sikh marriage ceremonies when the would-be-couple goes around Sri Guru Granth Sahib - provide exactly the detail that you're asking for, Bhai Sahib. The four Laavan, in fact, are the four stages which the Sikh bride has to attain for her wedding (union) with Waheguru. The Laavan, recorded on page 773 of Guru Granth Sahib, describe the process by which Waheguru-seeking Sikh advances from one spiritual stage to the other - similar to the five stages discussed a few minutes ago. Now, let's discuss the sacred writing - Laavan - by Guru Ram Das Ji.

LAAVAN: (Suhi Chhant M:4, 773)

There are four stages of preparation before the human bride gets married to Waheguru (qualifies to realize Waheguru). Again, as before, I'll simply paraphrase the holy writings in simple language and try to avoid any additions of my own.

The First Laav: Oh, Waheguru, dearer than my life! You have established the requirements of eligibility for human brides to be one with You. In the first stage, the human bride is advised to strictly follow the duties of the would be bride. She is advised to recite, and to act upon the holy Gurbani as a result of which all sins will be dispelled. The human bride does not have to follow the Vedas of Brahma, because for a Sikh Gurbani is supreme. The duty of the would-be-human bride is to sing the praise of Waheguru. This advice of the Guru to sing praise of Waheguru repeatedly is akin to the advice of Simritis (Hindu Religious books) to the Hindus. Worship the perfect Guru, and thereby rid yourself of all sins. The lucky ones find Waheguru sweet to their hearts. They enjoy bliss and their minds do not wander around. (Guru) Nanak, the servant of Waheguru, says that this is the first stage in the path of matrimonial union with Waheguru.

The Second Laav: Oh, Waheguru, dearer than my own life, by singing Your praise, the human bride attains the second stage in the matrimonial path. With Your grace, she meets the perfect Guru. Due to her meeting with the Guru, she becomes fearless of worldly pressures, and washes away the filth of selfishness. (When a person realizes that it is not his soul but only the body that dies, he starts imparting less and less importance to human body and its needs. As a result, he begins to feel detached from the world, and his needs become limited. When you attain that level, you're no longer afraid of losing anything, and don't feel the need to please or appease anybody. So, you become fearless). By singing the praise of Waheguru, the human bride finds the presence of Waheguru all around her, and develops a blissful fear of Waheguru. When she realizes that it is only the power of Waheguru that is sustaining the whole universe, and feels the presence of Waheguru in her own heart, she is overwhelmed, and sings the praise of Waheguru in the company of holy men. (Guru) Nanak says that in the second stage, the bride's heart gets filled with the ever fresh Divine Shabad.

The Third Laav: Oh Waheguru, dearer than my life, in the third stage in the path of the matrimonial union with You, the human bride loses all interest in worldly things, and she is overwhelmed with the excitement of being one with You. With kind blessings of the holy men, the lucky bride can realize Waheguru. By reciting the sacred Gurbani and singing praise of Waheguru, the bride can become one with the sacred and unblemished Waheguru. The lucky holy men narrate the story of the undescribable Waheguru (sing His praise), and realize Him. (Guru) Nanak says that in the third stage in the path of the matrimonial union with Waheguru, the bride loses all interest in worldly things, and her heart is filled with the praise of Waheguru and the lucky bride sings His praise all the time.

The Fourth Laav: Oh Waheguru, dearer than my life, in the fourth stage in the path of matrimonial union with You, the mind of the human bride ceases to wander around, and attains eternal peace. Through the grace of the Guru, she finds Waheguru very sweet to all her senses, and Waheguru appears in her heart. My Waheguru approved the hard labour of the bride, and now Waheguru is on her mind day and night Whom she finds very enjoyable. She realizes the most cherished goal of her life - Waheguru - and her heart is now overjoyed with the realization of Waheguru. Waheguru Himself initiated this task of matrimonial union for the bride who is very blissful now because of the appearance of Waheguru in her heart. (Guru) Nanak says that the bride realizes Waheguru in the fourth stage in the path of the matrimonial union.

In the four Laavan, Guru Ram Das Ji has very kindly explained the process to progress from one spiritual stage to the next as laid out by Guru Nanak Dev Ji. Mind you, I've only translated the holy Laavan into simple language, and haven't added anything myself. If something is not clear, please don't hesitate to ask again. Guru Nanak Dev Ji explained the results of each spiritual stage, which means He explained what happens in each stage, but Guru Ram Das Ji focused on the progression from one stage to the next. The fifth stage as explained in Jap Ji by Guru Nanak Sahib Ji is the description of Waheguru and His creation as the lucky a true devotee sees it when he becomes one with Waheguru. It is not progress from the fourth stage as described by Guru Ram Das Ji. So, There is no fifth laav. I hope I've answered your question, Bhai Sahib. If you need more detail, please let me know." Bhai Dalip Singh Addressed Bhai Chanan Singh.

"No, everything is perfectly clear now. Thank you very much for your detailed explanations." Bhai Chanan Singh thanked Bhai Dalip Singh.

Laavan and Wedding Ceremonies

"May I ask a question Bhai Sahib." Bibi Parkash Kaur

asked in a sweet voice. "By all means. Please, go ahead." Bhai Dalip Singh said encouragingly. "We recite Laavan as written by the revered Guru Ram Das Ji to perform wedding ceremonies. But as you explained, Laavan have entirely different meaning which has nothing to do with wedding ceremonies. So, is it appropriate to recite Laavan at wedding ceremonies? Some people are already suggesting that some other appropriate shabads than the Laavan be recited at the wedding ceremonies." Bibi Parkash Kaur asked curiously.

"It's a very appropriate question and demands deep analysis. Let us discuss this with open minds. There's no doubt that the "Laavan" describe the progress from one stage to the other in the spiritual path, but, let us not forget the objective of human life. As we discussed on the very first day of our gatherings, the objective of human life is to realize Waheguru. To do so, we must never forget Waheguru anytime, and must include Him in all daily activities. Guru Nanak Sahib advises us in very beautiful words that daily activities, like eating food, wearing clothes, sleeping, and even horse riding, become painful if we forget Waheguru while enjoying them. They are enjoyable only if we remember Him all the time. Please listen to this holy hymn carefully.

- Obeying Waheguru's Command (acting on Guru's advice) is like enjoying all the sweet foods. Listening to Waheguru's Naam with full concentration, and understanding its meaning is like enjoying all the savoury foods. Reciting Waheguru's Naam with your tongue is like enjoying all the tangy foods, and singing His praise is like enjoying the spicy foods. Continuous love for Waheguru is like enjoying all the thirty six varieties of foods; but all this happens only if He is kind to you. Without remembering Waheguru, the consumption of food leads to discomfort and produces impious thoughts in the mind. **(Siri Raag, M:1, 16)**

In the same holy Shabad, Guru Sahib also discusses the discomforts, rather than enjoyment, resulting from wearing expensive clothes, or pleasures of past-time like horse riding, or even from sleeping when we do not remember Waheguru.

Guru Amar Das Ji expresses similar thoughts as follows.

- The perfect Guru savours Waheguru's Naam as a sacred food which eliminates all appetite for worldly possessions. The person who consumes this sacred food loses all desires for wealth and other comforts of life, and Waheguru resides in his heart for ever. Taking of any other food (without worshiping Waheguru) leads to discomforts because man becomes a slave to desires very quickly.————**(Sarang ki Vaar, Sloak M:3,1250)**

Singing praise of Waheguru, not only leads to union with Him, but is also helpful in all aspects of life to achieve whatever you wish for. Listen to these sacred shabads:

- If you want to rid yourself of your troubles, sing praise of Waheguru all the time. If you want recognition and praise, get rid of your selfishness and ego in the company of holy men. If you are afraid of death and rebirth, join the company of holy men to sing Waheguru's praise. **(Sukhmani, M:5, 266)**
- Where none of your relatives - mother, father, brother, son, or friend - can be helpful, Waheguru is always there to help you. **And, Waheguru's Naam is the cure of all diseases. (Gauri Sukhmani, M:5, 264)**
- Waheguru is power for the powerless. If one is in some big trouble and has no one to help him or provide shelter, or his enemies are on the attack, and all his relatives have turned their back on

him; and if he has no other support or backing, he will come out unscathed if he remembers Waheguru. If some one is really frail, suffering from hunger and lacks clothing, and has no money and no one to support him; if he has no means to meet his needs, and is unable to do any other business, he would still enjoy ever-living satisfaction if he remembers Waheguru. **(Siri Raag M:5, 70)**

- If Waheguru's Naam resides in your heart, no pain ever comes near you. Hunger or thirst (of worldly things) would not bother you and the angel of death (spiritual) will stay away from you. **(Maru ki Vaar, Sloak M:5, 1102)**

There are hundreds of other holy hymns like these in which the importance of Waheguru's Naam in our everyday life has been highlighted. **So, we cannot afford not to include Waheguru in our wedding ceremony which is one of the most important events in our life. In fact, It is the most appropriate way for the new couple to start their life together to realize their main common goal - being one with Waheguru.** Even though, none of the matrimonial unions or other worldly relations is everlasting because they are terminated by death, yet the husband-wife relation has been acknowledged to be deeper than all others because all other relations are dependent upon husband-wife relationship. Describing the importance of women (and hence of husband-wife relationship), Guru Nanak Sahib writes:

- We are born from women, and our lives start with women. We are engaged to and then married to women. Women are our real friends and continuation of life is dependent on them. If your wife dies, you look for another, and all the bonds of life are due to them **(Assa ki Vaar, M:1, 473).**

Similarly, Guru Arjun Dev Ji writes:

- A woman who treats her husband like God (just like devotion to one God, she is fully devoted to her husband, and she does not even fantasize about other men, let alone having sexual relations with them), overcomes the fear of death. **(Gauri M:5,185).**

Describing the importance of this special relation, Guru Amar Das Ji writes:

- A man and a woman cannot be considered husband and wife simply because they are spending life together. They are real husband and wife only if they have one soul (identity of views through mutual respect) even though they have different bodies **(Sloak M:3, Suhi ki Vaar, 788).**

That's why all humans are referred to as the wives of Waheguru - the only Husband - in Gurbani. So, even though, "Laavan" describe the spiritual stages in the path of matrimonial union of human bride with Waheguru, it is highly appropriate to recite "Laavan" at wedding ceremonies because of two reasons. First, the holy Hymns teach the couple their prime goal in life - union with Waheguru - and how to achieve that goal. Second, using the "Waheguru - human bride union" as model, Laavan teach a couple how to have happy and successful marriage. Just as Waheguru is kind and initiates the union of the human bride with Himself, the husband must be kind, and mindful of the needs of his wife. That is the best prayer we can offer at weddings in the form of Laavan. Moreover, we sing the praise of Waheguru by reciting the Laavan thus taking His asylum and including Him in one of the most important events of our life. Also, I haven't come across any other holy shabad (hymn) in Guru Granth Sahib more suitable than the Laavan for weddings. So, I fully endorse recitation of Laavan at weddings. **However,**

we must explain the meaning of Laavan just before the actual ceremony starts so that the couple, and all others for that matter, understand what the holy Shabads mean.

If you still have some questions, I'll be very glad to share my thoughts on them." Bhai Dalip Singh concluded the discussion.

There was complete silence among the congregation and no further questions came forth. "That was highly educational Bhai Sahib. On behalf of all the Sangat, I thank you very much for enlightening us regarding stages of spiritual progress and the appropriateness of "Laavan" at weddings using the sacred Gurbani. I'm also very thankful to the Sangat (holy Congregation) who have listened to the brilliant and honest explanation of Gurbani from Bhai Sahib with respect and dedication." Bhai Kashmir Singh thanked Bhai Dalip Singh and all the Sangat. The session was adjourned until the following evening.

Unhad Shabad

"Waheguru Ji Ka Khalsa, Waheguru Ji Ki Fateh." Bhai Dalip Singh welcomed the congregation the following afternoon. It was another beautiful afternoon. It was a bright sunny day, and the birds were chirping on the trees in the surrounding fields. Smoke was rising from all the farm houses indicating that dinner time was approaching.

"May I ask a related question before we embark on a new topic, Bhai Sahib?" Bhai Balraj Singh asked.

"Absolutely." Bhai Dalip Singh said with his usual politeness. "Please, go ahead."

"Many people talk about "unhad shabad" which they claim can be actually heard when they concentrate using some yoga practices. They believe that hearing the 'unhad shabad' is akin to realizing Waheguru. So, their focus is on hearing the 'shabad' to realize Waheguru. Would you, please, explain unhad shabad and what its relevance in Sikhism, if any?" Bhai

Balraj Singh asked.

"A very good and pertinent question." Bhai Dalip Singh commented. "Unhad shabad is a very old thought, and has been mentioned in the Vedas and the Upnishadas. The Vedas posit that unhad shabad is an ongoing divine sound which started as the universe came into being. Some other religions or schools of thought also believe in some form of unhad shabad. Some people believe that God can be realized by listening to the 'unhad shabad', and as you pointed, their whole focus is on listening to the 'unhad shabad' through some kind of concentration. In Sikhism the focus is entirely on realizing Waheguru by singing His praise. The sole objective of the Sikh is to be one with Waheguru, and not to listen to the 'unhad shabad', (if there is any). There is a lot of mention of 'unhad' in Sri Guru Granth Sahib, but it simply means **'uniform' and everlasting,** and the term 'unhad shabad' means the **state of bliss where your mind seems to hear a melodious music and begins to dance.** But, the blissful state of mind has also has been described without using the term 'unhad' in which the mind seems to begin dancing on hearing five types of Divine musical notes.

According to Sri Guru Granth Sahib, Gurbani itself is unhad and leads to a state of bliss. Consider the following holy Shabads in which the term 'unhad' has been used to describe the state of mind.

- Hey yogi, rather than building a temple in a remote area for meditative purposes, my body of six circular centres is itself serving as a place of meditation. And rather than detaching the body, my mind is completely detached from the worldly affairs. Having been convinced by Guru's Teachings, I have dedicated my mind to Waheguru's Naam, **and unhad music is playing** in my connected mind now all the time........ I have realized the non-destructible Waheguru through the Guru's grace, and unhad music is playing day and night. **(Ramkali M:1, Ashatpadian 903)**

NOTE: The yogis believe that human body has six circular centres through which energy can be forced to flow to the brain.

- Sing regularly the sweet melodious unhud shabad (uniform and everlasting shabad of Waheguru's praise) in the company of holy men, oh my friend! Waheguru's Naam destroys all the evils and sins. ———— **(Ramkali M:5, Chhant, (925)**
- Play on such a banjo, hey yogi, which should connect you with Waheguru, and produce unhad music. **(Ramkali M:3, Ashatpadian, 908)**
- Waheguru's Naam equals the worth of the precious stones for me. ———— Waheguru's praise is the priceless diamond and is the source of all good qualities and all bliss. The **unhad Gurbani** is my wealth, but, it can be acquired only by Guru's grace.————**(Ramkali M:5, 896)**
- Sing the praise of Waheguru by reciting the unhad Gurbani, oh man! By doing so, you will become that swan (great soul) which is capable of recognizing the diamond (Waheguru). **(Assa Kabir Ji, 483) NOTE:** It is an old myth that swans eat diamonds or pearls only for food.
- A Great soul who can show the presence of Waheguru in the heart of a man, is the real and wise Satguru. When a man attains that stage, Guru's Shabad is the only prevalent force there. **He feels as if all the five musical instruments are playing there. (Malhar ki Vaar, Sloak M:1,1290)**

- ———Only that person is Satguru or Waheguru's beloved who gladly accepts
Waheguru's will. Waheguru embraces such great souls, and blissful **unhad music plays in the hearts of the great souls. (Ramkali ki Sud, Sunder Ji, 923).**
NOTE: Baba Sunder Ji was the great grandson of Guru Amar Das Ji. He wrote the Sud about Guru Ji leaving this world)
- If you sing the praise of Waheguru in the company of holy men, oh man, you will attain that blissful state of mind where it quits to wander, and acquires all the imaginable comforts. In that state, no worldly discomforts or anxieties impinge upon you, and even the fear of death and rebirth does not sting you. **In that state, you feel as if you hear all the five types of perfect music, and you are lost in the awe of unhad music.** The holy men feel blissful by connecting to Waheguru Who is completely detached from maya. **(Ramkali M:5, 888-9)**

It is perfectly clear from these holy shabads that **hearing of unhad shabad (music) is a feeling which comes automatically when a man is connected to Waheguru. So,**

hearing of unhad shabad (if there's any) is not the real objective of a Sikh. **The objective of the Sikh is to sing the praise of Waheguru by reciting Gurbani.** If there's still some doubt about this explanation of unhad music, please, pay attention to the following holy shabad by Guru Ram Das Ji which makes it perfectly clear that unhad shabad is only a feeling and not something real.

- ———By following Guru's Teachings a man who is blessed with the life-sustaining (Amrit) Naam of Waheguru, keeps reciting the life-sustaining Gurbani with his tongue. The utterings of the holy men are life-sustaining, oh my soul! If we listen to them with full concentration, they connect us with Waheguru from Whom we have been separated for a long time. Waheguru embraces us affectionately and begins to reside in our hearts. Because of the union with Waheguru, I, Nanak, feel very blissful **as if unhad music** is playing in my heart. **(Bihagara Chhant M:4 (538)**

Guru Amar Das Ji and Guru Arjun Dev Ji also describe the feeling of **bliss without using the term 'unhad'** when one realizes Waheguru.

- I am in a state of perfect bliss, oh my mother! I have realized Waheguru. I am in a state where my mind has quit wandering and has become completely satisfied. My mind is so blissful that there is a feeling as if all the ragas along with their raginis (families) have come to sing in my heart.— —**Ramkali M:3, Anand (917)**
- Nanak humbly describes that one acquires all his wishes when he realizes Waheguru. He feels Waheguru's presence all around him, and his mind is filled with bliss and he feels as if it is singing songs of joy. He also feels as if he is watching some joyful event. **(Bihagara Chhant M:5, 544)**

Guru Granth Sahib maintains that when one realizes Waheguru, let alone just one type of music, the individual is so blissful that he feels as if all the five types of musical instruments (wind, wire, drum, metal, and water containers) are being played. Listen to the following

holy Shabads:

- Hey formless and desireless Wahegru, Your slave, Kabir, has performed unconventional aarti by connecting himself with You! Now I feel so blissful that **all the five types of unhad musical instruments** seem to be playing in my heart. **(Parbhati Kabir Ji (1350)**

- I am a trader of Waheguru's Naam. I have realized Waheguru by singing His praise in the company of holy men whom I was able to please. Now I feel as if all the five types of musical instruments are playing in my heart. **(Assa M: 5, 408)**

Guru Nanak Sahib goes even beyond the number five and maintains that there are infinite musical notes that you seem to hear and which bring joy to your heart when you realize Waheguru.

- —— There are infinite Brahmas reading Vedas by the throne of Waheguru, and infinite Shivas meditating. ——— There are countless Dharam Rajs (the mythical justices) and countless angels of wealth. **There are infinite tones of unhand music which produce bliss, and there is no end to such blissfulness. (Sarang M:1, Ashatpadi, 1235)**

As we can see, Guru Sahiban are simply describing the blissful state of mind when one realizes Waheguru. So, the whole idea of 'unhad shabad' is about the feeling or the state of mind when one has realized Waheguru, and there is no real unhand shabad as such. As we discussed earlier, our goal is not to listen to any unhand shabad. Our goal is to be one with Waheguru. The state of bliss follows the union". Bhai Dalip Singh paused for a short while.

"Are there any questions?" Bhai Sahib asked. There was no response.

Everybody was listening to Bhai Sahib with such concentration that they had the feeling as if unhad shabad was ringing in their ears. They did not realize when Bhai Sahib finished his discourse. They were awakened only when

Bhai Dalip Singh called the traditional slogan, 'Waheguru Ji ka Khalsa, Waheguru Ji ki Fateh'. Hearing no questions, Bhai Kashmir Singh profusely thanked Bhai Dalip Singh and all those who were present. Lungar was served to everybody.

3

Huqum (Divine Command)

"Waheguru Ji ka Khalsa, Waheguru Ji ki Fateh to all of you - the beloveds of the Guru. I extend a hearty welcome to all of you on this lovely afternoon." Bhai Dalip Singh welcomed everyone with deep affection. The congregation was larger than before and there was a lot of enthusiasm. The congregation responded to the greetings by Bhai Dalip Singh with a loud roar of "Waheguru Ji ka Khalsa, Waheguru Ji ki Fateh". Everybody had settled down to their comfort in the courtyard of Bhai Kashmir Singh's farmhouse.

"Are there any questions before we start?" Bhai Sahib asked.

Hearing no question, Bhai Sahib continued, "In that case, I plan to discuss what the term 'Huqam' (Divine Command) means as used in Sri Guru Granth Sahib because there is a great emphasis on obeying the Huqam of Waheguru, and the term appears again and again. Very early in Jap Ji Sahib, Guru Nanak Sahib makes it perfectly clear that the only way to realize Waheguru is to obey His Huqam.

- How can one achieve Divine Truth and dismantle the wall of ignorance? (Guru) Nanak says that the only way to do so is to obey the Divine Huqam which is required of all human beings ever since the creation of the universe. **(Jap Ji, 1)**

There are hundreds of holy shabads (hymns) like this in Sri Guru Granth Sahib which emphasize obeying the Huqam.

Huqam is a Persian word and in everyday usage the term means an order or a command from a superior. Most of the Sikhs find it hard to identify the Huqam of Waheguru, let alone obeying it. It is easier for us to obey an order if it comes from an identifiable power (source) and in a language that we can understand. If there's some confusion about the order, we can seek clarification from the power issuing the order. For example, if I request a glass of water, I can easily get it because you can see the source making the request and the request (order) is very clear to you. However, we cannot see Waheguru - or even our revered Gurus now - and their Huqam or Commands are not evident to us. So, it is very difficult for us to obey them. Hence, it is very important that we understand the meaning of the term, and identify the Huqam.

Huqam as Orders

In some situations, the word has been used to mean command in Sri Guru Granth Sahib. But, when it is used in reference to Waheguru it has a slightly different meaning which we'll discuss in a few minutes. Let's consider a few examples in which the term, Huqam, means orders or command.

- Waheguru ordains as He wishes and nobody has the power to issue any **huqam** to Him. Waheguru is the King of all kings; the wise thing for a man to do is to live by His wishes. **(Jap Ji, 6)**
- You have lived your life following your mind, and issuing **huqam** to others for whatever you wished, oh man! But when you are presented before Waheguru after your death, you will have to go through stringent tests and all your past deeds will be evaluated very carefully. You will be judged and given the kind of life that you deserve based on your past deeds. **(Assa ki Vaar, M:1, Pauri, 470)**

- (Guru) Nanak says that you can only make a request to your master. You cannot issue **huqam** to him. **(Assa ki Vaar. Pauri 22, 474)**
- It is only Waheguru Who has created the whole universe and is the Provider for all His creation. He controls the whole universe according to His will, and nobody else has any power to issue any **huqam. (Raag Assa, M:1, wooden board written, 432)**
- When you ask enlightened holy men how to realize Waheguru, you will be advised to accept everything gladly whatever Waheguru is doing, and not to use your own intelligence, or to impose your **huqam**. You will also be told to set your mind on the feet of the Power (Waheguru) by Whose grace you would realize Him. **(Tilung M:1, 722)**

In all these holy Shbads, the term, **huqam,** has the commonly used meaning - orders. But the word 'huqam' has been used very few times in this sense in SGGS. Now consider the following holy Shabads in which the term huqam has been used in reference to Waheguru.

Huqam as the Will of Waheguru

- Only that devotee is rendering real service to Waheguru whom Waheguru makes obey His Huqam. The devotee who obeys Waheguru's Huqam wins His approval and is able to reach the Residence of Waheguru (becomes one with Him). **(Assa ki Vaar, M:1. Pauri 15, 471)**
- Those who have recognized Waheguru's Huqam, have realized Waheguru by getting rid of their selfishness through the Teachings of the Guru. Those are the ones who really worship Waheguru day and night and are always connected to Him. You too should obey Waheguru's Huqam so as to

attain the state of bliss and comfort, oh my mind! **(Malhar M:3, 1258)**

- All bodies come into being with the Huqam of Waheguru. However, the Huqam cannot be described. All living beings are born with His Huqam, and people earn respect and dignity with His Huqam too. ———— Waheguru's Huqam prevails everywhere and nobody is outside His Huqam. (Guru) Nanak says that if a person comes to recognize Waheguru's Huqam, he will never behave in a selfish way (will overcome his ego). **(Jap Ji, 1).**
- The devotees recognize Waheguru's Huqam, and accept whatever has happened. They recite Waheguru's Naam all the time and avoid taking credit for anything. ————— **(Gauri Sukhmani, M:5, 286)**
- You can realize Waheguru only by dedicating your body, mind and wealth to the Guru and by obeying His Huqam. Obey the Huqam of the Guru, oh my mind, and recite Guru's utterings to sing praise of Waheguru! **(Ramkali M:3, Anand Sahib, 918).**
- Things will happen as per Your Huqam, oh Waheguru! The duty of human beings is simply to accept Your Huqam. Those who have come to realize Your Huqam, will never have to cry. **(Goojri ki Vaar. Pauri, M:5, 523)**
- Great is the human bride who has realized Waheguru by abdicating her ego and by obeying His Huqam. She enjoys life while dedicated to Waheguru. **(Suhi M:5, 737)**

As is clear, the term 'huqam' as used in the holy Shabads just discussed, means the 'Will' of Waheguru. Whatever happens in his life, the devotee accepts that gladly as the Will of Waheguru.

Huqam as Laws of Nature

All the preceding holy Shabads (Hymns) emphasize recognizing the Huqam of Waheguru and on obeying it. Now the question is how do we recognize Waheguru's Huqam because He is not known to have ordered anyone directly to do something. If we don't know what His Huqam is, how are we going to obey it?. We know one thing for sure - Waheguru's Huqam has to be the same for everybody. If Waheguru were to issue different orders to everybody, there will be different standards for everybody, and Waheguru cannot be neutral. He will have some favourites and some others whom He doesn't like. (He does have favourites - His saints - but they too achieve that level by obeying the same Huqam as everybody else). Since Waheguru is perfectly neutral (without prejudice), and bears no enmity with anyone **(Jap Ji Sahib), His Huqam has to be His Law (or Constitution) which govern the universe and which applies equally to everybody without any discrimination.** This conclusion is supported strongly by the following holy Shabads.

- **All bodies come into being with the Huqam of Waheguru**. However, the Huqam cannot be described. All living beings are born with His Huqam, and people earn respect or disrespect with His Huqam too.—— **Waheguru's Huqam prevails everywhere, and nobody is outside His Huqam.** (Guru) Nanak says that if a person comes to realize Huqam, (s)he will never talk selfish or behave in a selfish way because recognition of Huqam helps them get rid of his haumein. **(Jap Ji, 1)**
- **Huqmi (The Ruler, Waheguru) runs the whole universe with His Huqam**, and He is always in a very happy and carefree state. **(Jap Ji)**
- Waheguru is capable of doing anything and everything, and has the power to motivate living beings.——— **He creates the universe with His**

Huqam which (the universe) stays in place without any visible support. The world comes into being with His Huqam, and vanishes with His Huqam as well. ———— **(Gauri Sukhmani, M:5, 276-7)**

- A person whose mind is imbued with Waheguru's Naam, treats all human beings as equal. He has found eternal peace and his mind quits wandering. He sees Waheguru all around him and realizes that it is **His Huqam which is running the whole universe.** He becomes fearless, and his dealings with all human beings are the same (fair and square). **(Parbhati Naam Dev Ji,1350)**
- The whole universe has been created by Waheguru alone, **and His Huqam is running the whole universe. (Raag Gauri, Ashatpadian, M:1, 223)**
- Everybody has come to this world as a part of Waheguru and with His **Huqam**. The whole world is functioning under His **Huqam**. The Master is everlasting, and the universe created by Him follows His everlasting laws. ———— **(Tilung M: 4, 723)**
- I have noticed a fascinating phenomenon of Waheguru, oh my dear friend! **Whatever Waheguru does is based on perfect justice and holy laws.** He has created this world as a wrestler's ring for human beings where they fight for the good or evil. He has also fixed birth and death for living beings. ————**(Bihagra M:5, Chhant, 541)**
- It is an **eternal Huqam** of Waheguru that no one can realize Him without the grace of the Guru. With the grace of the Guru, Waheguru takes abode in the heart of the individual because of which the individual stays connected with Him and remembers Him with every breath. **(Bihagra ki Vaar, Sloak M: 3, 556)**

- The divisions of earth and the galaxies are factual, and so are the planets and all heavenly bodies. All that You have done is for real and You have done this with real (careful) thought, oh Waheguru! Your Court and Your Rule is also real, and so are **Your Huqam and Your Orders** (message). **(Sloak M:1, Assa ki Vaar, 463)**

  NOTE: Some people believe that life is nothing more than a dream. All the creation is a dream and not a reality. Guru Sahib is simply dispelling that false belief and asserting that Waheguru's creation is not a dream - it is for real.

The above Shabads make it perfectly clear that the word 'Huqam' alludes to the laws of the universe. **In the last Shabad Guru Nanak Sahib has also made a distinction between huqam and order indicating again that Huqam implies laws.**

Also, Guru Sahiban have written quite a few times that Waheguru is always in a happy state and **He is carefree.** Please pay attention to the following holy Shabads.

- First Waheguru creates Himself, and then He creates Naam (laws). Then He creates the nature (universe), and now He watches His creation from His Throne. **(Sloak M:1, Assa ki Vaar, 463).**

  Note the term 'watches '. **He is not interfering, only enjoying.**
- **Waheguru is carefree**, and is beyond the comprehension of human senses. Worship Him round the clock, oh, my mind! **(Ramkali M:5, 896)**
- As the devotee attains the stage of Eternal Truth, he sees world upon world of Waheguru's creation. He 'observes' that the whole universe is following Waheguru's Huqam strictly, while Waheguru is watching the whole operation joyously. **(Jap Ji Sahib, 8)**

Waheguru can be carefree only if He doesn't have to worry about the normal operation of the universe. **And the only way He will not need to worry is if He had a set of laws to govern the universe. So, clearly Huqam means the set of laws.**

Will of Waheguru and His Laws

"Are there any questions so far?" Bhai Dalip Singh asked in a pleasant tone.

"Bhai Sahib, you explained 'Huqam' in terms of the Will of Waheguru and also as His Laws that govern the universe. Some of the holy Shabads that you quoted to explain 'Huqam' in terms of the Will of Waheguru were also used by you to explain 'Huqam' in terms of the Laws of Waheguru. Would you, please, further elaborate this distinction between the "Will and the Laws", if possible?" Bhai Kanwar Jit Singh asked hesitatingly.

Noticing a hesitation in Bhai Kanwar Jit Singh's voice, Bhai Dalip Singh replied assuringly, "Please, feel perfectly comfortable, Bhai Sahib. That's a very good question. I'll try to make the distinction clear. In fact, the Will and the Laws are strongly related. In some situations the word 'Huqam' may seem to mean the Will of Waheguru, but, the Will of Waheguru is NOT based on His fickle emotions. There has to be a good reason for His will or wishes otherwise **He cannot be just**. We reap the reward of our deeds. **So, even if the word 'Huqam' means Will, it is based on His Laws.** We may not understand His Justice or His Will right away because we do not have any information to base our judgment on. Only Waheguru has all the needed information, so, we may sometimes resent Waheguru's decisions when the outcome is not to our liking. That's why Guru Sahib advises us to accept Waheguru's Will because our resentment may be totally unfounded. Guru Sahiban have made it very clear many times through their writings that Waheguru is just, and if there is suffering for us, it is because of our own deeds. Consider the following holy Shabads (Hymns).

- Do not blame others when things go against your expectations oh, man! The outcome is the result of your own deeds. You reap the rewards of whatever you sow. You are caught in the net of your own deeds, and you will continue to go through the cycle of births and deaths because all the deeds you do for *maya* result in the cycle. **(Ramkali M:5, 888)**
- You should blame your own deeds and not somebody else if you do not like the outcome, oh man! You are harvesting only whatever you had sowed. So, do not blame others. **(Assa M:1, Wooden board Written, 433)**

So, clearly whatever we are experiencing in life is the result of our good or bad deeds. Sometimes we can see Waheguru's justice, but many times the justice is not evident to us especially if there is an untimely or unnatural death, or other big calamity in the family. Guru Sahib maintains that even that may be the result of our collective deeds or Universal Laws not apparent to us. Consider the following holy Shabad which Guru Nanak Sahib shared with Bhai Lallo about the impending attack by Babar on Emnabad.

- As revealed to me by Waheguru, I am going to share some future happenings with you which will take place in Emnabad, Bhai Lallo. The evil forces of Babar from Kabul will attack India mercilessly and thousands of innocent lives will be lost when bodies will be cut into pieces like fabric. ——— Waheguru, who has created the whole universe and has caused His creation to do different things, is watching His creation now while sitting totally aloof. The Master is perfectly Just, and so is His Justice. The Just will deliver true Justice. ———————**(Tilung M;1, 722-23)**

The reason for Babar's impending attack as given by Guru Sahib was to punish the corrupt Mogul rulers who were ruling Emnabad and other territories in India. Of course, some innocent people would also die. But, the point is everything happens by the Huqam of Waheguru.

Whatever is happening in the universe is all based on Waheguru's own planning, and is happening strictly in accordance with His Huqam (Laws). From the creation of the universe and the birth of living beings to the quality of life for them including all sorts of joys and grief, and to their death, everything is governed by Waheguru's Laws. From the universal law of gravity, and the formation of days and nights, to the fatal effect of poison, everything follows Waheguru's Laws.

Another term used for the Universal Laws by Guru Nanak Sahib is **'fear'**. When He writes that every object - living or non-living in this universe - is fearful of Waheguru, what He means is that each and every object is following His Laws.

- The air is moving constantly and hundreds of thousands of rivers are flowing because of the fear (Huqam) of Waheguru. The fire is obeying the orders out of fear, and the earth is held in place under weight **(does not leave its orbit)** because of the fear (Huqam) of Waheguru. ———————————**(Assa ki Vaar, Sloak M:1, 464)**
- Only Waheguru is fearless while countless Ramas are like the dust of Waheguru's feet. ——————— **(Assa ki Vaar, Sloak M:1, 464)**

From the two Sloaks, it is clear again that fear (or Huqam) means the Laws of Waheguru because when Guru Sahib says Waheguru is fearless, He means that the universal Laws do not apply to Him. **Nirbhau in the 'Mool Mantra' also means exactly the same.**

Waheguru has assigned different characteristics to different parts of His creation which never change, and keep the universe in order. For example, He created gravitation by which everybody in this universe attracts every other body. This law keeps all the heavenly bodies in their relative positions in space, and makes living possible for us. Having created this law, Waheguru does not have to track down the motion of any individual star or planet. Now, He is carefree about the motion of heavenly bodies. Likewise, He has created zillions of other laws to run the universe. As another example, He gave a powerful poisonous character to potassium cyanide. Now, if someone consumes that substance in sufficient amount, he is sure to die because that is the Law (Huqam) of Waheguru, and there will be no exception. Guru Nanak Sahib has made this perfectly clear in the following holy shabad:

- If you are proud of your higher caste in society, let us see if your higher caste can save you from the effect of poison, oh Pandit Ji! If you consume a poisonous substance, you are as sure to die as a person of lower caste. **(Sloak M:1, Maajh ki Vaar).**

A poisonous substance does not discriminate between people of higher or lower castes. Its poisonous effect is Huqam (a law of) Waheguru. When Waheguru's Laws (Huqam) apply to different situations, and the outcomes are unfavorable to individuals, **we usually call the outcomes the will of Waheguru.** But remember, as discussed shortly before, whatever Waheguru does is based on complete Justice, and is a result of our own deeds. Thus if a person dies of poisonous material, it may be his own fault. **This is not to say that some innocent people do not die when they are administered poison on purpose or otherwise.** The point is that the poisonous character has been created by the Huqam of Waheguru and has become a law for that substance.

Likewise, if someone contracts the virus of smallpox, he will get the disease. This is a law of nature (Waheguru's Huqam), and the **Huqam will not change**.

Incidents of Historical Importance

Now let's consider a few incidents of great historical importance. When Guru Arjun Dev Ji went to serve the suffering humanity in the smallpox-infested area of Amritsar district in 1596, He had to take his infant son, (Guru) Hargobind, with Him for Hargobind's safety reasons. Even though, the child Hargobind, was the son of the Guru - and later became Guru Himself- nature's law did not spare him, and he had a severe attack of smallpox. Everybody at that time labeled the illness of (Guru) Hargobind the Will (Huqam) of Waheguru, which really meant the Laws of nature (Waheguru) were taking their course. Now, it is a different story how the child Hargobind recovered, but the point is, what everybody called the 'Will' at that time, really meant the Law of nature.

Something similar happened to the Eighth Guru, Harkrishan Sahib. He was invited by Aurangzeb, the emperor India at the time, to visit the latter in Delhi. Guru Ji was only about eight years old. Delhi was under a severe attack of smallpox at the time. Guru Ji began to help and comfort the sick round the clock. Young as He was, He was also attacked by smallpox. The attack was so severe that Guru Ji left this world in a few days. Again, this very significant fact proves that laws of nature apply with the same gusto even to Waheguru's beloved ones. This was also the **'Huqam'** of Waheguru. **The more we study Guru Granth Sahib, the more we discover that the word 'Huqam' pertains to the laws of Waheguru and His Will."** Bhai Sahib paused for a while.

How to Obey Waheguru's Huqam

"Bhai Sahib, you said at the beginning that obeying

Waheguru's Huqam is very essential for us to be one with Him. If 'Huqam' implies Divine Laws - and many of which are not known to a common man - how do we obey Huqam?" Bhai Dilbag Singh asked.

"That was my next topic, but, thank you for bringing me on line. You are right when you said that to be one with Waheguru, it's a requirement that we obey His Huqam, and Guru Sahiban have made it very clear again and again. **There are four pauris (12 - 15) in Jap Ji Sahib** alone that explain the importance of obeying Guru's Teachings (or Waheguru's Huqam). But, I'll quote a few other holy Shabads (Hymns) as well, in which the significance of Waheguru's Huqam has been emphasized.

- Only that person gets Waheguru's approval who obeys His Huqam. By doing so, the individual becomes one with Him. **(Assa Ki Vaar, M:1, pauri, 471)**
- Grant me only that knowledge and concentration on Naam which You approve, oh Waheguru! Because Your real praise lies only in obeying Your Huqam. **(Majh M:5, 100)**
- ——As long as man does not realize Waheguru's Huqam, he suffers. But, when he recognizes the Huqam through the Guru, he becomes happy and content. **(Assa M:5, 400)**
- The everlasting Waheguru resides in every living being. Whatever is happening in the universe is His will. That person is dear to Him who recognizes His Huqam and 'sees' Him around everywhere in the universe. **(Parbhati Kabir Ji, 1349)**

There are hundreds more holy hymns that highlight the importance of obeying Waheguru's Huqam. Now the question is how do we obey His Huqam. The answer to this question is again provided by the holy Gurbani. Guru Arjun Dev Ji makes it perfectly clear that **obeying the Huqam means following the Teachings of the Guru and singing the praise of Waheguru all the time and staying content and never complaining to Waheguru if things do not turn out the way we wished.** Do your best to achieve your goal by fair means, but accept the consequences as they happen. Listen to the following holy Shabads.

- Sing the praise of Waheguru day and night, oh man!———— **The devotee recognizes Waheguru's Huqam, and accepts all happenings in life gladly as they take place. (Gauri Sukhmani, M:5, 286)**
- I am neither a pundit nor a wise or clever man. I do not claim to be knowledgeable, and do not comment or criticize (complain) much. **I have recognized Waheguru's Huqam by listening to the advice of the Guru.** That's why I have not lost my path of truthfulness, and I am in a very blissful state. **(Raag Gauri, Ashatpadian, M:1, 221)**
- ——What kind of gathering should be considered the company of the truth seekers (sadh sangat or sat sangat)? Sat Sangat is the gathering where only Waheguru's praise is sung. (Guru) Nanak says that the Guru has made it clear that **only the recitation of Waheguru's Naam in sat sangat is Waheguru's Huqam**.——Humans who are motivated to obey Waheguru's Huqam, internalize Waheguru's praise through Guru's Baani. **(Siri Raag, Ashatpadian, M:1, 72-73)**
- When I ask my Satguru whom I should serve, and what *baani* should I recite to shield myself from the attacks of sensual pleasures, my Satguru advises me that I should obey Waheguru's Huqam and rid myself of my ego (or selfishness). **Obeying Waheguru's Huqam is the real service to Him which is carried out by singing His praise through**

Guru's comforting Shabad. By doing so, Waheguru's Naam begins to reside in the heart of the devotee who then enjoys all the comforts.—— **——(Siri Raag M:3, 34)**

- Everybody belongs to the Master, and everybody is created by the Master. But only he realizes Him who recognizes His Huqam. **His Huqam is recognized by reciting His Naam using Guru's Shabad**. Also, an individual who, following the Teachings of the Guru, analyzes himself, and treats nobody as bad or evil, makes his life successful. **(Sarang ki Vaar, Sloak M:4, 1244)**
- Waheguru Himself is the earth and Himself the tiller (farmer). He is the one Who raises and harvests the crop. He cooks and serves food, and enjoys the food Himself. He serves water and toothpicks, and He Himself does swooshing. He Himself invites the devotees to religious congregations, and Himself sends them off. **He makes only those individuals accept His Huqam gladly to whom He is kind.** (And he is kind to those who sing His praise through Guru's Shabad) **(Bihagara ki Vaar, M:4, Pauri, 550)**
- ———With Waheguru's grace, if His Shabad (Naam) begins to reside in an individual's mind, all his desires are satisfied. **That individual begins to realize Waheguru's Huqam** and he plays the game of life just as an expert plays the game of cross-board checkers to ensure victory. **(Suhi, Kabir Ji, 793)**
- **Worship Waheguru by obeying the Teachings of the Guru, oh my mind!** By obeying the Huqam of Waheguru like this, you will get rid of your haumein and be one with Him. **(Wadhans M:3, 560)**
- ——Man is born by the Huqam (Will) of Waheguru, and he dies by His Huqam (Will). The man

following his heart is hand-cuffed by Waheguru's Will and taken to His Court where he is given appropriate punishment. **His Huqam is recognized through Guru's Shabad,** and a person who recognizes Waheguru's Huqam this way, is honoured in His Court. ——**(Sorith M:1, 636)**

- I am your slave, oh Waheguru! **Please issue Your Huqam (orders) to me so that I may serve you.** Please, assign the foolish me, Your great service. I wish to do the deeds as per the Teachings of the Guru if He is kind enough to lead me. **The Guru advises me that singing the praise of Waheguru in the company of holy men is the best service of Waheguru Who is completely without any desire. (Sorith ki Vaar, M.4, Pauri, 643)**

So, it is clear that obeying the Huqam of Waheguru means to mould our lives according to Guru's Teachings — which include singing the praise of Waheguru, and leading a life of contentment without complaining to Waheguru for things which are not to our liking. So, one should sing the praise of Waheguru and lead a life of contentment. That's how we obey Waheguru's Huqam". Bhai Dalip Singh concluded.

"Are there any further questions?" Bhai Sahib asked after a short pause.

No questions came forward. Bhai Kashmir Singh thanked Bhai Dalip Singh for a highly enriching lecture, and the gathering for being great listeners.

The congregation ended with a loud slogan of "Waheguru Ji ka Khalsa, Waheguru Ji ki Fateh". A delicious meal was waiting for all of them.

4

Waheguru's Naam: Panacea For All Ills

"You're such an enlightened group of people that I've learnt a lot from your deep and thought-provoking questions. Many questions that you've asked of me over the past few days have impelled me to think and study more because nobody has ever asked those questions before. I think I can serve you better by responding to your questions rather than me just lecturing routinely. So, I've decided that from now on, I'll just answer your questions." Bhai Dalip Singh started the afternoon session after welcoming an overflowing gathering with the traditional Sikh Slogan, "Waheguru Ji ka Khalsa, Waheguru Ji ki Fateh." The gathering had been growing at a phenomenal rate everyday. It started with about a hundred people, but now the number had grown to more than four hundred. Luckily, Bhai Kashmir Singh's farm house was big enough to accommodate about a thousand people in its yard. The weather had been good, and no precipitation was expected for the next two months or so.

"Let's start with some new questions." Bhai Dalip Singh looked around smilingly.

"I'll ask a question, Bhai Sahib. Some preachers and some self-proclaimed saints recommend specific holy shabads from Sri Guru Granth Sahib to cure specific diseases. For example, they claim that everyday recitation of Jap Ji Sahib for two months cures such and such disease, and two months' recitation of Sukhmani Sahib cures such and such disease. Now there is a new booklet of Sukhmani Sahib which claims that the holy Baani can cure almost any disease provided it is recited in a certain ritualistic way. Could you, please, comment on that?" Bibi Parkash Kaur asked.

"I'm very glad that you asked this question, Bibi Ji. This is an extremely important issue for all of us, and demands a good open discussion. Most of the problems facing us result from stress in everyday life. There's hardly a thing in life that is stress-free. The stress could result from a number of problems such as financial hardship, the inability of your children or yourself to get a meaningful job, not getting a suitable matrimonial relationship for your children, job-related problems, non-cooperation from some family members or colleagues, injustice done to you by someone, or simply a challenge to your ego. Also, your perception of some situations can cause stress. Thus, there are millions of sources of stress. All of us face some degree of stress in life on regular basis.

Different people have different capacities and different skills to handle stress which may vary from no skill at all to excellent skills to handle almost any situation. But, there will be very few people who have the skills to handle all stress. Most of us can deal with common stress in life, but will get crushed beyond a certain limit. Some people are better skilled to handle certain kinds of stress, but have almost no skills to handle other kinds of stress. They buckle completely under some specific kinds of stress to the extent that they are either driven insane or commit suicide - which is so unfortunate. In most people, a high degree of stress can cause loss of appetite and/or loss of sleep which, in turn, can result in body malfunctioning ranging from constipation and insomnia to high blood sugar, high blood pressure (eventually heart attack) or reduced resistance to many other diseases. More advanced countries have professionally trained people who provide counselling to the victims of stress. Stress counsellors are now available in limited areas in India too. **I'm NOT saying that stress is the cause of all diseases, but stress does reduce**

your resistance to fight diseases. There are many other forms of diseases or discomforts which do not originate from stress. For example, any wound caused by some accident, infectious diseases that you acquire when exposed to certain bacteria, and some genetic diseases that you acquire from your parents. **Selfishness and ego (or conceit) are also diseases, albeit mental, and so are lust, greed, rage, and possessiveness.**

But, before I answer your question whether a particular baani is capable of curing diseases or not, let us search for the importance of Naam in relation to diseases from Guru Granth Sahib. According to Gurbani all sorts of diseases can be cured by Waheguru's Naam. Listen to the following holy Shabads.

- Waheguru's Naam is the cure of all diseases, and singing the praise of Waheguru is a source of comfort. **(Sukhmani M: 5, Ashatpadi, 9)**
- Where ever I apply the medication of Waheguru's Naam, all discomforts and ills are gone in a moment. Whoever applies Naam medication with respect and affection, will not suffer from any disease even in his dreams. ———— **(Gauri Bawan Akkhari, M: 5, 259)**
- I have taken the medication of Waheguru's Naam. As a result, the source of all discomforts has been eliminated, and I have all the comforts now. With the help of the Perfect Guru's Shabad, all burning and agony are gone, and I feel very blissful ——— **(Assa M: 5, 378)**
- My physician is my Guru, my Waheguru, Who administers the medication of His Naam to cut the noose of (moral) death. Waheguru's Naam nurtures the dead mind and dispels the agony of many incarnations.————**(Sorith M: 5, 618)**
- ———— My forehead is hurting, my whole body is burning, and my heart is aching. The pain is

very severe and no medication is working to alleviate it. But, Waheguru has taken over to be my physician. He has given me His Naam as the holy liquid of immortality which serves as the panacea for all the troubles in the world. Bheekhan (Ji) says that with the grace of the Guru, I have found salvation. **(Sorith Bheekhan Ji, 659)**

- Your Naam is the killer of all ills, oh Waheguru! We ought to meditate twenty four hours on the Divine Knowledge imparted to us by the Perfect Guru. The heart in which Waheguru's Naam resides, is a beautiful place. Reciting His Naam keeps the agents of death away. ————**(Gauri Maajh M: 5, 218)**
- ————Waheguru is the destroyer of all the three types of agonies - physical, mental and conflictional. He kills all your discomforts whereby you acquire mental peace and comfort. A person who prays to Waheguru with full faith, does not suffer from any of the discomforts. ————**(Todi M:5, 714)**

As is clear from the above holy Shabads, Waheguru's Naam is panacea of all ills. However, the holy Gurbani doesn't say that a particular baani will cure a specific disease. It is the Naam that is the destroyer of all ills." Bhai Dalip Singh emphasized.

What is Naam

"That's another question that has been on my mind for a long time, Bhai Sahib. What exactly do we mean by Naam?" Bibi Parkash Kaur asked another related question.

"This is another very important question, Bibi Ji, which requires a detailed explaining." Bhai Dalip Singh reacted. "The word 'naam' in ordinary usage means the name of an object, just like my name is Dalip Singh, and you have a name, and so on. The term has been used in this sense a few times in Guru Granth Sahib. For example, there are countless names used by people for the Supreme Soul - Waheguru. The most popular name used for Waheguru in Guru Granth Sahib is Ram, but many other names have also been used including Kartar, Mohan, Gopal, Niranjan, Truth, Dayo, Krishan, Bishan, Gobind, Murari, Gosaeen, Vaas Dev, Narain, Damodar, Sarang Paan, Banwari, Chatarbhuj, Beethul, Allah, Raheem, and so on. Naam has also been used synonymously with Waheguru. Listen to the following holy Shabads (Hymns)

- All the living beings are supported by Naam as are all the stars and the galaxies. The sky and the under worlds are also supported by Naam. ———— **(Gauri Sukhmani, M:5, Ashatpadi 16)**
- Naam is the source of all treasures oh my mind! Drink the Naam - Amrit (the liquid of immortality) in the company of holy men. The Naam - Amrit quenches the thirst of all desires, and we feel blissful. ————————**(Gauri ki Vaar, M:5, 318)**

as is clear from the above two holy Shabads, Naam has been used synonymously with Waheguru. There are many more holy shabads like this in which Naam has been used in the same sense. **But when it comes to realizing Naam, it means singing the praise of Waheguru as per the Teachings of the Guru to the extent that your heart becomes the dwelling of Waheguru.** In other words you worship Waheguru so much that He is on your mind all the time. And the best way to sing the praise of Waheguru is through the recitation of Gurbani with love and respect, preferably in the company of holy men. Singing of Gurbani with devotion is another name for 'Naam'. Listen to the following holy Shabads.

- The liquid of immortality (Waheguru's Naam) is there in your heart, oh man, but can be realized only with the grace of the Guru. ———— Waheguru's Naam sprouts from the Shabad of the Guru (Gurbani), and a person who recites

Guru's Shabad with devotion becomes one with Waheguru. People who do not recite Guru's Shabad are ignorant and are wasting away their human life aimlessly. **(Sorith ki Vaar, Sloak M:3, 644)**

- You can worship Waheguru through His grace only. ——(Guru) Nanak shares this thought that you can find salvation only if you love (and recite) Gurbani which is written in the praise of the everlasting Waheguru. ————**(Dhanasari M:1, 661)**
- You are given this human life to listen and to recite Gurbani, oh man! But you are wasting away your life in the greed for worldly objects and forgetting the Naam. However, only those devotees worship Waheguru's Naam who are liked by Him. ——————All the wisdom, effort and the energy required to recite the Naam are granted by Waheguru alone. **(Sarang M:5, 1219)**
- Only Gurbani and Gurbani alone is the Guru, and only the Shabad of the Guru needs to be the focus of human thought (to realize Waheguru). Guru's store is everlasting and so is the merchandise in the store which is full of invaluable precious stones of Waheguru's Naam. You can access those precious stones only through the grace of the Guru.—— ——**(Sorith ki Vaar, Sloak M:3, 646)**
- Come on all the dear Sikhs of the Guru and recite the Gurbani which is the praise of the everlasting Waheguru. Recite the Gurbani which is the supreme of all other baanies. The hearts which are blessed by Waheguru become the dwellings of Gurbani (Waheguru).————**(Ramkali, M:3, Anand, 920)**
- The faces of the devotees who have internalized the treasure of Waheguru's Naam by reciting Gurbani shine with a special glow in the Court of Waheguru. Those who are so blessed never forget Waheguru whether they are standing or sitting

(whether working or resting). ————**(Sloak M:4, 1422)**

- Guru's words are the liquid of immortality. Whoever recites Guru's Baani, and thus worships Waheguru's Naam, attains the highest spiritual level. When Waheguru's Naam has taken residence in the heart of an individual (through the recitation of Gurbani), all types of his agony in this world of selfishness are dispelled. ————**(Suhi M:5, 744)**

It is perfectly clear from the above holy Shabads that (Waheguru's) Naam is realized through the dedicated recitation of Gurbani." Bhai Dalip Singh clarified the link between Gurbani and Naam.

"Recitation of Gurbani with devotion does two things. First, it has a very soothing effect on you which takes your mind away from your problems thereby lowering the stress. Also, you realize that you are not the only person in the world with problems; the whole world faces similar problems. This realization gives you the strength to fight problems. Second, and more important, it connects you to Waheguru - the source of all energy and all comforts. With closer connection with Waheguru, your mind becomes stronger and stronger and gets more and more confidence and assurance that there is the Supreme Power, Waheguru, to help and protect you. Like stress, which is mental, recovery from other diseases is also controlled by mind. **Stronger the mind, the greater is the ability to fight diseases and to recover.** With a strong mind, you acquire so much energy to deal with the situation that all the body discomforts, whether stress-related or otherwise, are gone, and you feel healthier and cured.

Sri Guru Granth Sahib is full of praise of Waheguru or His Naam. **So, reciting any Baani (composition) with devotion will purify your mind and connect you with Waheguru,**

which will of course, treat all your ills. But the sad thing is that some irresponsible people misguide the innocent devotees by declaring that only a particular Baani is good to treat certain illnesses. Their idea is nothing more than making money or get publicity that the idea is coming from such and such 'saint'. There are certain Baanies which are simpler to understand than others and easier to recite, and they may also affect your state of mind in different ways. For example, when you recite 'Laavans' which are normally recited at weddings, your state of mind will be very different than when we recite 'Allahanian' which are normally recited at the death of someone. **However they all connect you to Waheguru, which is the main objective.** Guru Sahiban have written baanies for almost all occasions in life, but, the basic idea is the same - to connect people to Waheguru no matter what the occasion is. The Sikhs are allowed to celebrate all occasions in life within limits as long as they don't go overboard and keep Waheguru in mind all the time. When they remember Waheguru in all their activities, the Sikhs will not go wild in happy occasions, and will not be depressed in sad occasions. You may recite, Jap Ji Sahib, Sukhmani Sahib, Anand Sahib, or any other Baani. All of them are perfect medicines. So, don't be restricted by the claim of some irresponsible business people." Bhai Dalip Singh took a few sips of water. "Are there more questions?" Bhai Sahib asked.

Is There a Special Way to Remember Waheguru?

"Would you clear up another misgiving, Bhai Sahib? Is there some special way to remember Waheguru, or to recite the holy Baanies, as some people claim?" Bibi Pritam Kaur asked politely.

"That's another sad story when self-proclaimed 'saints' misguide innocent people advising them to recite Waheguru's Naam (holy Gurbani) in some ritualistic way. Love for Waheguru is no different from the love of a mother for her child, or the love for wealth of a money-minded person, or the love of an addict for opium or any other intoxicant. Does it require some special ritual for an addict to love opium, or for a mother to love her child? When her son is away, does the mother sit down or lie down in some special way to miss her son? Isn't he on her mind most of the time? When she cooks some food, wouldn't it be automatic for her to wish that her son were there to eat the food? Every little incident reminds her of her son. If she is talking to someone, she will use any excuse to talk about her son in one context or the other. That happens with everybody when they love someone or something. A businessman will love to talk about some aspect of business, and so on. **Just as a mother or a businessman does not require some special body postures or some special occasions to love their respective objects, we do not need any special ritualistic way to love Waheguru.** There are some holy shabads in Sri Guru Granth Sahib that teach us how to love Waheguru. As you will notice, there's absolutely no requirement of any special way.

- Show the same intensity of love for Waheguru as does a lotus flower for water, oh my mind! Even though water waves hit it hard, yet the flower flourishes even more. ———Show the same level of love for Waheguru as does a fish for water, oh my mind! As the volume of water increases, the fish enjoys more and more - physically and mentally. ————Show the same level of love for Waheguru as does water for milk, oh my mind! When put on fire, the water takes all the heat (and boils off) leaving the milk unscorched. ——— **(Siri Raag, M:1, 59)**
- Just as a hungry person loves food, or a thirsty person loves water, and just as a simpleton person loves his family (for dependency), Naam Dev loves his Lord (Waheguru).—————Just as some men love other women, or a greedy person loves money, and just as a lusty person loves women, Naam

Dev loves his Waheguru. ——————**(Bhairon Naam Dev Ji, 1164)**

- Just as a cow feels uncomfortable without her calf, Naam (Dev Ji) begins to feel nervous without his Lord. Just as a fish feels out of water, so does Naam (Dev Ji) without his Lord. ————Just as people feel uncomfortable in the strong heat of the sun, so does poor Nama without his Lord. **(Goand, Nam Dev Ji, 874)**
- If You don't break off with me, I have no desire to break off with You, oh my Lord! I have nobody else to rely on. My love for You is just like the love of a peacock for mountains (clouds), or like the love of a chakor (a bird) for the moon. My relationship with You is similar to that of an oil lamp and the wick, or that of a holy place and a pilgrim. I have broken off all my bonds with 'maya', and my true love is for You alone. —————— **(Sorith, Ravidas Ji, 658-59)**
- Show the same intensity of love for Waheguru as does a deer for enchanting music of the poachers. He lays down his life for his love for music. Offer your mind to Waheguru (remember Him) the same way as a devoted wife does to her husband and remembers him all the time.————**(Assa M:5, Chhant, 454)**

As you can see, there is absolutely no mention of any special ritualistic way by which a person should remember Waheguru. Only the level of dedication has been stressed.

On the contrary, there are many holy shabads in which the use of any special effort to remember Waheguru has been discouraged. Listen to the following holy Shabads.

- Why would anyone look for anklets and musical instruments to worship Waheguru? These things require some time to get ready. Rather than wasting time on those things, I will simply remember my Waheguru. ———Why would anyone dance by spreading their arms and legs to please Waheguru. It takes some time to do those actions, I will simply remember my Waheguru during that time too. ———You do not need to show off. Remember Waheguru in your heart all the time. Every body will praise you (for not showing off). **(Assa M:4, 368)**

Note: Some people worship their gods with dance and music.

- You do not please Waheguru when you dance for Him or play music for Him or even read religious books. You do not please Him either when you practice the Yogic way of concentration or are engaged in a discussion of knowledge. ———You do not please Him by pilgrimage or by wandering naked. Nor you please Him by donations to Brahmans or by other acts of charity.——— Waheguru is pleased only when we sing His praise with clean mind and dedication. **(Sarang ki Vaar, Sloak M:1, 1237)**
- Quit cheating, and acts of show off, and sing only the praise of Waheguru, oh my dishonest mind! None of the acts like hard self-discipline by suspending yourself upside down in Kashi (Varanasi); ending your life at holy places; torturing yourself in surrounding fire etc. come even close to Waheguru's Naam (Singing His praise). You may perform a horse-sacrificial *yaga* or donate gold secretly to Brahmans, or donate thousands of cows at holy places by the banks of the Ganges, Godawari or Gomti, and undertake pilgrimage millions of times, or freeze yourself to death in the Himalayas, you will not be able to please Waheguru. None of

those sacrifices is equivalent to singing the praise of Waheguru.——— The only and the best thing to do is to drink the Naam-Amrit. (Sing the praise of Waheguru selflessly). **(Ramkali Nam Dev Ji, 973)**

Bhagat Naam Dev Ji of Maharashtra was a washerman by profession. He was well known in the whole country as a devoted bhagat. Once, Bhagat Trilochan, also from Maharashtra, and a neophyte devotee, went to visit Bhagat Nam Dev Ji for guidance. Bhagat Naam Dev Ji was applying imprints on fabric at the time. Bhagat Trilochan was disappointed to see Naam Dev Ji busy in worldly affairs. He had expected Naam Dev Ji to be sitting in some isolated place and worshipping Waheguru. When Trilochan Ji shared his feelings with Naam Dev Ji, the latter explained how to really remember Waheguru. Kabir Sahib has narrated this conversation in the following beautiful sloaks.

- Naam Dev is overcome by maya, says Trilochan. Why is he putting imprints on fabric rather than remembering Waheguru? **(Sloak Kabir Ji, 1375)**
- Naam Dev advised: Recite Waheguru's Naam with your tongue, hey Trilochan! Use your hands and feet to earn your livelihood while your mind is in unison with Waheguru. **(Sloak Kabir Ji, 1376)**

There is another shabad in Sri Guru Granth Sahib in which Naam Dev Ji has a similar advice for Trilochan Ji, and in fact, for all of us.

- Young boys buy paper to make kites and fly them in the sky. They talk to one another, but their mind is always on the string (the kite). Likewise, my mind is stitched with my Lord exactly the same way as that of a goldsmith who always keeps his mind on the molten gold (to make ornaments). The young city girls go to fetch water from the river and carry the water-containers on their heads. They share jokes with one another, but keep their minds focussed on the containers so that they don't fall off. ————Just as a mother, seemingly busy with house chores, always keeps her child in the cradle in mind, Naama always keeps his lord in mind, hey Trilochan! **(Ramkali, Naam Dev Ji, 972)**

As you can conclude beyond any doubt, there is no special way to sing the praise of Waheguru, and no other act of charity or of sacrifice will please Him until it is for some noble cause as approved by the Guru. Of course, the company of the holy men has always been emphasized because that's where you develop love for Waheguru and have your doubts and questions answered. The environment in that gathering is full of praise for Waheguru, and according to Gurbani, Waheguru resides there. There are many holy shabads in Sri Guru Granth Sahib in which the importance of Sadhsangat (a gathering of holy men) has been emphasized.

- ———If you are looking for eternal comfort, attend a gathering of the holy men, oh my friend! This is the advice of the Guru. Only Waheguru's praise is sung in such a gathering, and that will emancipate you from the bonds of maya.————**(Basant M:5, 1182)**
- ———Everybody talks about going to paradise. I have no idea where that paradise is. ———— How can I explain to the people that the gathering of the holy men is the Paradise, oh Kabir! **(Gauri Kabir Ji, 325)**

Other than that any ritualistic way to recite the holy Gurbani is totally against the Teachings of Guru Sahiban, and should be totally disapproved. The Sharomani Gurduara Parbandhic Committee should put an immediate ban on all such claims." Bhai Sahib concluded. "Is there any other question?" Bhai Sahib asked after a pause.

Hearing no further question, Bhai Dalip Singh thanked the congregation and took his seat on the carpet. Bhai Kashmir Sing thanked Bhai Dalip Singh profusely for his informative lecture, and the congregation for their patience. The session was adjourned with the traditional slogan: Bolle so Nihal, Sat Sri Akal. Lungar was served soon after.

5

Are There Different Paths to Realise Waheguru?

"Waheguru Ji Ka Khalsa Waheguru Ji ki Fateh." Bhai Dalip Singh welcomed the congregation with his usual big smile after everybody had taken their seats on the carpet. The congregation responded to Bhai Sahib's salutation with equal enthusiasm.

"Are there any questions before I start on something new?" Bhai Dalip Singh asked.

"I've a question, if you don't mind." Bhai Harpal Singh said politely while rising.

"Please go ahead, Bhai Sahib." Bhai Dalip Singh signaled courteously.

"I've heard many times people saying that all religions lead to the same God - only paths are different. They maintain that religions are like rivers which merge into the same body of water - ocean - even though they follow different paths. I'm not very sure of that. Would you, please, clarify that for all of us?" Bhai Harpal Singh sat down.

"I'm enjoying this holy congregation very much. You folks ask excellent questions. This is an extremely important question, and I had plans to address this question in one of my discourses. Since you've asked this question, we'll discuss it today. Let me comment on the analogy of rivers and the ocean first. I would like to say that not all rivers end up in the ocean - some of them go only as far as a lake. And you may be surprised that a few never reach a large body of water - not even a lake. For example, Mojave river in Mojave desert in California reaches nowhere. It simply disappears in the desert. Dams have been built on many rivers now leaving the rives almost dry for most of the year. So, the river-ocean analogy may not be the best for comparison of religions." Bhai Dalip Singh said smilingly.

"Anyway, as with every question on theology, let's seek the answer to this question from Sri Guru Granth Sahib and find out what the holy Gurbani has to say on this issue.

As far as putting religious labels is concerned, Gurbani has no problem at all with that. One can call himself a Hindu, a Sikh, a Muslim, a Christian, a Buddhist or belonging to any other faith. Guru Sahiban request Waheguru for the well being of the whole humanity and for the salvation of all mankind no matter what their faith is.

- Oh merciful Waheguru! the world is burning (suffering) from the heat (burning desire for maya - discontentment, jealousy, wants etc.). **Please, salvage everybody no matter what their faith is (what church they go to)**. There's none other than Waheguru I can think of who is capable of forgiving. The True Guru demonstrates the real comfort if you contemplate Waheguru's Shabad, oh man! **(Sloak M:3, Bilawal ki Vaar, 853).**
- **Look after all humanity, and provide enough food and water for everybody** so that all misery and all poverty are eradicated, oh my Lord! **Sarang ki Vaar, M: 5, 1251)**

Everyday in our prayer, we pray to Waheguru for the well being of all humanity - not just for the Sikhs.

- (Guru) Nanak says that Waheguru's Naam leads to such a high spiritual level that the devotees pray for the well being of the whole humanity. **(Sikh Prayer)**

The fact that Sri Guru Granth Sahib contains compositions of holy men of many different faiths clearly shows that Gurbani does not care what religious label you put on yourself. However, all the holy men whose compositions are included in SGGS, profess the same fundamental principles to lead a good life and to realize Waheguru. Whether Guru Sahiban advised a Hindu, a Brahman, a Yogi, a Muslim or a Jain, the Teaching was always the same. **Let's first list the main Teachings of Guru Granth Sahib for the whole humanity.**

- There is only one God - Waheguru. Have an unshakable faith in Him. DO NOT worship any other god or goddess
- The objective of human life is to purify the soul by singing Waheguru's praise and leading a pious life as per the Teachings of the Guru so that it reunites with Waheguru. However, Waheguru **CANNOT be realized without Guru's Grace.** This is the most fundamental Principle of Guru Granth Sahib and has been reiterated again and again
- Do not try to gauge the limits of Waheguru, or His Creation
- Treat all human beings as equal
- Earn your livelihood by honest means and never lay claim to the belongings of others
- Develop a good moral character by controlling powerful urges of lust, rage, greed, possessiveness and conceit. A fickle mind under the influence of the above mentioned powerful urges can be controlled by connecting to Waheguru and by singing His praise through the recitation of Gurbani

- Do not believe in rituals and superstitions
- Do your best to achieve your noble goals against all odds, but accept the Will of Waheguru gracefully
- Be kind to everybody and help the needy
- Be forgiving and help the needy. Pray for the well being of everybody

Now let's find out what Guru Sahiban and the Bhagats (holy souls whose compositions have been included in Sri Guru Granth Sahib) have to advise people of all faiths. But before we do that, let me remind you that **according to Guru Granth Sahib, Hindu philosophy of worshiping and realizing God, includes the following.**

- Full faith in three gods - Brahma, Vishnu, and Shiva (Mahesh) - and their idol worship. In addition to these three gods, there are many other gods and goddesses, like Rama, Krishna, Ganesh, Hanuman, Durga, Luxmi, Kali, and many more whom they worship.
- There are also gods for almost every natural phenomenon, like, god of fire, of rain, of wind, of wealth, of intelligence and so on.
- Donations to the Brahmans - as much as one can afford including cash, gold, land, cows, and even women
- Pilgrimage of one or more of the 68 holy places in India.
- Full faith in caste system, and leading one's life according to the caste in which one is born, and following all the rituals associated with the caste
- Torturing your body in many different ways to please gods and goddesses, and to control your sensual pleasures. This could include standing on one foot for a long time, sitting in cold water in severe winter or sitting on ice, surrounding yourself

with fire on hot summer days, going on fast for many days, keeping your mouth shut for weeks or even months, and finally getting sawed off at Benares or trampled over by a huge chariot of Jagannath

- Performing many special rituals for the dead
- Following the custom of 'Sati' whereby widows were expected (even forced) to burn themselves on the pyre of their dead husbands

At the time of Guru Nanak Dev Ji, the major faith prevalent in northern India was that of Sidh Yogis. They were seen in large numbers everywhere in Punjab during winter. During summer, they went to the mountains.

The Sidh Yogis' path to realize God involved:

- Belief in Lord Shiva as their saviour. They worshiped God by reciting word 'Alakh Niranjan' which means formless power on which 'maya' has no effect. They focused their mind between the two eyebrows when reciting the Word.
- Leaving their home to live in jungles because staying at home got them involved in worldly attractions
- Staying unmarried all their lives, and performing some daily practices (rituals) to keep the internal parts of the body clean to control sensual desires. The practice included cleaning the nose and sinuses with a thread. Raising the air to the brain and holding it their for a long time. Cleaning the stomach by thrusting water in through the anus. Churning the intestines by sucking in and blowing out, and giving a rotatory motion to the stomach, etc.
- Covering the body with ash to look ugly with the belief that they will not be attractive to women
- Going from door to door for food, again with the belief that this brought humility in them and their

ego was subdued

- They carried a few trade marks of their faith which included saffron robes, big glass earrings, a quilt of many pieces of fabric of different colors, a wooden dish for food and alms, and a stick to ward off vices

Islam, another prevalent religion in India at the times of our Gurus and with ever increasing following, believed in one God and considered Muhammad Sahib as their savior. Their other beliefs include:

- Reciting holy hymns (praying) from the Koran five times a day at specific times. They call the prayer, 'Nivaj' or 'Namaj'. They always face Mecca when they offer nivaj.
- Every Muslim must go to Mecca (perform Haj) at least once in their life time. Mecca, in Saudi Arabia, is the birth place of Muhammad Sahib, and is their holiest shrine. While there, they are required to kiss the 'black stone' - part of a wall of Kaaba - and throw rocks on another wall, supposed to represent Satan.
- The Haj is not complete until they offer a sacrificial animal - a cow, a goat, a lamb etc. - to please Allah.
- They fast for a full month - called Ramadan or Ramzan - when they do not eat between the sun rise and the sun set. According to their belief, this practice purifies the mind
- They do not cremate their dead with the belief that a body that is burned suffers in hell. They also believe in the Judgement Day when all the dead will rise from their graves. A body that has been burned will not be able to rise
- Like Christians, they also believe in Satan as an

independent power who can force people to do bad deeds. They also believe in Hell and Heaven as special places where people are sent after the Judgement Day to be punished for their bad deeds or rewarded for their noble deeds.

- They believe that Islam is the only acceptable path to realize God. All other faiths are condemned as nonbelievers or infidels, and are unable to realize God.

Another religion prevalent at the time was **Jainism. Jains believe in nonviolence as the path to their salvation.** They are so overcome by this belief that they rarely bathe so that they do not kill or hurt water life. They walk in queues with one man leading the way who has a whisk in his hand to clear the path of all living beings. They uproot the hair from their heads so that no life (lice) will have a chance to develop. They never seem to be happy in life. They rather always seem to be depressed. Thus, their life style seems to be very unhealthy.

Even though there are scores of holy shabads in Sri Guru Granth Sahib which sre addressed to people of different faiths, but, let us first consider a few holy Shabads which address the whole humanity in general, and the **Hindus and the Yogis in particular**, and find out what the Teachings of Guru Granth Sahib are for all of us.

- ——— No matter how hard one tries, one cannot realize Waheguru through rituals. The only way to serve the Guru, and thus realizing Waheguru is through the Guru's Shabad. You can rid your *haumein* only by the Shabad whereby the sacred Naam will begin to reside in your heart. The best thing in this world to do is to internalize Guru's Shabad by which you can make Waheguru's Naam a permanent occupant of your heart. Without the

Shabad, everything else is darkness of attachment to worldly things. **(Parbhati M:1, Ashatpadian, 1342)**

- A man whose fast is **Waheguru's Naam**, and contentment is his pilgrimage; his concentration on Waheguru's Shabad is his cleanliness, kindness for others is his godliness, and forgiveness is his rosary, is the leader in Waheguru's Court. There are only a few such people who make noble life style their dhoti (a long cloth worn around the waist and the head), their attention in Waheguru's Naam their kitchen, their high character the tikka (mark on the forehead), and affectionate dealing their food. **(Sarang ki Vaar, Sloak M: 1, 1245)**
- **Only Waheguru is capable** of freeing the man from all worldly attachments (so, worship Him alone). No ritual or practice can help. So, I am seeking Your refuge, oh Waheguru! **(Bilawal M: 5, 815)**
- All other activities without **Waheguru's Naam** are useless, oh man! All the acts of meditation, self-discipline, and forced controlling of your sensual pleasures do not take you very far on the path of Waheguru. You are robbed of their credit only a short distance away. You have been busy in regular fasting and forcibly controlling your sensual desires, which carry insignificant value. The rules of the next world are completely different. Such activities are of no use there. **(Gauri Mala, M:5, 216)**
- Sing the praise of Waheguru with affection following Guru's Shabad, oh man! ——— Donning scarlet clothes and roaming in the world (that is what yogis do) will not get you salvation. No matter how many different things you try, you will not get contentment. **Only the people who are imbued in Waheguru's Naam get the really**

blissfulness. Without Waheguru's Naam, people suffer in the fire of *haumein.* **(Basant M: 3, 1175)**

- A person who worships Bhairon (a Hindu deity who is quite scary in looks) can, at best, achieve his looks of a devil, and a person who worships the goddess Seetla (the goddess of small pox) can, at best, be a donkey to spread dirt (the goddess rides a donkey). **But I wish for Waheguru alone. I will gladly forsake all the gods and the goddesses to get Waheguru.** A man who worships Lord Shiva by reciting his name, can at best, ride a bull and play on a small drum (that is what Shiv Ji does). Likewise, a man who worships the great goddess, Parbati, will be reborn as a woman.——— Naam Dev pleads that worship only Waheguru following the Teachings of the Guru, oh my friend! Because that is what even Geeta says. **(Raag Goand, Naam Dev Ji, 874)**
- You read religious books, studied the Vedas and did all the required rituals of the Sidh yogis, but could not rid yourself of the five demons (lust , rage, greed, attachment, and conceit), oh my friend! On the other hand, your ego became much bigger. I have done all these things, but you cannot realize Waheguru like this, my dear! I finally took refuge at Waheguru's doorsteps and begged Him for wisdom to realize Waheguru. Even if you stayed mute, ate food held in your hands only, and stayed naked in the jungle. Even if you visited all the holy places, and roamed the whole earth, you still will not have full faith in Waheguru. Even if you gave gold, even your wife, high quality horses and elephants in charity, you will not realize Waheguru. ——— **The only way to realize Waheguru is to sing His praise in the company of holy men because this is the best of all the**

efforts. But only those who are predestined by Waheguru, do so. ——— **(Sorith M: 5, Ashatpadian, 641- 42)**

- Make contentment your earrings and hard labor the dish to receive alms (earn your own living by honest means), oh yogi! Focus your mind on Waheguru and use that as ash to cover your body. Remembering death all the time should be your quilt, and keeping your body protected from sensual pleasures should be your code of ethics, and your faith in your efforts should be your stick. If you treat all human beings the same, then that is the best class of the Yoga faith. A person who can control his mind is capable of controlling the whole world. That is the best yoga. Now, salute Waheguru Who is the origin of everything, Who is unblemished, has no beginning, is unperishable and is never changing throughout all the yugas. That is the way to realize Waheguru. **(Jap Ji, M:1)**

As you can clearly see, in all of the above holy Shabads, Guru Sahiban have disapproved any approach to realizing Waheguru other than singing His praise using Guru's Shabad. This also enables you to control your sensual pleasures, and free yourself from all the bonds of maya. **There are many shabads that point out the weaknesses of the practices followed by our Hindu and Muslim brothers to realize Waheguru.** Pay attention to the following holy Shabad by Naam Dev Ji.

- I, Naama, saw God (was one with Him) today (in this life) oh, Pundit! Let me explain why you cannot realize Him, oh fool! You recite holy Gayatari (a Hindu hymn) to achieve salvation, but, at the same time you also believe that she was cursed for some reason to be a cow and was kicked out of Paradise and sent to the earth. When she was grazing in a farmer's field, he hit her so hard that she became lame and was walking on three legs. You worship Lord Shiva, but, at the same time you also maintain that he cursed the son of his host to die because the Lord did not like his (the host's) food. You say less than respectful things about your other god - Rama - who fought with Ravana because he had abducted Lord Rama's wife, Seeta. For lack of real knowledge, the Hindu is blind of both eyes and the Muslim is blind of one eye. The person who has acquired complete Divine knowledge is wiser than both. The Hindu worships statues in the temples and the Muslim in Mosque (Kaaba), but Naam Dev worships the all powerful Lord who resides neither in the statues nor in the Mosque. **(Goand Naam Dev Ji, 874)**

Is it possible that our Hindu brothers ridicule their gods because they may not be real and may only be mythical? Gurbani maintains that there are countless Brahmas, Vishnus, Shivas, goddess Durgas and so on, in the Court of Waheguru. This will imply that they are mythical only. Even if they are real, they carry no significance because there are not just one of each, rather there are millions of them.

- There are countless gases, countless water-like liquids, and countless types of fire. **There are countless Krishnas and Shivas. There are countless Brahmas** who are "creating" bodies of different colors, shapes and dresses. ——— **(Jap Ji Sahib)**
- There are millions of suns in Waheguru's creation who light up the universe. There are millions of Shivas and millions of Kailash mountains (the residing place of Lord Shiva). There are millions of goddess Durga who apply massage to Waheguru. There are millions of Brahmas who utter Vedas.

But I have no business with any of these gods or goddesses. I wish for Your Naam only, oh Waheguru! —— (Bhaion Kabir Ji, 1162)

Not only that there are millions of each type of god and goddess, but, they are also unclean and suffer mentally because like anybody else, they are victims of *haumein*.

- The suffering caused by *haumein* is a serious and a bad disease, oh Nanak! When I look around in the world, I see people suffering from this disease everywhere. **Only those are healthy who are connected to Waheguru through the Guru's Shabad by Waheguru's grace.** Haumein is so powerful that the gods of wind, of water and of fire, are all sick, and so is mother earth. It does not end there, **being in the grip of haumein, even Brahma, Vishnu, and Shiva are sick. ——— (Bhairon, Ashatpadian, M: 1, 1153)**
- Brahma is unclean and so is god Inder. The sun and the moon which provide light to the earth, are unclean. (The sun and the moon are considered and worshiped as gods by the Hindus). The whole world is unclean and impure. **Only boundless Waheguru is pure and clean.** ———(Only a clean object can make you clean. How can an unclean substance make you clean?) **(Bhairon Kabir Ji, 1158)**

As you can see clearly from these two holy Shabads, the topmost gods - Brahma, Vishnu and Shiva - are themselves victims of haumein. So, how can they relieve you from the clutches of *haumein*, and how can you be one with Waheguru? Only singing the praise of Waheguru can rid you of your haumein, and can you be one with Waheguru. In other words, the only path to unite with Waheguru is to worship Him following Guru's Word (Gurbani)

There are many hymns which are addressed to different faiths teaching them how to realize Waheguru. And as we will see, they too, say exactly the same thing no matter what the faith is.

- If you want to realize Allah, make kindness your mosque, contentment your mat, and honest earnings your Koran, oh my Mussulman brother! Shielding yourself from vices should be the circumcision, and pleasant nature your fasting. You are a Mussulman only, if you follow this recipe High character should be the Kaaba, Allah your guru, and good deeds your nivaj. This is the kind of rosary (the life style discussed above) that is approved by Allah, and you will be honoured in the Court of Waheguru. **(Maajh ki Vaar, Sloak M: 1, 140)**
- Our Mussulman brothers offer five nivajes a day at five different times, and each has its own name. For a real Mussulman, the first nivaj should be his truthful living. Honest earning should be the second nivaj, and praying for the well being of all humanity should be the third nivaj. Keeping your thoughts and your mind pure should be the the fourth nivaj, and singing the praise of Allah should be the fifth nivaj. Buillding high character should be the final prayer. You are a real Mussulman only if you follow these nivajes, otherwise it is all a show off which does not earn you any respect (in this world or in Allah's Court). **(Maajh ki Vaar, Sloak M: 1, 141)**

These two holy Shabads are addressed to our Muslim brothers. But when you compare the teachings of Guru Nanak Dev Ji here in these two hymns to the list of teachings of Sri Guru Granth Sahib, you can see the that they are exactly the same. There are many more holy shabads in SGGS which teach the same path to realize Waheguru again and again no matter what your faith is. In the following two holy Shabads, Guru Sahiban have made it clear without the slightest doubt that there is only one path to realize Waheguru, and there has always been only one and the same path.

- ———The perfect Guru has revealed that the only True Knowledge is praise of Waheguru Who does not need any support. The only real passport to reach Him is the recitation of His word as revealed by the Guru (Gurbani). One should sing only His praise. ————**(Basant M:1, Ashatpadian, 1188)**
- Waheguru is the only likable Master and the Provider, oh Nanak! His doorstep is the real dwelling for all of us. **The Guru-Ladder is the only straight path that leads to the doorstep of Waheguru.** Reciting Waheguru's Naam (using Guru's Shabad) is the source of all comforts.——— **(Malhar ki Vaar, Sloak M: 1, 1279)**
- You can read the Vedas, the books of the Western faiths (the Bible, Torah etc.) the Simritis, and any other religious book, you cannot find salvation. But, if you recite the Naam of Waheguru following the Guru, you will enjoy a sacred respect. **The teaching for all the four major castes - Brahman, Khattri, Vaish, and the Untouchables - is the same that Waheguru resides in every human heart, but can be realized only by worshiping Waheguru's Naam through the Guru. (Suhi M: 5, 747)**
- The Sidh yogis claim that their path is sweet and is the only path to realize Waheguru. There is no other path like theirs. The shaven- headed Jains and the one-wordy recluses of Gosaeen faith who utter 'undescribable, undescribable' claim that they are the only ones who have achieved success. But, they are completely blind and misguided because

they have forgotten Waheguru. ————The whole world is deluded into using outside symbols only as the right path to realize Waheguru. The pundits, the skilled, the chivalrous, the philanthropist, and the like, all claim to be supreme because their's is the only right path. But only the ones who are guided by Waheguru Himself realize that worshiping Waheguru following Guru's word is the only real path to be one with Him because that is the only way to get rid of haumein. ———
—(Gauri Kabir Ji, 334)

These last holy Shabads prove unequivocally that **there is only one way to realize Waheguru, and that is internalizing Waheguru's Naam following the advice of the Guru and singing His praise using Guru's Shabad. It does not matter what faith you belong to or what your religion is.** It has to be that way because there is only one Waheguru and the requirement to be one with Him cannot be different for different people. **Since the objective for all us is the same - to realize Waheguru - and the requirement is the same (to get rid of our haumein to cleanse our bodies which can be done only by acting on the advice of the Guru), how can the paths be different? So. there has to be only one path.** That 's why Guru Arjun Dev Ji declares in no uncertain way that He is neither Hindu nor Mussulman, and is a believer of only one ubiquitous Power - Waheguru.

- I have severed all the spiritual relations with Hinduism and Islam, both. I believe only in one Lord whom Hindus call Gosaeen and the Muslims, Allah. Unlike Hindus, I have no faith in undertaking fasts, and unlike Muslims I do not fast for the whole month of Ramzan. I worship only one Waheguru Who saves everybody at the end. ——
— I am neither a Hindu nor a Mussulman.———
(Bhairon M: 5, 1136)

If there were another major religion in India at the time, Guru Sahib would have said exactly the same thing about that religion too that He does not belong to that either. The point is that there is only one path to realize Waheguru."

Bhai Dalip Singh gave his final analysis fully supported by the holy Gurbani.

"Are there any questions?" Bhai Sahib asked after a brief pause.

Nobody had a question. They seemed completely satisfied. Bhai Kashmir Singh thanked Bhai Dalip Singh richly for his analysis, and the congregation for their patient listening.

The congregation left for the Langar after the daily slogan: Waheguru Ji ka Khalsa, Waheguru Ji ki Fateh.

6

Pilgrimage and Charity: Bibi Rajni

"Waheguru Ji ka Khalsa, Waheguru Ji ki Fateh". Bhai Dalip Singh greeted the congregation with his usual smile. The gathering responded to the salutation with a loud roar.

"Does anyone have any questions before we start the day?" Bhai Sahib asked.

"Yes, Bhai Sahib, I have one, if you don't mind." Bhai Aman Deep Singh, a young student, showed interest.

"Please, go ahead, Bhai Sahib." Bhai Dalip Singh signalled affectionately.

"Some religions put a great emphasis on pilgrimage and charity. How important are they in Gurmat? Would you please, give your thoughts on that?" Bhai Aman Deep Singh asked.

"This is a very good question, young man. And I'm sure most of you would like to know more about pilgrimage and charity. Spiritual rewards for most of the actions depend upon the motives behind them. If the motives are selfish to boost your ego or to achieve some kind of worldly gain, there is absolutely no spiritual gain in pilgrimage or even in charity. But, if you could acquire some Divine Knowledge and develop devotion for Waheguru, and help the needy, pilgrimage and charity could be useful. But, that happens very rarely. To give you an example of such rare opportunities, consider the visits of Guru Nanak Sahib and Guru Tegh Bahadur Sahib to the perceived holy places when They visited them to disseminate Divine Knowledge. The people, who were lucky enough to listen to the Teachings of Guru Sahiban at the 'holy' places, made big spiritual gains. Similarly, if some holy saint is delivering Divine Message at some 'holy' place, the listeners could gain a lot. But, normally, people undertake pilgrimage due to mistaken beliefs that a visit to a perceived holy place, or a dip in perceived holy waters washes their sins away, and they become eligible to go to paradise after death. Such visits to holy places are, in fact, more harmful than useful because as Guru Sahiban have explained, the pilgrims become conceited about their pilgrimage and complacent about the perceived results. They believe that now their sins have been washed away and they don't need to do any other noble deed to achieve salvation. In fact, they are more likely to commit bad deeds now because of the false hope that they can again undertake pilgrimage to wash their sins away.

As far as charitable donations are concerned, they are useful in spiritual advancement only if they meet the following conditions:

(a) They are given out of your honestly earned income. If someone makes one million rupees by cheating, stealing, or robbing others of their earnings, and then donates two hundred thousand rupees out of that, he is still a big cheat in Waheguru's eyes, and gains no spiritual advancement. He is cheating again because not only his donations are not from his honest income, but also because he wants to be a well known philanthropist among people. This is an act rooted purely in ego no matter how large a donation is.

(b) The recipient of the donations must be a genuinely needy individual or organization. If you are making donations to rich people so that you could get something in return, the donations carry no weight in Waheguru's Court. Some people make contributions to people in power so that they could win their favours. Such contributions are not acceptable donations according to Guru Granth Sahib.

(c) Even if the donations are given to the rightful needy people, and they come from your honestly earned income, they are still not acceptable if there is ego involved, and you are giving them because you want to earn the respect of people as a donor. To be acceptable to Waheguru, the donations must come from your honestly earned income, must be given to the needy, and there must not be any personal interest or ego involved.

The following few holy Shabads from among the hundreds appearing on the two subjects in Guru Granth Sahib, clarify the point.

- **Pilgrimage, hard self-discipline, kindness to animals, and charitable donations are worth very little, if at all, in Waheguru's Court.** A person, who listens to the Guru's Teachings with full dedication and then acts on them gladly and bears love for Waheguru, attains a high spiritual level. His inner-self becomes a place of pilgrimage where he bathes and washes away the filth of all sins. **(Jap Ji, M:1)**
- ————If I cut my body into extremely small pieces, and burn each piece individually to please Waheguru; if I make my body and my soul firewood to be burned in *heavn* (a ritual performed by Hindus to please gods where they keep a fire going by burning butter oil while rendering hymns from the Vedas), and I do this everyday; and if I perform

millions of other such rituals, none can come even close to reciting Waheguru's Naam. ———— If I donate forts of gold, many top class horses and elephants, donate land and many cows to please Waheguru, He is not pleased because all these donations will enhance my ego. ———— **The best thing to do to please Waheguru is to worship Him by reciting Guru's Shabad and acting on it.————(Siri Raag, M: 1, Ashatpadian, 62)**

- ————People perform millions of rituals to please Waheguru, but, He is not pleased by any of such rituals. Some people go mute for very long periods of time while some others use only their hands rather than dishes to hold food and eat it. Some others wander naked in forests, while some others undertake pilgrimage of holy places. Some are just travelling all over the earth, but, no such ritual is able to win Waheguru's approval.————Some people donate gold, their wives, topnotch horses and elephants, food, clothing and land to realize Waheguru, but, fail to please Him. ————The only way to realize Waheguru is to sing His praise in the company of holy men. But, only the blessed, who are destined to do so because of their noble deeds in their previous incarnation, worship Waheguru. ——— **(Sorith M: 5, Ashatpadian, 641)**
- All the recognized religious rituals other than worshipping Waheguru are useless, oh my friends! The recitation of some *mantras* to please gods, the self infliction, or the tough acts of hard self-discipline carry no weight in Waheguru's Court, and your soul is stripped of them even before it is taken to Waheguru.————**Undertaking of pilgrimage of holy places and bathing in perceived holy waters** or travelling all over the earth because

you have renounced the world, are not recognized in Waheguru's Court. No such effort is of any value there. All such efforts lead only to personal satisfaction that you are a 'religious' person. **(Gauri M: 5, 216)**

- Quit all the acts of deceit, and recite Waheguru's Naam all the time, oh my dishonest mind! Reciting gods' mantras in Benares, killing yourself by suspending yourself upside down at some holy place, or self immolation to purify your soul, don't even come close to Waheguru's Naam. Even performing yags of horses or donating gold secretly to religious charities have no worth in comparison to Waheguru's Naam. ———Even if you donate thousands of cows in charity at holy places on the banks of the Ganges, Godavri, or Gomti, you get very little reward, if at all, in comparison to reciting Waheguru's Naam. ———— **(Ramkali Naam Dev Ji, 973)**
- Being able to make your heart a home for Waheguru is equivalent to taking baths at millions of holy places and donating millions of rupees in religious charities. Singing the praise of Waheguru purifies you all over. Taking Guru's refuge washes away all the sins. Reciting Waheguru's Naam with your tongue is million times better than tough self-infliction for self-discipline or achieving some other profitable objectives. ————**(Gauri M: 5, 202)**
- Pilgrimage to holy places, fasting for self-discipline, and charitable donations, are all useless in the path of spiritual advancement, and are like the bath of an elephant (because soon after the bath, the elephant covers himself with mud or dirt), oh Nanak! All such acts of perceived spirituality lead to conceit and ego. **(Sloak M: 9, 1428)**

- You acquire mental peace only by reciting Waheguru's Naam with affection. Worshipping gods, undertaking fasting, wearing religious symbols, pilgrimage to holy places, making expensive donations, or just uttering sweet words without real devotion to Waheguru, do not earn Waheguru's approval for you, oh man! ———— —— **(Dhanasari M:5, 674)**
- ————————Waheguru is not pleased by pilgrimage even if you visit holy places completely naked. He is not pleased by your donations either. He is not pleased even if you meditate in remote isolated places. ———— He is pleased only if you worship Him selflessly with dedication. **(Sarang ki Vaar, Sloak M:1, 1237)**

All these holy Shabads leave no doubt that any perceived religious rituals including pilgrimages to holy places and donations to religious charities carry no value (or very little, if at all) for spiritual advancement. They may even be harmful because they boost people's ego. Only reciting Waheguru's Naam with full devotion brings you closer to Waheguru. Of course, as discussed earlier, your donations to the needy are rewarded if they are given without any expected return, and are in the name of Waheguru." Bhai Dalip Singh explained.

Darbar Sahib (Harmander Sahib), Amritsar

"Are there other questions?" Bhai Sahib asked after a brief pause.

"What about a visit to Darbar Sahib, Amritsar and a dip in the holy Sarovar, Bhai Sahib? Isn't that considered a worthy cause?" Bhai Bikram Jit Singh asked. He seemed a little confused.

"Darbar Sahib Amritsar is the centre of Sikhism, and the holiest place of Sikhs in present India. We are all attached very emotionally to the holy place and it is much different and holier than any other perceived holy place in India because of the Divine Light of the holy Sri Guru Granth Sahib there, and because of the recitation of the immortal Gurbani and singing the praise of Waheguru there for almost eighteen hours a day. Darbar Sahib has also a special reverence for the Sikhs because the holy place was built personally by three Guru Sahiban - Guru Ram Das Ji, Guru Arjun Dev Ji and Guru Har Gobind Sahib Ji - Who also held holy congregations there for a long time. However, even though I don't want to hurt anybody's feelings, but I'm afraid, my response is going to be the same as for any other place of pilgrimage or any other ritual. It is the objective behind your visit and what you do when you are there which is important and not just the visit itself. Remember, thefts and other crimes and sins like discrimination, and women teasing are still committed by some unscrupulous individuals at Darbar Sahib. Such sinners do not make any spiritual advancement there. In fact, they fall down even further from their present spiritual level because of their shameful acts. Also, don't forget that evil Mannu, the highly infamous governor of Lahore, also stayed at Harmander Sahib for several weeks, and committed evil acts of drinking, smoking and dances by prostitutes, thereby desecrating the holy place. Do you think the evil governor gained anything spiritually by being there while he was committing all sorts of evil things?

Then there are people who make money by selling their services within the Darbar Sahib Complex. No matter how many times they bathe there, would they make any spiritual gains if they did not listen to Gurbani with devotion?

The only way to gain spiritual advancement is If you go there, listen to the holy Gurbani, and start moulding your life according to the Guru's Teachings. But if you are there, and your mind is still wandering around worldly attractions, you do not gain anything even if you spend a lot of time there and bathe in the holy Sarovar several times a day.

The situation is no different when Guru Sahiban were enlightening the world in human bodies and millions of people visited them. Not everybody gained spiritually from their visits. Guru Sahiban have written several times that a *maya*-minded man does not gain anything even in the company of the holy Guru because he is always thinking about *maya,* and how to advance his selfish interests. No place of pilgrimage is holier than the Guru Himself. So, if a person is unable to gain anything spiritually from the Guru, where else can he improve? The following few holy Shabads explain the point.

- Hypocritical people cannot spend any time in Guru's company because the Guru promotes high moral values and truthfulness which are not to the liking of the maya-minded people who feel out of place there. They somehow force themselves to spend a little time in Guru's company, but soon rush to join the company of other non-devoted (maya-minded) people. ————The non-devoted enjoy the company of like-minded people while the Sikhs spend time in Guru's company. **(Gauri ki Vaar, M:4, Pauri, 314)**
- Even if the non-devoted (money-minded) people go to bow before the Guru, they are still dishonest at heart and think about *maya* all the time. When the Guru calls the Sikhs to be alert, like a heron, they too pretend to be devoted and join the Sikhs in the congregation. However, they don't have their mental food there, so like the sheep, they go somewhere else for their food. But, at the time of judgement they are taken apart even though they try to hide among the Sikhs and be a part of the religious congregation. They are readily recognized because the Sikhs have the Guru residing in their hearts while *maya* houses the hearts of the money-minded people. **(Gauri ki Vaar, Sloak M: 4, 312)**

- How can a person who is spiteful of the Guru find salvation? Such a person is bound to go to hell. Even if he bathes in all the sixty eight holy waters and worships all the twelve *Shivalings;* and even if he digs wells and pools of water for needy people, he loses all the credit if he bears malice for the Guru. If such a malicious person goes to Kurukshetra during solar eclipse to take a bath in the perceived holy pool, and donates his wife along with the jewellery to the Brahmans, he gets no reward and loses the credit of all his efforts. ——————**(Goand Ravi Das Ji, 875)**
- ————You cannot teach anything positive to malicious people. You should stay away from people who have been deprived of His worship by Waheguru. Such people never listen to Waheguru's praise, nor do they ever sing it. However, they can talk enough even to bring down the sky. They don't help the needy even with a drop of water, but are eager to denounce the ones who provide a full river of water. —————— They always plan immoral activities. ————Kabir is ashamed of their behaviour. **(Gauri Cheti Kabir Ji, 332)**

There are many more holy shabads like these which clearly illuminate that a non-devoted and maya-minded person does not gain anything spiritually by going to the Guru, let alone a holy place. So, if a person goes to Darbar Sahib Amritsar and bathes in the holy Sarovar, his sins are not automatically washed away. A person has to listen to the Guru's Teachings with devotion and start acting upon them to change his life. His sins will be washed away over time only if he is able to change his life to be honest and recites Waheguru's Naam regularly with devotion. Otherwise, you don't gain much." Bhai Sahib concluded.

"That makes perfect sense, Bhai Sahib. But we recite a holy shabad written by Guru Arjun Dev ji that if we bathe in the holy sarovar of Guru Ram Das Ji, all our sins are washed away. How do you explain that, Bhai Sahib?" Bibi Kulwant Kaur asked.

"That's an excellent question, Bibi Ji. But the holy Shabad does NOT mean what most people think it does. Also, the wording of the shabad is not 'Guru Ram Das Ji's Sarovar', it is 'Ramdas Sarovar', which is very different from Guru Ram Das Ji's Sarovar as we interpret it. 'Ramdas', as used in this holy Shabad, is not a proper name, and is not used for Guru Ram Das Ji. It is an adjective, and means devotees of Waheguru or noble souls atuned to Waheguru - not that Guru Ram Das Ji was not atuned to Waheguru. 'Ramdas sarovar' means a holy gathering of the devotees of Waheguru (Sadh Sangat). The term has been used by Guru Arjun Dev Ji in some other Shabads in which the meaning becomes very clear. Let's listen to a few of those holy shabads.

- Maya-gripped man thinks that his body is going to last for ever and has continuous attachment with it. But as long as the man is attached to his son, his wife, and his family, he has the noose of attachment around his neck, and cannot be a ramdas (devotee of Waheguru). ————**(Gauri Guareri, M; 5, 179)**
- I recite 'Guru, Guru and Waheguru, Waheguru' with my tongue only, but, have no knowledge of worshipping Waheguru, my friends! Because people hear me reciting 'Waheguru', they think that I am a devotee of Waheguru, and they have started to call me a ramdas (devotee of Waheguru). Now, protect my dignity and bless me with the gift of Your Naam, oh Waheguru! ———— **(Sorith M: 5, 612)**

- The lazy Pundit recites the Vedas loudly only to earn his living. ——— Some other people wear religious robes and symbols as a show off only to earn their living. They undertake fasting, perform rituals with great regularity and wear bells around their ankles to look like a ramdas (a devotee of Waheguru).——— **(Maru M:5, 1003)**
- I have visited all places, but, none of them is as good as you are (oh gathering of the holy men)! You look adorned because Waheguru Himself has created you. The boundless and the unrivalled city of ramdas pur (the gathering of the devotees of Waheguru) is having a huge population (of noble qualities). Nanak says that all the filth of the unholy deeds or thoughts is washed away by taking a dip in the **sarovar of ramdases** (The Naam - liquid of immortality produced by singing Waheguru's praise in the company of holy men). **(Funhe M: 5, 1361-2)**
- An individual is a true ramdas (devotee of Waheguru) if his heart has become a place for Waheguru to reside. ——— Seemingly living in the family, such a ramdas is unattached to the everything. **(Gauri Sukhmani, M:5, 274-5)**

It is perfectly clear from these holy shabads that the word 'ramdas' as used in these and other shabads does not refer to the Revered Fourth Guru. It means the bhagats (devotees) of Waheguru. As a consequence, even though the Sarovar of Darbar Sahib at Amritsar is extremely holy for the Sikhs, the sarovar referred to in the holy Shabad in question, does not mean the Sarovar of Darbar Sahib. It means the Naam - liquid of immortality produced in the company of the holy men when they sing the praise of Waheguru. The meaning will become perfectly clear when we discuss the whole holy Shabad by the Fifth Master.

- An individual who saves all his good qualities (from being destroyed by evil actions or impious thoughts) by acting on Guru's advice, wins Waheguru's approval and is blessed with all comforts and everlasting peace of mind. All the sins of the individuals who bathe in the sarovar of ramdases (in the Naam - liquid of immortality in the company of the holy men) are washed away. By taking such a bath, their minds become perfectly clean. But all this happens only with the grace of the Guru. **The filth of all evil deeds is washed away in the company of the holy men** and Waheguru becomes their supporter. Oh Nanak! whoever sings the praise of Waheguru in the (sarovar of ramdases) is able to realize Waheguru, Who is the creator of the whole universe and Who is omnipresent. **(Sorith M:5, 625)**

As you can notice from the holy hymn, Guru Sahib has made the meaning of the 'sarovar of ramdases' perfectly clear in second last sentence where He says that the filth of all evil deeds is washed away in the company of holy men. **So, clearly, it is the company of holy men and not the pool of water at Darbar Sahib, Amritsar, where sins can be washed away. Also the emphasis is on singing praise of Waheguru and to follow the Teachings of the Guru.** The importance of Sadh Sangat in realizing Waheguru has been emphasized over and over again in Guru Granth Sahib. Only a few such Shabads will be quoted as follows.

- ————A man can cleanse his unholy thoughts in the company of the Guru, oh my friend! Like wise, a filthy man can become holy. **One can wash away all his sins by taking a dip in the sarovar of ramdases. If we sing the praise of Waheguru in the company of the holy men** everyday, and thus keeping the Teachings of the Perfect Guru alive in our heart, we can achieve anything we wish for.——————— **(Sorith M:5, 624)**

- ————The sarovar of ramdases is very holy, oh devotees! Whoever takes a dip in this sarovar, finds salvation not only just for himself, but also for the members of his family of many generations. ————Whoever takes a dip in the sarovar of holy people, attains the highest level of spirituality. **By worshipping Waheguru (in the company of the holy men)**, an individual is able to break the cycle of death and rebirth.————**(Sorith M:5, 623)**
- Everybody talks about going to paradise, but I have no idea where the paradise is! These people have been unable to unravel themselves, but, talk about the paradise a lot. ————Kabir says how can I explain to these people that there is no paradise other than the company of holy men **(where Waheguru's praise is sung). (Bhairon Kabir Ji, 1161)**
- ————Remember Waheguru all the time, oh my mind! Watch out, lest you forget him because of your involvement in *maya.* But, you can realize Waheguru only with the grace of the Guru. So, take refuge of the Guru. ————But you cannot have access to the Guru without an honest devotion, and you do not develop affection for Waheguru without predetermined fate. **Likewise, without your predetermined fate, you cannot attend the company of holy men where you can realize Waheguru.** All this happens with the grace of Waheguru only ———— **(Basant Hindole M: 1, 1171)**
- Without the Naam of Waheguru, all the worldly materials are tasteless, oh my friends! Only praise

> of Waheguru provides the real taste of (spiritual) life. One must sing praise of Waheguru alone, and an individual who does it, feels highly blissful and feels as if Divine music is playing in his heart all the time.———**But Waheguru's praise can be sung best in the company of the holy men only.——————(Sarang M:5, 1219)**

These holy Shabads leave no doubt that 'the Sarovar of ramdases' refers to the holy congregation of the devotees and not to the Sarovar at Harmander Sahib in Amritsar. Let me emphasize one more time that I am NOT downplaying the importance of the holy Sarovar at Harmander Sahib. That sarovar has a special significance as discussed earlier and deserves our utmost reverence. I'm only saying that in the holy Shabads (hymns) just discussed, the sarovar of ramdases refers to the gathering of holy men where Waheguru's praise is sung. I hope I have made my point clear. Are there other questions?" Bhai Dalip Singh provided another opportunity to seek clarification.

Bibi Rajni (The Dukhbhanjani Berry)

"Your rationale is very plausible, Bhai Sahib, and makes complete sense. But there's a story connected to the holiness of the Sarovar at Harmander Sahib where a leper was cured completely of his leprosy after he took a dip in the holy Sarovar. I'm talking about the story of Bibi Rajni which is said to have happened at the time of Guru Amar Das Ji or Guru Ram Das Ji. Would you, kindly, examine that story too?" Bhai Bikram Jit Singh asked.

"You're absolutely right, Bhai Sahib. This story does need examination, and we sure will examine this. I'm very thankful to you for asking this question." Bhai Dalip Singh was pleased with the question.

"In case some of you have not heard the folk story of

Bibi Rajni, she was the youngest of the seven daughters of a big landlord, Duni Chand, of Patti, about 55 km from Amritsar. As per the story, her father got really irate with her because unlike her sisters who wanted to please their father to win his favours, Rajni did not acknowledge that her father was the provider of all her needs. She believed that it was Waheguru who looks after the needs of everybody. To teach her a 'lesson', her father married Rajni to a leper who was also lame. Rajni accepted the Will of Waheguru, put her husband in a basket, and walked to a village near Amritsar while carrying her husband on her head all the way. She laid down the basket with her husband inside it, near a small pond, and herself went to beg for food in the nearby village. On returning, she found a handsome young man sitting on the basket with no trace of her leper husband. On being questioned, the handsome young man convinced her that he was her husband indeed who had been cured by the water in the pond. He told her how he had seen a couple of crows changing into swans when they took a dip in the pond. So, he did the same, and to his great amazement, he was cured of his disease. That's the pond where the holy Sarovar (pool of water) of Harmander Sahib is radiating its fragrance now." Bhai Dalip Singh narrated the story very briefly.

"Now let's examine it. Most of the Sikhs are delighted to hear the story because the leper got cured by the water in the pond which is now the holy Sarovar at Amritsar. But, even without discussing the spiritual flaws and their incongruence (negative implications) with the Principles of Gurmat, the story is rife with other flaws as follows:

- It is highly unlikely for her father to have Rajni Ji married to a leper, not because some people won't do it, but, because of the fear of exposure of his own evil nature. Everybody would have cursed him for such a big and unjust punishment - and for what reason? Innocence?

- Patti is about 55 km from Darbar Sahib and the area in between was very thinly populated those days. The city of Tarn Taran came into existence later and so did the city of Amritsar. There was not even a dirt road between Patti and the present city of Amritsar, and travelling was very unsafe even for men, let alone young pretty girls. Human thugs aside, the journey was also very unsafe due to carnivores in the jungle through which she had to pass. Moreover, why would Bibi Ji go that far when there was no known refuge there at the time? Did she go there to find some job or what?
- Carrying such a heavy load on the head over such a long journey (55 km) for a pampered and delicate young girl who was raised in luxury was almost an impossible task.
- The area along the banks of Beas River was comparatively more thickly populated. Khadoor Sahib and Goindwal Sahib were well known places those days in Patti area because of the Second and the Third Guru Sahiban Who lived there and Whose fame had spread far and near. Also Patti was much closer to both Khadoor Sahib and Goindwal Sahib than Amritsar which did not even exit then. It is highly unlikely that Bibi Rajni had not heard about the Divine Guru, Amar Das Ji. Supposing she had not heard about the kind Third Guru, she would still have earned many sympathisers who would have guided her to go to Guru Amar Das Ji in Goindwal. **What other place could be better to go for help than Goindwal Sahib where the perfect Guru, Amar Das Ji (or Guru Ram Das Ji in case Guru Amar Das Ji had left this mortal world) was radiating the Divine Light and showering love on the needy like Bibi Ji?**
- There were two villages - Tung and Sultanwind -

close to the pond where Bibi Ji could have gone for food. But each was more than 5 km away and Sultanwind was on her way from Patti to the pond. Two serious questions arise. First, she should have hit Sultanwind before she could have reached the pond. Why did she overshoot the village and then went back to it? **Second, but more important, was it safe to leave her defenceless invalid husband that far away from population in a deserted place in the bush where there was a big risk of being attacked by carnivores who were there in plenty those days? Did she do that on purpose!**

- Begging for living is strictly disapproved in Gurmat. When Bibi Ji had such a deep faith in Waheguru as the provider, why would she go begging? She should have settled down in some safe place and waited for Waheguru to help her." Bhai Sahib discussed some very valid weaknesses in the story.

"Now, if we discuss the story from spiritual aspects, it has so many flaws and serious negative implications that our leaders should be shocked and ashamed that they are still promoting it." Bhai Dalip Singh became a little emotional now. He took a few sips of water before continuing.

"The story claims that the crows turned into swans because there was amrit (liquid of immortality) in the pond. Now, I've a few simple questions about this claim as follows:

- First, Gurbani does **NOT** believe in any other amrit than Waheguru's Naam because only Waheguru's Naam can make you immortal.
- Nanak says (Waheguru's Naam) is the only Amrit . There is no other Amrit. (Sarang ki Vaar, Sloak M:2, 1238)
- Waheguru's Naam is the Amrit and is the source of all comforts. Gather together my friends, and

drink this Amrit.————(Gauri ki Vaar, Pauri, M:5, 318)

- **Wonderful! Wonderful! is the True Master (Waheguru) Whose Naam is Amrit. Those who serve Waheguru are rewarded. I wish to offer my life to serve them.———— (Gujri ki Vaar, Sloak M:3, 515)**
- **Amrit is falling all the time, but, only the lucky ones with awareness realize that. Those who have recognized by the grace of the Guru, house the Amrit in their hearts. ———— Amrit is Waheguru's Naam and falls by His kindness. — ————Malhar ki Vaar, Sloak M:3, 1281-82)**
- ————Your Naam is the Amrit, oh Waheguru! Only that individual is living a moral life who worships Your Naam. An individual who receives this Amrit by Your grace, leads a pious and clean life. ————(Sorith M:5, 616)

There are many more holy Shabads like these which teach us that only Waheguru's Naam is Amrit, and no other substance can be amrit. **So, there could not have been any amrit in the pond.** But let's believe for a second that there was some kind of amrit there. That raises the following questions.

- By definition, amrit is a liquid that will make people (or may be all living beings) immortal. **But in this case the crows are not said to have become immortal, they turned into swans! Is that how Waheguru creates swans?** At the same time that amrit had a very different effect on the leper. Even though he was cured of leprosy, he remained a human being and did not turn into some fairy or cherub! What kind of amrit was that?
- If the crows did get turned into swans, they are birds of water. They should have stayed in the

pond, especially when the water of the pond was so wonderful. Why did the swan-turned crows leave the pond as soon as they got turned? Did they leave to tell other crows of the secret?

- What is the intended lesson to learn from the story? I suppose the story is intended to affirm faith in Waheguru. The young Bibi had a strong faith in Waheguru, so Waheguru brought an end to her misery. But in this case, like an insecure politician who is afraid of losing votes, Waheguru seems too eager to please His devotee lest she should change her mind. There is no doubt that Waheguru does protect and help His highly dedicated devotees but only when they face some extremely tough situations. The Bibi did not have to wait even a few days!
- Where did that amrit go now? Why don't the crows turn into swans now, or the fish which are there in the holy Sarovar now turn into some thing more interesting like mermaids? **What unholy thing has happened now? Don't our leaders realize that the story is a big blasphemy to our Holy Harmander Sahib?** If the pond was so holy with some mythical amrit before, obviously something unholy of big magnitude must have happened to undo the effect after the Holy Sarovar was built there by Guru Ram Das Ji! What possible unholy event could that be, particularly when the praise of Waheguru is sung there for more than eighteen hours a day, everyday of the year! My body begins to shiver when I think of this kind of unholy implication of the story. **Aren't we ashamed of ourselves when not only we believe in such fake stories which bring a big disrespect to one of our holiest places, but also promote them!"** Bhai Sahib paused for a short while. His voice was cracking now.

"Are there any questions at this point?" Bhai Sahib asked after a brief pause.

"You are doing a super good job at dispelling all the misconceptions, Bhai Sahib. We used to feel very proud of our Harmander Sahib that a leper was cured there. I'm very thankful to you now that you have opened my eyes which were shut due to my stupid ignorance. Just a little further clarification. Is it possible that curing the leper was a miracle performed by Waheguru to save His devotee, Bibi Rajni, from big misfortune?" Kaka Satinder Bir Singh asked.

"Protecting His devotees in trouble is Waheguru's grace from times immemorial. He does that all the time. If Waheguru were to help Bibi Rajni, rather than just helping her on one score only - that too in a very weird way - He would have simply directed her to Goindwal Sahib to take refuge at Guru Amar Das Ji's feet who would have taken care of everything for the Bibi. **If Waheguru was to help His devotees, why would he ignore His best devotee - Guru Amar Das Ji (or Guru Ram Das Ji) - and not send Bibi Rajni to Him for help, especially when the Guru was so close!** If Waheguru must help Bibi Ji without involving Guru Amar Das Ji, He could have simply cured her husband in a few weeks or some other reasonable length of time rather than playing that unreasonable drama and bypassing His topmost devotee - Guru Amar Das Ji." Bhai Sahib explained.

"How could have that story started, Bhai Sahib?" Bhai Gur Bhagwant Singh wondered. "I can only speculate, Bhai Sahib. It is a very clever story which seems very credulous unless you examine it really carefully. Superficially, it seems to enhance the importance of Harmander Sahib. That's why many Sikhs including our leaders promote it with great enthusiasm. But, it's like a poisonous pill that is coated with honey, and is probably fabricated by someone (or a group of people) who was very jealous of the popularity of Guru

Nanak's Dynasty. He couldn't do anything to stop the ever growing popularity of Harmander Sahib, so he contrived something to attribute the importance of Harmander Sahib to something Brahmanical in nature. **He carefully misguided the ignorant Sikhs to accept the literal meaning of the holy shabads in which a man with evil qualities (manmukh) is referred to as a crow and a man with noble qualities (Gurmukh) as a swan. Listen to the following holy Shabads.**

- If Waheguru casts His kind sight even on a heron (an imposter of good qualities) How difficult is it for him (the heron) to become a swan (a person with noble qualities)? (Guru) Nanak says that let alone a heron (a man who looks noble from outside at least), Waheguru can turn even a crow (a man who has bad qualities inside and does not look noble even from outside) into a swan (man with noble qualities) if He so chooses. **(Siri Raag ki Vaar, Sloak M:1, 90)**

The fabricator of the story used this holy Shabad in particular, to misguide the ignorant Sikhs. There are some other holy shabads in which the word crow has been used for evil qualities (or men with evil qualities) and swan for a Gurmukh or good qualities.

- The people who worship Waheguru find every place pleasant (because they feel blissful all the time). But the bodies of the people who have forgotten Waheguru are attacked and weakened by the crow (immoral or evil qualities). **(Sarang ki Vaar, Sloak M:5, 1247)**

As we were discussing, the creator of the story cleverly misled the people to believe that the pond which existed there before it was converted into the holy Sarovar by Guru Ram Das Ji (and later Harmander Sahib built inside by Guru

Arjun Dev Ji) had amrit in it as proved by the conversion of crows into swans. **So, according to this highly illogical story, the importance of the Golden Temple is not due to the fact that it was built by Guru Arjun Dev Ji and that Waheguru's praise is sung in the presence of Guru Granth Sahib all the time, but because of some funny 'amrit' that was there before in the pond! The sad thing is that our leaders embraced the totally illogical cock and bull story with great enthusiasm and are still promoting it."** Bhai Dalip Singh sighed before making a short pause.

"Are there more questions?" Bhai Dalip Singh asked

Nobody had further questions. The congregation seemed to be mesmerized by Bhai Sahib's explanations based on the holy Gurbani to demystify some popular but very dangerous stories about Darbar Sahib.

Bhai Kashmir Singh thanked Bhai Dalip Singh for his deep analysis of the stories.

The session had already become too long. Everybody was feeling hungry too. So, the session was adjourned with the traditional slogan.

7

Puzzle of the Universe, Heaven and Hell, Confession

"Waheguru Ji ka Khalsa, Waheguru Ji ki Fateh" Bhai Dalip Singh welcomed the congregation warmly to which the congregation responded with a warm enthusiasm. "On some previous occasions people have asked me about the origin of the universe as described in SGGS (Sri Guru Granth Śahib). The subject may also be of interest to you. So, I'd like to discuss that if you permit." Bhai Dalip Singh wanted to discuss a new topic today.

"Sure, we'd love to hear that. Please, do so." Many voices came from the congregation.

"According to Sri Guru Granth Sahib, Waheguru has two manifestations - formless, and the visible universe. The universe has been created and been folded an infinite number of times. When the universe does not exist, and Waheguru is all by Himself in His meditative state, it is all fog and darkness. Nothing can be described about that state. Both states - the existence and the nonexistence of the universe - last for an infinite length of time. The following holy Shabads (Hymns) describe these facts.

- Before the universe came into existence, there was complete darkness for an infinite length of time (who could measure the time then?). There was no earth, sky, nor expressed laws of the limitless

Waheguru. There was no day or night, and no moon or sun. At that time Waheguru was all by Himself in a meditative state. He had not expressed Himself in a visible form yet. ——— When He wished, Waheguru created the universe and stretched the sky without any support. He created Brahma, Vishnu and Shiva, and the attraction for *'maya'* in the universe. Waheguru imparted Divine Knowledge to some rare individual who came to realize that it is Waheguru alone who has created the universe, and is looking after it. It is His Huqam (Divine law) that is running the whole universe. Waheguru, Himself, **started the creation** of the solar systems and the galaxies as His own manifestation from the invisible state. It is only through the perfect Guru that man comes to realize that no one can ever determine the limits of Waheguru. **(Maru Solhe, M: 1, 1035)**

- Waheguru has created and folded the universe infinite number of times. When the universe is folded, Waheguru is all by Himself, and nothing else exists. **(Gauri Sukhmani, M: 5, 276)**
- The Waheguru, who is all by Himself and there is nothing beyond Him, has created His own power. That limitless Waheguru needs no support. He Himself creates the state where there is no universe, and He is all by Himself. He creates the universe out of Himself. ———— **(Maru Solhe, M: 1, 1037)**

These holy Shabads illuminate that Waheguru stays in a meditative state for an infinite period of time, and then as per His wish, He creates the universe from Himself. As will be clear from the following Shabads, Guru Nanak Sahib has also described the process by which the universe is created. He describes that after illuminating Himself, Waheguru creates the Divine Laws. He then creates gases part of which is converted into water and the rest into three dimensional solids to create the universe. Listen to these holy Shabads.

- ———Waheguru creates gases from Himself which produce water and three dimensional solids. Waheguru then creates the universe from these elements, and His light sustains all forms of life. **(Siri Raag, M: 1, 20)**
- Waheguru created the air and water from Himself, and after creating the universe, He created fort-like bodies and infused life into them. ——— Waheguru created the moon, the sun and the sky (stars) all from Himself alone, and His Divine light is sustaining the whole universe.——— **(Maru Solhe, M: 1, 1037)**

So, a few things become clear from the above holy Shabads (Hymns).

(a) The universe is NOT everlasting. Like it has happened many times before, it will eventually come to an end, and Waheguru will be again all by Himself.

(b) Waheguru creates the universe in an orderly fashion with His Huqam (laws). The term, **'started'** used in the very first hymn that we discussed, is very significant. **What it means is, the universe did not come into existence with a bang. It developed slowly.**

(c) Waheguru created gases first from Himself, which partly changed into water and solid matter. These three 'elements' resulted in the universe. The most recent science confirms this scheme of universal development. Scientists are saying now that the whole universe has developed slowly from gases.

Guru Nanak Sahib and Guru Arjun Sahib make it very

clear that the sun, the moon, and everything else in the universe is perishable and eventually comes to an end.

- (Guru) Nanak tells the eternal truth that the day, the sun, the night, the moon, and the millions of stars, are all perishable. Only Waheguru is everlasting. **(Siri Raag, M: 1, Ashatpadian, 64)**
- Beauty declines (is perishable), the continents decline (are perishable), and so do the sun, the moon, the stars in the sky. The earth, the high-peaked mountains, and the trees are all perishable. —— The only everlasting thing is Waheguru and His holy men. **(Sloak Sehskriti, M: 5, 1354)**

Are there any questions so far?" Bhai Dalip Singh asked.

"Bhai Sahib, how many skies are there? Is that true that there are fourteen skiesl - seven above the earth and seven below the earth?" Bhai Gulwant Singh, an elderly gentleman asked.

"Bhai Sahib, Guru Nanak Sahib has given us a universal fact about Waheguru's creation which maintains that we will NEVER be able to find the limits of Waheguru or His Creation. Everything about Waheguru's Creation is beyond human imagination. There are countless galaxies as per Guru Nanak Sahib. Listen to the following holy Shabads.

- There are millions (countless) of galaxies above the earth (which we can see) and millions more below the earth (which we cannot see because they are obscured). Many Hindu ascetics, including the authors of the Vedas, who tried to find the limit of the universe, admit that they failed to find the limits, and that there are millions of them. The holy books of the Western World - the Koran, the Bible the Torah, and the Tanakh - claim that their eighteen thousand learned holy men are also unable to find the extent of the universe. In fact, we cannot count the number of worlds (skies) because there are so many of them that we run out of numbers to count them. **(Jap Ji, 4)**

- There are countless earths (planets), countless Meru mountains (a mythical mountain in Paradise which is supposed to be full of gold and other precious metals) ——— countless gods like Inder, countless moons, countless suns, and countless galaxies. — — **(Jap Ji, 7)**

Peir Dasatgeer of Baghdad asked Guru Nanak Dev Ji Who visited Baghdad on His way back to India from Mecca, that according to the Koran there are fourteen skies (seven above, and seven below the earth), but He (Guru Nanak Dev Ji) maintained that there were countless of them. Who was right?. Guru Ji answered that Muhammad Sahib must have seen fourteen only, but He (Guru Sahib) saw millions. So, to answer your question, Bhai Sahib, according to Guru Nanak Dev Ji, there is no limit to the universe, and again the recent advances in science are confirming it." Bhai Dalip Singh explained.

"How about different life forms, Bhai Sahib? Are there really 8400000 of them?" Bhai Gurdeep Singh, an elderly gentleman, asked?

"I have to go back again to Guru Nanak Sahib's fundamental principle of Waheguru's limitless Creation to answer this question, Bhai Sahib. Just like the number of skies, Guru Nanak Sahib has put no limit on the number of life forms. The number quoted by you comes from the Hindu religious books. This number, like many other numbers, has been used in Sri Guru Granth Sahib simply to sing praise of Waheguru, Who is beyond numbers. To give you an example, it has been mentioned many times in Sri Guru Granth Sahib that there are four different ways of reproduction, but, when describing the Stage of Divine Knowledge in Jap Ji, Guru Nanak Sahib maintains that there are infinite ways by which the living beings reproduce.

- —— there are countless gods, countless demons, and countless ascetics who never talk (for whatever reason). There are countless seas of jewels, **countless ways of reproduction,** and countless ways the living beings can communicate (not just four as listed in Hindu religious books), and there are countless kings.———— **(Jap Ji, 8)**

Now, if there are countless ways of reproduction - and the biologists agree that there are many, many ways of reproduction (World Book Encyclopaedia) - how can we count the number of life forms? There are many such huge numbers given in the ancient religious books without any proof. So, again, as you already got the answer, the number of life forms is unknown. It could be more or less. Who could find the end to Waheguru's Creation?" Bhai Dalip Singh tested the question on the yardstick of Gurbani.

"While expressing His grief and heartache at human misery brought about by the barbaric attack of the army of Baabar on Emnabad, Guru Nanak Sahib wrote that the Nawab of Emnabad had detained **millions** of holy men to pray for his victory and to cast their magic on the advancing forces of Baabar so that they would go blind.

- ————When the Nawab heard about the imminent attack by Baabar, he detained **millions** of holy men (to pray for his victory and to cast their magic on the forces of Baabar). But no army personnel of Baabar was distracted, or turned blind. On the contrary, the fort-like buildings and palaces were burned down, and the princes were cut down in small pieces and their bodies were left in dust to rot. ———— **(Assa M:1, 417-18)**

Do you think that the number, "millions", used in this holy Shabad was an actual count? Of course, not! It has been used to emphasize the desperation and the highhandedness of the Nawab for which he was so infamous.

Although in different contexts, but while talking about the gestation period of human beings, Farid Sahib writes "six months", while Kabir Sahib writes "ten months". Listen to the following holy Shabads by these two Great Souls.

- The mortal human body will be housed in a humble grave one day, and will turn into dust. So, Sheikh Farid advises you to remember Allah, oh my dear friend!. ———Remember always that the mortal will have to leave this world! It takes **six months** for a human body to develop, but only a second to come to an end. ———**(Assa Farid Ji, 488)**
- Why are you wasting the precious human life in greed, oh man? You have ignored the kind Waheguru who created your body in **ten months** in the womb of your mother just from a sperm of your father.———**(Assa Kabir Ji, 481)**

Is one of these two highly revered holy men right, and the other wrong? Definitely, not! As you can easily conclude, the period of gestation is not the issue here. The issue here is to sing praise of Waheguru, and both the Great Souls are emphasizing the importance of that by reminding the man of the mortal nature of human body.

We were talking about the authenticity of different numbers which have been quoted in Guru Granth Sahib. As, you can clearly see from the above holy Shabads, accuracy of numbers is NOT the issue in Guru Granth Sahib. The numbers may or may not be real. They have simply been used to highlight certain aspects of spiritual world." Bhai Dalip Singh explained.

"Bhai Sahib, I already kind of expect the answer now, but based on Gurbani, can you discuss **how the very first human being appeared on earth?** Was Baba Adam the first human being ever to set foot on earth?" Bhai Jasvinder Singh asked smilingly. He did not seem to be very serious about his question.

"I know full well that you already know the answer because you have understood the fundamental principles of Guru Nanak Sahib. If we believe that Baba Adam was the first human being ever to appear on earth because he was driven out of Heaven for disobedience, then what caused all other life forms to appear on earth? Did all the other life forms appear on earth because of some punishment as well? Nobody has ever said anything about them. Also, if all of us are descendants of the same father, Adam, and the same mother, Eve, how can we explain the existence of so many different races of human beings on earth? Furthermore, if other life forms can appear, why cannot humans appear on earth? **Guru Nanak Sahib says in Jap Ji that Waheguru's Huqam cannot be described.** How Waheguru looks after His world, cannot be known. So, we do not know how the very first man appeared on earth; but by the same token, we don't know anything about other life forms either. It is a puzzle very well articulated by the popular question: who came first - the chicken or the egg? Can anyone answer this question?" Bhai Sahib asked with a smile.

Heaven and Hell

"Talking about Heaven, are there really such things as hell and heaven, Bhai Sahib?" Bibi Balwinder Kaur asked.

"That is an interesting question, Bibi Ji. Some religions believe that heaven and hell are real places where people are rewarded or punished after death depending upon their deeds on the earth. **But according to Gurbani, heaven and hell are NOT real places, but are situations or states of mind where**

one feels either very blissful or miserable. Everyone can have their own definition of heaven or hell in which they feel very happy or wretched. One thing is common to the concept of Heaven in almost every religion that it is a place where Waheguru or God resides. **According to Gurbani, Waheguru is present where the holy men sing His praise. So, that is Heaven.** Even though Waheguru is present in every little particle of the universe, He can be realized only in the company of holy men. There are hundreds of holy shabads that define Heaven like this. Please listen to the following.

- I am looking for Waheguru everywhere, oh my mother! I am searching my mind and my body and seeking help to find Him. I am going to attend the company of holy men to search for Waheguru because **He is known to be there. (Maajh M:4, 94)**
- Waheguru's Naam is the real Amrit (liquid of immortality), oh my friend! Keep this Amrit and its taste safely in your heart. But, it can be realized only by listening carefully (internalizing) to Guru's Shabad in the company of holy men. **(Kanra Ki Vaar, Sloak M: 4, 1314)**
- People who claim that they have realized the inaccessible and unimaginable Waheguru, and have accessed Heaven, do so only in words. I have no idea of that heaven where everybody says they have to go. ——— Kabir says how can he explain to such people that Waheguru is present only in the company of holy men. **(Gauri Kabir Ji, 325)**
- Salvation, enjoyment of comforts, and good life style, are all achieved when one serves You, oh Waheguru! But, only that person can serve You whom You are kind to. It is Heaven where Your praise is being sung, but it is You alone Who inculcates that affection and devotion in the heart of the devotee. **(Suhi M: 5, 749)**

- All the sixty eight holy places are contained in the spot where the Sadhu (Guru) sets His foot. (Listening to the Guru with devotion is much more useful than a pilgrimage of all the sixty eight Hindu holy places). And the **place where Waheguru's Naam is recited becomes the Heaven. (Ramkali M: 5, 890)**
- Everybody says that they have to go there, but, I do not know where the Heaven is, and have no concept of the door to the Heaven. ——— Kabir says, how can I tell people that **Heaven is housed in the company of the holy men. (Bhairon, Kabir Ji)**
- I am looking for the place where Your Naam is never forgotten, and where Your praise is sung twenty four hours a day to purify the body (mind), oh Waheguru! After looking carefully, I have found out that that place is the company of holy men. I have taken their refuge now. **(Suhi M: 5, 747)**

As is perfectly clear from the above holy Shabads, Heaven is not a dedicated special place where you see beautiful flowers and get all the comforts of life. Waheguru is present where His praise is sung with devotion, and that is where the Heaven is. Likewise, hell is the situation where people forget Waheguru completely and commit sins.

As far as rewards for noble deeds (heaven), and punishment for the evil (hell) are concerned, people receive them in the present life - right here on this earth. **So, if we use reward and punishment as the definition for heaven and hell, they are right here on this earth. People who enjoy all the luxuries of life are in heaven and the people who are suffering, are already in hell."** Bhai Dalip Singh wrapped up the topic.

"Are there further questions?" Bhai Sahib asked.

Confession

"Bhai Sahib, some faiths believe that if a sinner confesses his sins before a priest, all his sins are forgiven. How far is that true? Are the sins of a Sikh forgiven if he confesses them before Sri Guru Granth Sahib?" Bhai Jasvinder Singh asked.

"Everything is possible, Bhai Sahib, but, it is NOT as simple as some faiths believe. A verbal confession without any change in character means nothing at all. If that were possible there would be no sinner in this world. You could commit some heinous acts, go to a priest and confess them; and you would be clean! I don't believe so! According to Gurbani, nobody else can wash away your sins. You, and you alone, are responsible for cleansing them. Gurbani maintains that let alone forgiveness by way of confession before a priest, even if you recite Waheguru's Naam all the time, but your mind is full of treachery and evil thoughts, you cannot be forgiven. Listen to the following holy Shabads.

- What do people with unclean minds and theft-committing bodies gain by pilgrimage? They may wash off dirt and grease from their bodies by bathing, but they add twice as much filth to their souls. They wash the exterior of their bodies, but they carry fresh venom inside. The holy men are better off without bathing because the cheats will stay cheats, and will continue to cheat. **(Suhi ki Vaar, Sloak M: 1, 789)**
- You cannot worship Waheguru without the grace of the Guru, oh enlightened man! If you recite Waheguru's Naam everyday but deceive people, your heart cannot be clean for Waheguru to appear. No matter how many rituals you perform to cleanse your heart, you will never experience comfort even in your dreams. ——— **(Suhi M: 4, 732)**

- Some people try to please Waheguru by singing, by playing music, or just by reading religious books, but Waheguru is not pleased by any of these efforts because if you harbour deceit and guile at heart, your fake crying (praying) is not going to help. No matter how hard you try to hide your craftiness, the Creator Wahguru knows everything. **(Assa M: 4, 450)**
- A person with unclean mind will not be able to go to paradise even if he undertakes pilgrimage many times. Simply by impressing people, such a person will not be able to please Waheguru because Waheguru is not ignorant. (He knows all our intentions and deeds full well).———— **(Assa Kabir Ji, 484)**

It is perfectly clear from the above holy hymns that confession before a priest does not cleanse your sins, and you are as guilty as ever. **Actually, confession encourages a person to commit more sins because he has the false security of being forgiven through confession every time he commits a sin.**

However, Gurbani also maintains that if you commit sins, and you are honestly remorseful about them, pray to the Almighty to give you the strength to recite His Naam with devotion, and vow never to commit any crime again, you can be forgiven. If you take Guru's refuge, and continue to sing Waheguru's praise, and serve humanity in some constructive way, and try never to commit a sin again, your soul will become clean slowly and Waheguru will embrace you. The following holy Shabads (Hymns) will clarify the point.

- Just like the filth on your body can be washed away with water; and just like the filthy clothes splashed with urine can be cleaned with soap, the sinful and dirty mind can only be cleansed with Waheguru's Naam ———— **(Jap Ji Sahib)**

- You honour those people who have never been honoured by anyone else, oh my dear Waheguru! I would love to sacrifice my life for Your power and Your kindness. Just like a father who scolds his child for disobeying and disciplines him, but later embraces affectionately, Waheguru also forgives his devotees and guides them in the future. ————**(Sorith M: 5, 634)**

- Oh Source of grace, Waheguru! Please be kind to us so that we may always sing Your praise. I always pray for Your kindness and wait for the time when You would embrace me, oh Waheguru! We are foolish, and are like a child who is always prone to making mistakes, but, You always guide us, oh Waheguru!. We make mistakes again and again, but, You still love Your children.———— **(Kalyan M:4, 1321)**

- Oh my Sovereign Waheguru! I take pride in being totally dependent upon You. I know You are mine. It is very easy to say that we obey Your Will, but, it is a very difficult task. I have wasted away my whole life taking pride in Your affection and Your support, oh my dear Father! I am sure, being my mother and my father, You will forgive my mistakes.———— **(Siri Raag, M: 5, 51-2)**

- Oh my Waheguru! Oh my Lord! You are the creator of the universe and You possess all the powers in the world. I am a sinner who has come to your asylum. Please, do not expose my sins. You know and watch all my bad deeds everyday, and I have no way to deny them; but, I still keep doing them and try to hide them from You, oh my Lord! I have heard that You are capable of all powers, and Your Naam can destroy zillions of sins. Please,

bestow Your Naam on me too, oh Waheguru!——
———— **(Bilawal M: 5, 828)**

As is clear from these holy Shabads, the emphasis is on the 'Naam' to wash your sins away. There is absolutely no other way to cleanse your sins. So, according to Gurbani, a simple confession before a priest is incapable of cleansing your sins. And as discussed earlier, there is actually a big risk that the sinner will sink deeper into committing more sins." Bhai Dalip Singh explained.

"Are there other questions?" Bhai Sahib asked after a short pause.

Hearing no further question, Bhai Kashmir Singh thanked Bhai Dalip Singh, and the congregation was adjourned with the traditional Sikh Slogan: Bolle so Nihal, Sat Sri Akal. Langar was served as usual.

8

Maya: Satan and Reincarnation

People are beginning to assemble at Bhai Kashmir Singh's farmhouse to listen to Bhai Dalip Singh's discourses which are gaining more and more popularity. People are also bringing milk, butter, sugar and other needed items for the langar (common kitchen) to feed the ever growing congregations. There is great hustle and bustle at the Farmhouse.

"Waheguru Ji ka Khalsa, Waheguru Ji ki Fateh". Bhai Dalip Singh greeted the congregation as he appeared on the stage. There was a big smile on his face as usual. The huge congregation responded the salutation with a big roar.

"Is there any question before we start?" Bhai Sahib asked.

"Yes, Bhai Sahib, if you don't mind please." Preet Pal Singh, a young student, said politely.

"By all means, young man." Bhai Sahib encouraged the young student.

Satan

"Some religions believe that all the bad things that people do, are caused by a controlling power called Satan. They conclude that they are not responsible for their evil actions because Satan makes them do the bad things. How far is that true Bhai Sahib? Is there such a thing as Satan? Would you, please, comment on that? I'm not convinced that we can blame Satan for our bad deeds." Preet Pal Singh wanted to be reassured.

"That's a very good question, young man. People always look for someone else to lay the blame on for their bad or evil actions. Gurbani makes it clear again and again that we solely are responsible for our own actions, and cannot blame someone else.

- The comforts and the discomforts that you experience are the results of your deeds in your previous life (incarnation), oh man! But, only Waheguru alone Who has given you these comforts or discomforts knows this secret. You cannot blame someone else for your deeds, so suffer the tough consequences now. **(Maru Solhe M: 1, 1030)**
- You cannot blame someone else for your discomforts, oh man! You are reaping the seeds of whatever you had sown. Man is caught in the net of maya due to his own deeds, and as a result he stays in the birth-death cycle.——— **(Ramkali M: 5, 888)**
- Why do you blame the Lord for your discomforts or misery, oh ignorant and foolish person! Your comforts or discomforts are the results of your own good or bad deeds. ———**(Dhanasari Trilochan Ji, 695)**
- You cannot blame anyone else for you problems. The deeds of your previous incarnations are causing the problems and you cannot find peace of mind. I am suffering the consequences of my previous deeds day and night. ——— **(Suhi M:5, 744)**
- With whose support other than that of Waheguru do you think you are living in this world, oh foolish man! Who else can be your best friend than Waheguru, oh fool! Not realizing this, you have mad friendship with the five robbers - lust, rage, greed, emotional attachment and conceit. ——— —You are busy in things which are not going to

be of any help to you, and then you will reap their rewards. ———**(Ramkali M: 5, 898)**

There are many more shabads like these which clarify the point beyond any doubt that man himself is responsible for his deeds - good or bad - and there is no such power as Satan in the world. Man makes his own choices. He can be slave to his sensual pleasures or can lead a moral life. Of course, as we discussed the other day, Waheguru has created the world in such a way that man loves ***'maya'***. Maya doesn't mean just money, but, everything in the world that affects our senses including *haumein*, lust, greed, ego etc. The following holy Shabads will clarify that Waheguru Himself sowed the seed of love for maya among people.

- It is only You and You alone all the time, oh Waheguru! This seemingly different world from You, is Your Own creation. **You sowed the seed of *haumein*, ego, and greed among the living beings.** They are now performing as programmed by you. Please, protect them by whichever way You may please.——— **(Maajh ki Vaar, M: 1, Pauri, 139)**
- ———Waheguru has created this world and **injected the poison of haumein (maya) among its living beings.** A person whose heart becomes home to Waheguru's Naam can get rid of this poison. ———**(Maru M: 1, Ashatpadian, 1009)**
- A person who makes his heart home for Waheguru to reside, realizes that the formless Waheguru created the whole world from Himself first. He then created love for maya among the living beings in His Huqam (as per His wish). He himself is playing the game of the world.———**(Maru Solhe M: 3, 1065)**
- Maya is so attractive and powerful that it has enslaved every living being (by Waheguru's

Huqam), oh my friend! The fishes in water are stung by maya, and so are the moths burning themselves on light. ———The gods are completely overcome by maya, and so are all the living beings in the ocean and on the earth. Kabir says that all living beings with stomach are suffering from maya.———**(Bhairon Kabir Ji, 1160)**

- ———Making emotional attachment its foundation, the Creator has created this world. Living beings are lost in the false (mortal) attraction for the world. ———**(Bhairon M: 3, 1128)**

As you can see clearly from these holy shabads, Waheguru Himself has created attraction for maya among the living beings whose lives revolve around maya. They do all the bad (or good) deeds under the influence of maya. So, they are alone responsible for their acts. Now, if someone wants to call their weakness for maya, Satan, they have the right to do so. But, it is still their own choice, and no hidden power other than their own weakness, is responsible for their actions. People commit huge frauds everyday, accept bribes to do injustice, and then may kill someone to hide their evil deeds. They cannot blame any Satan for their crimes and sins. They do such crimes only to gratify their own lust. So, to answer your question in brief, young man, Guru Granth Sahib does not believe in any independent power other than Waheguru in the world." Bhai Sahib concluded.

Reincarnation

"Bhai Sahib, while quoting holy shabads, you've mentioned several times that the suffering of human beings is the result of their previous incarnations. Does that mean that reincarnation is a reality? If so, why do some major religions not believe in reincarnation. Would you, please, clarify that?" Bibi Harleen Kaur, another young student asked. She seemed to be surprised.

"I know Bibi Ji that some major religions do not believe in reincarnation. It is their right not to believe. But, Guru Granth Sahib believes strongly in reincarnation. There are hundreds of holy hymns certifying reincarnation. But before I quote a few of them, let's assume for a second that there were no reincarnation. All religions believe in the existence of soul in some way. So, what happens to the soul after death if there were no reincarnation? Where does it go? There are only two possibilities. First, it could go to hell or heaven as the religions with no belief in reincarnation believe. Second, it could just wander around. There are quite a few problems with either of the two possibilities.

- If the souls go to hell or heaven, there have to be some kind of structured places where the souls go. Where are those places? Are they right here on earth or in some other galaxy? Also, do all souls in hell get similar treatment? And likewise, do all souls in heaven also get similar treatment?
- If they get similar treatment in their respective places, there is no justice or fairness because people with different degrees of evilness and nobleness will be getting the same treatment. Can God be that unfair!
- Aren't some people already spending their lives as if they were in hell, while some others are already in heaven? Millions of people in Africa and in Asia are so poor that they do not get even clean water to drink let alone good food, clothing and shelter. On top of that they are also suffering from vicious diseases like leprosy, blindness, AIDS, tapeworms and so on. Aren't they already in hell? **Will that be justice if they have to go to hell again because they did not get any opportunity to do some noble deeds due to poverty and poor health?**

- Also, how do we account for such wide differences in living standards? Why should some people deserve extreme riches while some others wretched misery?
- How do the mythical hell and heaven differ from life here on earth?
- **To enjoy the comforts of heaven or to suffer the punishment in hell, souls need bodies. Enjoyment or suffering is not possible without bodies. So, do the souls get temporary bodies when they are in hell or heaven?** What kind of bodies would those be! Wouldn't that be some kind of reincarnation!
- How long does the soul stay in hell or heaven? Is there any time limit, or it stays there indefinitely? If there is a time limit then what happens to it after that time is over?
- If there is no time limit, then again, it is injustice of the highest order. A person with a small theft on his record going to hell will suffer there to the same extent as another who has tortured thousands of innocent human beings mercilessly. How do you justify this kind of Divine planning?
- **What kind of life did a baby have who died within a few days after his birth? Whether the death was accidental or due to some disease, wasn't that already hell for the baby as well as the parents? Should life be over for the baby? What kind of justice is that?** Also, How does that compare to a millionaire who had a luxurious life of over one hundred years? Will God be that prejudiced without any good reason?
- How do we account for the huge differences in personalities and in talents of different people? Some of us are born artists, scientists or leaders? What causes those differences? **I recently watched**

on TV that a four-year old boy wrote a book! How do we explain that if this was his only life?

- What about the souls who had a balanced sheet of good and bad deeds? Where do they go?
- And finally, if souls do not go anywhere and just keep wandering, will not the universe be a chaotic place? If they are not subject to any judgment, and all the evil and the noble souls are wandering alike, what incentive is there for anyone to do noble deeds and fear of punishment for bad deeds? Then we might as well say that there is no God.

If we cannot answer these valid questions, we cannot simply reject the fact of rebirth". Bhai Dalip Singh raised many convincing objections to the idea of no life after death.

Are there any questions so far? Bhai Sahib asked. Hearing no question, Bhai Sahib continued.

"Let's listen to some of the holy Shabads which clearly maintain that there's life after death.

- Body and soul are united and get separated, and they are united again. In other words living beings are born to die and die to be born again. This cycle of life and death is so long that living beings become fathers of many, and sons of many others.——— —Nobody can keep account of all these lives and nobody knows what their previous life was and what the future life will be. ——— **(Sarang ki Vaar, Sloak M: 1, 1237)**
- ————Because of the countless ill qualities in us, we go through a lot of life forms, oh Waheguru! What can we tell about the length of time for which we have had different mothers, and different fathers (the point in time when we started life in some form). And what can we tell about the life

forms we had to go through before we were given the present human form.————We must have gone through an infinite varieties of life forms including vegetation and animals. For countless number of times, we must have been born as reptiles, and for infinite times we must have flown around as birds.————**Gauri Cheti M: 1, 156)**

- You have been given the human body after a long, long time, oh my friend! Now, dedicate yourself to realize the Master of the universe - Waheguru - because human form is the only life form in which you can realize Him. You have been in the life forms of bugs and insects for a long time, and an elephant, a fish and a deer for many other lives. Many times you were born as a bird, as a snake, as a horse and as an ox to be used for farm work.———— **(Gauri Guareri M: 5, 176)**
- Forgetting Waheguru's Naam, man carries a big load of serious sins and crimes which cause his spiritual death. He is awakened from his sleep in maya in a moment when the agents of death grab him by the hair, but, then it is already too late. Because of his sins, man is punished and given life forms of other animals such as a camel or donkey etc. ————**(Sarang M: 5, 1224)**
- The people who think or talk ill of Waheguru's saints enjoy no spiritual bliss, my friend! Because of the false accusations levied against the saints, the evil malevolent becomes mentally sick and goes through a long cycle of life and death in various life forms. ————**(Bhairon M: 5, 1145)**
- How can a troublemaker for Waheguru's saints get across the ocean of maya (worldly attractions), my friend! He is leading a hellish life for sure. Even if such an evil man does a few good things such as worshipping idols, donating land in charity,

and is visibly a good Samaritan to win praise in society, he does not gain anything spiritually, and is recycled in a number of low life forms.———— - **(Goand Ravi Das Ji, 875)**

- The malevolent of Waheguru's saints bears enmity with the saints and friendship with the evil. Such people never get comfort either in this world or the next (after death) and are born again and again. ———**(Sorith ki Vaar, Sloak M: 3, 649)**

These holy shabads are only a few of the hundreds that clarify beyond any doubt that there is life after death - a man may be born as a man again, or may take some other life form. But he continues to be trapped in the death - birth cycle until he finds salvation through Guru's Teachings - which he eventually does. But the fact is that life is not over in one incarnation alone." Bhai Sahib concluded .

"Is there any other question?" Bhai Sahib asked with his usual politeness.

Judgment Day

"It may sound naive, Bhai Sahib, but is there such a thing as the judgment day?" Bibi Harleen Kaur asked another related question.

"That's another good question, young lady. Some major religions strongly believe that a day will come when all souls will be united with their respective bodies and will be presented before God Who will deliver His judgement on the deeds of all the people - dead and alive. The day is called the Judgment Day. According to the belief of one religion, good souls (people) will take control of this earth, while all the bad souls will be sent to hell, while according to another, the Judgment Day will also be the Dooms Day and every body will leave this earth to go to hell or heaven. Since bodies will be united with the souls on the Judgment Day, the believers of the Faith do not cremate their dead so that they can preserve their bodies. They are all awaiting the arrival of the Day.

Guru Granth Sahib does not believe in any particular judgment day. We are being judged continuously for our deeds. If Waheguru were to wait to pass the judgment for an indefinite period which could run into millions of years, what kind of judgment would that be? Even in our everyday lives we denounce strongly if governments and courts don't decide on matters of importance in reasonable time. For such delays, we use a common and popular cliche, **'justice delayed is justice denied'**. If that's what our reaction is even about the worldly affairs, how can we be satisfied with Waheguru's delayed justice? Also, even if dead bodies are not cremated and are buried to preserve them, they too begin to rot after sometime, and are only a pile of a few bones which turns into ash over a period of time unless they change into fossils.

Moreover nobody - absolutely nobody - knows Waheguru's plans about creation or destruction of the world. So, how can someone say that the Judgment Day will be the last day of life on this earth? The following few holy Shabads explain these points.

- Because it is more pliable, sometimes the soil of graves is used by potters to make earthenware. When the pottery is baked in kilns, the bones of the dead bodies, which have already turned into dust, burn in fire leaving no body frames. (How can such frameless bodies of ash be united with their souls?) —— Only Waheguru, the Creator of the world, knows the secret (Where the souls go and how they are treated). **(Assa ki Vaar, Sloak M: 1, 466)**
- Some dead bodies are cremated, some are buried while some are devoured by dogs (wild animals). Some dead bodies are thrown in (running) water

and some exposed to vultures in a big dry dugout. But, nobody knows where the souls go after the bodies are disposed of in whichever way, oh Nanak! **(Sorith ki Vaar, Sloak M: 3, 648)**

- Who has died? Who is dead? Discuss this issue with the Guru because this is beyond the comprehension of a common man. When an individual dies, air inside him (breath) is absorbed by the atmosphere, his soul goes to Waheguru, and the body is mixed with the dirt of the earth. Nobody knows where the dead go.———— Nobody really dies because the soul which was a part of Waheguru goes back to Him.———— **(Ramkali, M:5, 885)**
- Because nobody can stop an individual from being born, by the same token, nobody can also stop that individual from dying. Only the Creator knows what happens to the living beings because all of them go back to him (where they are taken care of). ————**(Parbhati M:1, 1329)**

These holy Shabads maintain beyond any doubt that it is impossible to reunite the dead bodies with their respective souls for two reasons. First, the bodies will not survive in their original form for any reasonable length of time even if they are buried on the assumption that they will be reunited with their respective souls. Second, nobody knows where the souls have gone regardless of what happens to the bodies left behind. As we discussed earlier, Gurmat strongly believes in reincarnation. So, a particular soul may already have been through many other life forms. In that case which body will that soul be united with?

Also, according to Gurmat, the judgement of one's deeds is taking place continuously, and there is no waiting for some particular day, called the Judgment Day.

• Having created the living beings, **Waheguru has appointed Dharam Raj as the record-keeper to keep continuous records of all the good and the bad deeds of living beings.** The living beings are judged totally impartially in the Court of Waheguru, and the guilty are sorted out separately. The dishonest find no room there, and are shipped to hell with their faces blackened. The people who are imbued in Waheguru's Naam are honoured as successful while the cheats lose in His Court. ———**(Assa ki Vaar, M: 1, Pauri, 463)**

• ———When a living being runs out of all the breaths given to him by Waheguru (he breathes his last), he is required to leave this world by Waheguru's orders. All the comforts of life including food are withdrawn, and the living being is shackled to be taken to Waheguru's Court. ———**Each living being is held accountable for his each and every deed.** There is no escape and you have to reap the rewards of your deeds, oh living being! ——— **(Tukhari Chhant M: 1, 1110)**

These holy Shabads prove clearly that each human being is being judged continuously for his deeds, and let alone the Day, every second is the Judgment time for his actions as they are committed.

Also, nobody knows Waheguru's plans for the universe. It is He alone Who creates or destroys the universe. Absolutely nobody knows what will happen to the world at any time in the future. Listen to the following holy Shabads.

- It is Waheguru Himself Who talks in living beings, and it is also Him Who is the listener. He has created the whole universe from Himself alone. When He chooses, He creates the world, and folds it whenever He chooses to do that. ——— **(Gauri Sukhmani, M: 5, 292)**

- Worship the Waheguru Who creates the world in no time, oh man! He is capable of destroying the stretched skies in the twinkling of an eye, and recreate them in no time. He creates the world all by Himself and looks after His creation all by Himself. ———— **(Malhar ki Vaar, M:1, Pauri, 1280)**

There are many more holy shabads like these that clearly state that Waheguru alone knows what He is going to do with the world. Nobody else can make any prediction about the future of the world. So, how can anyone talk about the mythical Judgment Day? Gurmat does not believe in any judgment day". Bhai Dalip Singh explained.

"Are there further questions?" Bhai Sahib asked.

There was no further question. As always, Bhai Kashmir Singh thanked everybody, and the session was adjourned with a loud Slogan of "Waheguru Ji ka Khalsa, Waheguru Ji ki Fateh."

Everybody left for the kitchen where Lungar was going to be served.

9

Living Guru

"Waheguru Ji ka Khalsa, Waheguru Ji ki Fateh". Bhai Dalip Singh welcomed the large gathering warmly. The people had been waiting eagerly for him. They were mesmerized by Bhai Dalip Singh's knowledge of Gurbani and with his style of sharing knowledge.

"May I ask a question before you start, Bhai Sahib?" Bhai Gulwant Singh asked eagerly. He seemed to have something important on his mind.

"Please, do so, Bhai Sahib. That makes my job easier because questions from the audience give me direction." Bhai Dalip Singh smiled.

"Some people believe very strongly that they need to have a living guru who could listen to their problems in person, and guide them in their day to day affairs. We have tremendous respect for Guru Granth Sahib, but, we cannot get any visible response to our problems. Sometimes I also feel convinced that, may be, we do need a living guru. What is your valuable advice on that, Bhai Sahib?"

"From what you've said, I understand that what you need is not Guru, but someone with magical powers who would be able to find a quick solution to your immediate problems, Bhai Sahib." Bhai Dalip Singh said smilingly.

"Don't mind, Bhai Sahib. I was just joking." Bhai Dalip

Singh became serious. "In fact, you have a very pertinent question that may be of interest to all of you. But, before I disclose my position on the subject, let us first be clear about our expectations of the Guru. In other words, what the Guru does for us or for humanity at large. Once the expectations are clear, may be you will have a different view on the subject.

Role and Message of the Guru

As per Guru Granth Sahib, the following is the invaluable role that the Guru plays, and the Divine Message that He brings to the people.

- **Waheguru definitely exists - there is absolutely no doubt about it.**

  If I say million times that Waheguru exists, and million times million again and again, and continue saying that all the time without any break; and if Waheguru blesses me with enough energy that I never get tired of reciting His Naam and there is no hindrance in my recitation, I still will not have said enough in His praise. In fact, it will be only an insignificant fraction of the Truth. **(Sarang ki Vaar, Sloak M:1, 1241)**
- **Connects the people to Waheguru.**

  (i) I have realized Waheguru, and now I feel fully contented (I have no wants or desires left) oh, holy men! It is the Guru Who has connected me to Waheguru - the source of all the good qualities - and I wish to dedicate my body and my soul to the service of the Guru. Bravo to the great Guru!. The Guru is really great who has enlightened me with the Divine Knowledge.——— **(Suhi M:4, 776)**

  (ii) ———Let nobody be under the false impression; only the Guru is capable of salvaging you. The Guru guides all the misguided people and brings them on the right path. He connects you to the Almighty by breaking your bonds with *maya* ———**(Goand M:5, 864)**

(iii) I have realized the inaccessible and the limitless Waheguru by the grace of the Perfect Guru, and now I am trading in the life-sustaining Naam of Waheguru. I feel extremely blissful to see my Guru because it is He who has created a strong bond between me and Waheguru. ——— **(Sarang M:4, 1202)**

- **Emphasizes earning your living by honest means and helping the needy.**

  Only the person who earns his living honestly and helps the needy, recognizes truly the path to union with Waheguru. ———**(Sarang Ki Vaar, Sloak M:1, 1245)**

- **Emphasizes hard work to make life comfortable, but also on obeying Waheguru's Huqam. In other words, follow the Teachings of the Guru which include detachment from worldly attractions.**

  (i) An individual who recognizes the Huqam of Waheguru by the grace of the Guru, is able to control his mind. He harbours the precious Naam of Waheguru in his heart thereby leading a life of detachment from the worldly attractions.——— **(Maru Solhe M:3, 1054)**

  (ii) Do not feel grudgeful or jealous of the rich possessions of others, oh man! Why don't you work hard and acquire similar possessions by honest means? It is true that some people enjoy all the riches in life, while others have next to nothing, but, in addition to working hard, you must also accept the Will of Waheguru. ——— **(Assa Kabir Ji, 479-80)**

- **Asserts that Waheguru's Naam is the cure for all**

human suffering, particularly the mental suffering due to jealousy, discontentment, hatred, rage, lust, greed etc etc.

(i)The individual who sings the praise of Waheguru in the company of holy men is protected from all suffering———**(Gauri Sukhmani, M:5, 281)**

(ii)Waheguru's Naam is the panacea for all diseases (suffering). **(Sukhmani, M:5, A:9)**

There are many more Teachings of the Guru, but the major emphasis is on connecting people to Waheguru, and thus controlling wants, desires, sexual pleasures and other worldly attractions. Now that we have summarized the role of the Guru, let's find the definition of the Guru from Sri Guru Granth Sahib.

The Perfect Guru

There are hundreds of holy shabads (holy hymns) in Sri Guru Granth Sahib that assert that Guru is, in fact, Waheguru's Shabad (Divine Knowledge). Listen to the following holy shabads:

- ————It is Your Huqam that is running the whole universe, oh Waheguru! Even the part of the universe below the earth is alive with Your Naam. **Waheguru is present in the form of Shabad in everybody,** but can be realized only through His grace. **(Malhar M:1, Ashatpadian, 1275)**
- Waheguru Himself is the **Shabad**, and He Himself is the banner. He Himself is the listener, and Himself the know-it-all.—— **(Bilawal M:1, 795)**
- Waheguru Himsef disseminates knowledge and He Himself is the Knowledge. He Himself is the Perfect Guru and Himself the **Shabad**. He Himself is the narrator. **(Bilawal M:3, 797)**

- Sidh Yogis: Who is your guru whose disciple you are, hey Nanak! Guru Nanak Dev Ji: **The Shabad is my Guru**, and reciting the Shabad with full concentration is being disciple. **(Sidh Goshit, M:1, 939. Conversation between the Sidh yogis and Guru Nanak Sahib)**
- —— You are infallible, and never make a mistake, oh Waheguru! —— You reside in the **Shabad,** oh Great Master! Nanak's mind feels blissful when he sings Your praise. **(Basant, Ahatpadian, M:1, 1188)**
- ———Kabir says that I have realized the Guru whose name is Knowledge **(Shabad)**. **(Suhi Kabir Ji, 983)**
- You are the Perfect (everlasting)Truth, and You have disseminated Perfect Truth, oh Waheguru!.—— —— Lord Brahma is known as a great god, but even he could never find Your limits.——— You have placed Yourself in the Guru, and disseminated the **Shabad. (Malhar ki Vaar, M:1, Pauri, 1279)**

The above holy shabads (hymns) leave no doubt that the bodyless form of Waheguru is the Shabad (or the Divine Knowledge). Guru Nanak Sahib has written several times, particularly in the **'Sidh Goshit', that the Shabad is His Guru.** Waheguru places the Shabad in the body of some sacred soul (enlightens the soul) - the soul which is always connected to Him. **When Guru Nanak Dev Ji appeared on this earth, He possessed the Divine Knowledge, and was the Guru.** When He enlightened Bhai Lehna Ji with the same Knowledge, Bhai Lehna Ji became the Guru - Guru Angad Dev Ji - and so on. **Now, the same Divine Knowledge is in the form of the holy Guru Granth Sahib. So Guru Granth Sahib is our Guru now.**

We can control our sensual pleasures, and get rid of our *haumein* by reciting the holy Gurbani from Guru Granth Sahib with full concentration and pondering over the meaning. As we continue to recite Gurbani and mould our lives according to the golden principles of Gurbani, we can realize Waheguru and put an end to all our suffering. Once you attain that level of spirituality, you realize that the worldly attractions that you thought were very important to you at one time, have very little value, if at all. **Above all, you have realized the real objective of life - to be one with Waheguru. So, why would we need any living guru who may himself be a victim of *haumein*, and thus may be highly imperfect?**

The Guru is Created by Waheguru

But, if some other noble soul becomes enlightened because Waheguru has revealed the Divine Knowledge to him, he will be the Guru, and I will be the first to bow at his feet and worship Him. **However, no one can become Guru by self proclamation. It is Waheguru Who creates the Guru.** Guru Amar Das Ji testifies this fact in the following holy Shabad which seems to have been recited at the time of passing the Guruship to Guru Ram Das Ji.

- Why should not the belonging of someone else, held by you in trust, be passed on to the rightful owner? You feel relieved only when the belonging has been returned. **The Shabad (Knowledge of Waheguru) stays only with the Guru, and will Not enlighten anybody else. ——— (Sarang ki Vaar, Sloak M:3, 1249)**

So, the Guru is created by Waheguru. No one can just claim to be the Guru even though thousands of individuals are doing just that these days. Such fake gurus are a lot more harmful than helpful because they themselves are victims of *haumein*, and are captivated by *maya*. How can they rid your haumein when they are tightly gripped by it themselves? Name a single so called 'saint' who is not engrossed in *maya*. They live in mansions, have all the modern luxuries not available to most people, collect huge donations, and do not earn their livelihood by honest means - a fundamental requirement of all Sikhs, let alone the 'saints'. **Most people go to them not for spiritual reasons, but for the fulfilment of their worldly wants.** The 'saints' 'bless' the 'devotees' for the fulfilment of their wishes which statistically have a 50% chance of success, anyway. Those who have their wishes fulfilled serve as a major source of advertisement for the 'saints'. The worldly wants keep people visiting the 'saints' who have no clear concept of Waheguru and Gurbani. A true saint (Guru) will rarely grant your worldly wants. He will most likely advise you to accept the Will of Waheguru, and worship Him so that you realize Him and recognize the **insignificance** of the perishable worldly attractions, and lose interest in them. By worshipping Waheguru and controlling your worldly desires, you will also recognise the importance of the union with Waheguru - the main objective of human life. Guru Sahiban always advised their Sikhs (disciples) to accept the Will of Waheguru, and to sing His praise at the same time as a cure for their suffering, and to attain a spiritual level whereby their wishes would become unimportant to them and they would lead a life of contentment. A well documented example is provided by the life history of Guru Angad Dev Ji, the Second Guru. There was a serious drought in Majha (central Punjab) one year. The earth was parched and the crops were withering away. Heat was unbearable for all living beings, and ponds and pools were running dry. Even the supply of drinking water was low. Everybody was desperate for rain. Many farmers got together and went to Guru Ji in a group requesting Him to use His supernatural powers to cause rain to alleviate their problems. Guru Ji was living in Khadoor, a village, in the present district of Amritsar. Guru Ji listened to their problem very sympathetically, but, advised them to accept the Will of Waheguru and wait for His Grace. He also advised them to sing Waheguru's praise and pray to Him. Where things are beyond human control, accepting the Will of Waheguru is one of the important Principles of *Gurmat*. The farmers left satisfied, but the suffering caused by drought was unbearable.

There was also a yogi living in Khadoor who was very jealous of the reverence accorded to Guru Ji by the ever increasing number of people. He had claimed to possess some supernatural powers in the past. Some people went to him for help. He told them that he would use his powers to cause rain provided they made Guru Ji leave Khadoor. People were hesitant to do that, but the need for rain was so strong that they forgot all the reverence for Guru Ji, and asked Him either to cause rain or leave the village. **Guru Sahib chose to accept the Will of Waheguru and not to use His powers to cause rain.** He left the village to go to a neighbouring forest. This is an example of extreme humbleness on the part of Guru Sahib. He was fully capable of causing rain, and would have won the praise and glory of many more people. However, winning glory of people was NOT an objective of the Perfect Guru? Guru Nanak Sahib strongly disapproved the false and short-lived admiration by people which simply boosts ego and causes gap between Waheguru and the glorified individual.

- Burn admiration by the world in fire, oh Nanak! It causes you to forget Waheguru, and not even a small part of it accompanies you after death.
  (Malhar ki Vaar, Sloak M:2, 1290)

Guru Angad Dev Ji recited this holy Sloak at the time of leaving Khadoor. It is extremely tough to overcome ego of this magnitude. How many so called saints or living gurus do this? They are very eager to please people to win their admiration.

If a rare individual does visit the 'saints' for spiritual reasons, the 'saints' whisper a few select words very secretively in the ears of the Truth- seeker, and tell him to recite them in a very ritualistic way. They strictly forbid the devotees to share their 'words' with any one else. This process prompts a few questions. First, why are those words given secretively? Anything that's for the goodness of the people, should not be kept secret. Guru Sahiban never used secrecy to deliver the Divine Message to masses. We do not keep the holy Gurbani a secret either; we rather disseminate it on air waves so that it may reach millions of people, and benefit them. **Second and more important, are those 'words' more sacred than the holy Gurbani or the Mool Mantra?** Did Guru Sahiban forget to think of those secret words? Obviously, something is NOT right about the 'words' and the process. Therefore, the recitation of those secretively given words is incapable of bringing you any closer to Waheguru.

The self-proclaimed 'saints' are unable to guide you honestly in any aspect of life. They rather leave you more confused. On the other hand, they have already robbed you of some wealth, your intellect, and your dignity - and that's not all. When you realize that you have been cheated, you become alienated. You don't trust anyone else, and lose faith in religion. The gap between you and Waheguru becomes wider, and you are farther removed from the real objective of life. **Guru Nanak Sahib maintains that a fake guru is not capable of getting salvation for you.**

- I have been through countless lives before. I have no idea how many fathers, mothers, sons and daughters I have had. I must have had many gurus whose disciple I was. The reason I had to go through so many lives is because my fake gurus were unable to get salvation for me. **(Ramkali M:1, Dakkhni, Onkar, 932)**

  Kabir Ji also has a similar view.
- If you love Waheguru and want to realize Him, search for the Real Guru, oh my friend! Just like

grinding unripe mustard produces neither oil nor mustard meal, (a fake guru is incapable of guiding you spiritually or morally).
(Sloak Kabir Ji, 1377)

- People who sermonize others only, get sand in their mouths (gain no spiritual advancement), oh Kabir! While trying to teach spirituality to others, they lose their own. **(Sloak Kabir Ji, 1369)**
- Such gurus should be condemned strongly who cannot enlighten their disciples, oh Kabir! They are drowned completely in the four Vedas (are in complete dark because they have acquired no enlightenment) and are causing their followers to drown too. **(Sloak Kabir Ji, 1370)**

Only Waheguru Connects You to the Guru

But, even if a real living guru were there, and even if you could visit him, yet, according to the holy Gurbani, you will not be able to benefit from him until you have Waheguru's grace. You can be connected to the Guru only by Waheguru's grace. Waheguru Himself creates opportunities for the deserving people to be connected to the Guru. Listen to the following holy Shabads.

- I found the Satguru just as I had heard about Him. He is your advocate in Waheguru's Court, and He connects the disconnected people to Waheguru. ——**But only those people are connected to the Guru who are predestined to do so by Waheguru. (Ramkali ki Vaar, Sloak M:5, 957)**
- ———The Guru bestows upon you the Naam of Waheguru which is the real Amrit (liquid of immortality). **The Guru Himself reaches the lucky people who are predestined by Waheguru for the meeting. (Suhi M:1, 729)**
- People, who have searched for Waheguru in their

innerselves by reciting the pleasing Shabad of the Guru, and have thus worshipped Waheguru, get all their wishes fulfilled. **But only those get connected to the Guru, and thus worship Waheguru, who have won the kindness of Waheguru.**

(Maru ki Vaar, M:3, Pauri, 1090)

- ———The source of everything in the universe - Waheguru - Himself bestows gifts on you, oh man! You should always say 'victory to Him' (sing His praise). **When He is kind to you, He will arrange for you to be connected to the Guru**, and then you will be able to acquire Waheguru's Naam in your heart.

  (Bhairon M:3, 1129)

- ——— Recite the name of Waheguru all the time, oh my mind! It is Waheguru Who has connected you to the Guru by His grace. **(Bhairon M:4, 1134)**

There are hundreds of holy shabads like these which claim that only Waheguru's grace makes it possible for someone to be connected to the Guru. So, you will not be able to connect to the real Guru even if you tried on your own. Only Waheguru will make that connection. Remember, Baba Amar Das Ji (later Guru Amar Das Ji) was a very religious man who went to river Gunga (the Ganges) - the perceived holy river for the Hindus - every year for twenty years, but surprisingly, he never went to see Guru Nanak Dev Ji even though he was contemporary of Guru Nanak Dev Ji, and did not live too far from Guru Ji's place. He was able to come to Guru's refuge (Guru Angad Dev Ji's) only when Waheguru had wished. **So, we should also wait for Waheguru's grace Who would surely make arrangements for us to meet with the Guru.** However, to be eligible for Waheguru's grace, you have to start reciting Waheguru's Naam first with clean and focussed mind using Gurbani, and start living your life based on the Teachings of the Guru. With continuous hard work, you will become eligible for Waheguru's grace, and realize Him through Guru Granth Sahib. Waheguru will NOT connect you to an imposter. He will connect you to the real Guru. So, as discussed shortly before, we should work to earn Waheguru's Grace, and leave the union with the Guru to Him. We do not need any fake living guru. Did Guru Gobind Singh Ji make a mistake by not appointing a living individual as His successor?" Bhai Dalip Singh became a little emotional. He also paused for a short while to solicit questions.

"That's all very well said, Bhai Sahib, and is very convincing. But, there is a great praise for saints even in Guru Granth Sahib. We hear again and again that we should touch the feet of the saints, and sing Waheguru's praise in their company. Guru Arjun Dev Ji advises us in Sukhmani Sahib to wash the feet of the saint and offer your soul to him. So, aren't those holy hymns true then? Bibi Kulwant Kaur asked in an uneasy tone?

"May Waheguru burn my tongue if I ever said that. Only a big sinner could show such a profanity. The only secret here is to recognize a true saint as defined by Guru Sahiban. There are hundreds of holy shabads which define a saint. In Sukhmani Sahib alone, there are two full ashatpadis (about 3 full pages) that define a saint. According to the holy Guru Granth Sahib, a saint has the same spiritual level as the Guru, and many a time the two have been used interchangeably. Let's refresh our memory on the definition.

- Man is engrossed in *maya*. Therefore his mind is greedy and unwise. It is always preoccupied in greed, and shows no interest in Guru's Shabad. If he can be connected with the **Saint-Guru,** he will be able to realize Waheguru Who is the source of all good qualities. **(Siri Raag, M;1, 21)**
- I am as good as the dust touched by the Guru's

feet. —— You can attain contentment and rid yourself of all your sins and discomforts if you could meet the **Saint-Guru. (Sarang M: 4, 1198)**

- Oh Waheguru! Please be kind and connect me with the **Saint-Guru.** I may make my mouth the home of Guru's Shabad thereby ridding myself of the poison of vices just as snake's poison can be gotten rid of by injecting the appropriate herbal extract. We are Guru's slaves - His servants - and we can change our obnoxious nature to be sweet and pleasant in His company. **(Gauri M:4, 171)**
- I salute the formless Waheguru who Himself is the **Sadhu-Guru,** and Who alone was there at the beginning of the universe, is still here, and will be there even at the end of the universe. —— **(Gauri Bawan Akkhri, M: 5, 250)**
- Only those eyes are considered noble which see the **Saint-Guru**, oh my soul! **(Bihagara, M: 4, Chhant, 540)**
- Who has the ability to describe the greatness of the Sadhu (Saint) oh, Nanak! Just as no one can describe the greatness of Waheguru, so can nobody describe the greatness of the Sadhu - the two are comparable. ———— Even the Vedas cannot describe the greatness of the Sadhu because it is the highest and the greatest of all. Only the Sadhu deserves that greatness because there is no difference between the Sadhu (Saint) and Waheguru, oh Nanak!

  (Gauri Sukhmani, M: 5, Ashatpadi, 7)
- Whoever takes shelter of the Saint is protected from the claws of *maya* oh, Nanak! Whoever talks ill of the Saint is born again and again.

  (Gauri Sukhmani, Sloak, M: 5, 279)

As we can see from the above holy hymns, Guru Sahiban

have defined the 'Sadhu' or the 'Saint' the same way as the Guru, and just like the Guru, have called the Sadhu a form of Waheguru (A body fully enlightened with the Divine Light) . In the first five hymns, Guru Sahiban have used 'Saint - Guru' as one word making no distinction between the Saint (Sadhu) and the Guru. In the fourth Shabad (Gauri, Bawan Akkhri), Guru Arjun Dev Ji has called Waheguru 'Sadhu-Guru' leaving absolutely no doubt that just like the Guru, the Sadhu is also a form of Waheguru. So, Sadhu or Saint are just different words for the Guru. So, it is not a surprise when Guru Sahiban advise us to sing the praise of Waheguru in Sadh Sangat (the company of the Sadhu) because Sadhu means Guru.

Now, if you can show me a Sadhu or a Saint who fits this definition, I will consider myself the most lucky person to touch his feet. An individual cannot be a Sadhu or a Saint simply because he calls himself (or others call him) so. He has to be one with Waheguru all the time. But, if we don't have an individual of that calibre, it is no use to treat him like the Guru. In fact, as discussed earlier, it is very, very harmful to have that much faith in the fake sadhus, and accord them the level of respect as innocent people are according now. **Being the source of Divine Knowledge, Guru Granth Sahib is the only perfect Guru. So, I'll say: no, we don't need a living guru."** Bhai Dalip Singh made a brief pause to have a sip of water, and to catch breath.

"You've made it very clear, Bhai Sahib, and thank you very much for that. But, I have a slightly different question. Since the holy Gurbani is not that simple to understand for a common man, don't we need a guru to explain the Gurbani?" Bhai Hardev Singh asked.

"Sure, we need some knowledgeable scholar to explain Gurnbani to us. But, the scholar that explains the holy Gurbani is not the Guru. He may have a thorough knowledge of the language, but he is not 'enlightened' with the Divine Light, and thus cannot replace the Guru. For purpose of explaining Gurbani to us, we are lucky to have scholars of the calibre of Prof Sahib Singh who has done a marvellous job. He has translated the Revered Guru Granth Sahib, and where needed, has provided a convincing rationale for the conclusions drawn by him. His complete translation is available in ten volumes at a very reasonable cost. I'll urge all of you to buy that collectively, if not individually. That's what you need - a good explanation of Gurbani. But, people like Prof Sahib Singh, are scholars only - which we badly need - but they should NOT be mistaken for Gurus. **Our Guru is only and only Sri Guru Granth Sahib which is the soul of Guru Nanak and the other Gurus, and which is also the bodyless form of Waheguru."** Bhai Dalip Singh concluded.

"Have I answered your question to your satisfaction, Bhai Sahib?" Bhai Dalip Singh asked Bhai Hardev Singh.

"Most definitely, Bhai Sahib. Thank you very much for that. You have enlightened a large number of ignorant people like me. I hope people will have more faith in Sri Guru Granth Sahib now, and will quit wasting their time and money to seek the blessing of the so called saints." Bhai Hardev Singh was also emotional.

There was no further question. Bhai Kashmir Singh thanked Bhai Dalip Singh heartily for a highly informative discourse. There was a long and loud applause from the congregation which headed for the kitchen after the traditional Slogan: Waheguru Ji ka Khalsa Waheguru Ji ki Fateh.

10

Gurmat and Meat

Bhai Kashmir Singh's courtyard is full with people who are greeting each other with enthusiasm, and who are waiting eagerly for the arrival of Bhai Dalip Singh on the stage. Cooks are busy preparing food for the congregation, and there is a great hustle and bustle at the farmhouse. Bhai Dalip Singh appeared on the stage with a big smile on his face. He greeted everybody with the traditional slogan, "Waheguru Ji ka Khalsa, Waheguru Ji ki Fateh" in a sweet and warm voice to which everybody responded with the same warmth.

"What's the question for today?" Bhai Sahib asked smilingly.

"Would you mind answering a controversial question which has been dogging me for some time, Bhai Sahib?" Bhai Piyara Singh asked politely. He was a middle-aged pleasant-looking gentleman but was not wearing all the five K's.

"Please go ahead, Bhai Sahib." There was an equal politeness in Bhai Dalip Singh's voice.

"People are not clear about the verdict of Gurbani on the issue of eating meat. Different people have different opinions on the subject. Some Sikh "leaders" profess that eating meat is strictly prohibited while some are confident that eating meat is allowed in *Gurmat*. Yet some others maintain that meat is allowed under special circumstances only. All these people who are known to have a public opinion on the subject are well known in the Sikh world. How can different scholars draw different conclusions based on the same holy Gurbani? Would you please, clarify the issue?" Bhai Pyara Singh was genuinely concerned.

"Bhai Sahib, I cannot speculate why different scholars would draw different conclusions from the sacred Gurbani because there is no contradiction in Gurbani. There may be many reasons for different people to draw different conclusions on the subject. Such people may have their own agenda about the subject, or may follow their hearts rather than the Gubani, or may honestly be naive about the real meaning. I'll share with you what Gurbani has to say on the subject.

Before I share the verdict of the Gurbani on the subject, let's discuss how much has been written on the subject in Guru Granth Sahib.

There are about ten very important issues which are discussed in the sacred Guru Granth Sahib again and again. They include:

- Purpose of human life
- Having unshakable faith in Waheguru alone, and in no other god or deity.
- Reciting holy Naam and following the Guru's Teachings
- Importance of the Guru, and the company of holy men
- Leading a life of contentment, and obeying Waheguru's will.
- Earning one's living by honest means and not encroaching upon the rights of others.
- Controlling one's sensual pleasures, and not be attracted to the beauty of others

- Controlling one's rage
- Controlling one's ego or selfishness
- Equal treatment of all human beings, and helping the needy
- Not hurting the feelings of other human beings
- Avoiding strong attachment with the worldly things
- Having no faith in rituals or superstitions, etc. etc.

There is hardly a page among the 1430 pages of the holy Guru Granth Sahib where one or the other of the above mentioned issues is not discussed. The reason for the discussion of such issues is that they are very vital. But there are only about 6 or 7 holy Shabads (hymns) that discuss the subject of meat. If eating or not eating meat were so important, there must have been a lot more mention on the subject and an unequivocal emphasis on whether to avoid meat. But clearly, that emphasis is missing. Also, out of the 35 holy great men whose compositions have been included in Guru Granth Sahib, only two Great Souls - Guru Nanak Dev Ji, and Kabir Ji discuss the subject. Again, if the issue were that important, why would not the other Gurus or Bhagats discuss it? In terms of volume (the number of shabads and other holy writings), Guru Arjun Dev Ji has the most contribution to Guru Granth Sahib; but there is not even a couplet by Him on the subject. This conspicuous absence of the topic in Guru Arjun Dev Ji's compositions clearly shows that the issue is not important at all.

The issue of eating or not eating meat stems from the centuries old principle of being kind to animals, and therefore not killing them. But let's discuss the law of nature on the subject.

Law of Nature: The world has been created by Waheguru in such a way that one animal (or life form) is the food for some others. This principle ensures a healthy balance in nature. If no animal ate others, and all animals ate vegetation only, there would not be enough food for everybody, and soon all living beings will begin to die. But, there is even a much bigger concern. With all living beings consuming vegetation, it will begin to disappear quickly, and there will be an acute shortage of oxygen which is produced by the plants. At the same time, there will be huge surplus of carbon dioxide, resulting in less and less supply of oxygen for any life to be possible on the planet.

As all of us know, chickens eat small worms, and chickens are a favorite food for cats and dogs. Cats can be killed by dogs or other bigger animals, and this cycle continues. Likewise, ticks feed on animals, but birds love to have a feast on ticks. There are many predators of birds including the birds of prey and other carnivores. Guru Angad Dev Ji has expressed this fact of nature beautifully in one of His couplets.

- Don't panic over the lack of food, oh man! The Creator, Waheguru, is concerned about your needs. ————He has arranged for food for the living beings even in water. ————He has created the world in such a way that one life form is food for some others. **(Ramkali ki Vaar, Sloak M:2, 955)**

Will you believe that there are some varieties of plants that devour small bugs or insects! They trap the insects in their leaves and inject enzymes to digest them. **So, even innocent-looking plants can be meat eaters.** Such plants include pitcher plants, sun dew and Venus' flytrap. If some animals did not feed on others, and every life form were to survive on vegetation, there will be a shortage of food very soon on this planet resulting in starvation, death and destruction for all life forms.

Some Killing Almost Unavoidable

• We burn wood and animal dung cakes to build fire; but, all of us know that there are living bugs and worms in both, which are killed during burning. When sugar cane is squeezed in big steel rollers, many bugs which remain sticking to the canes get killed. The same is true when wheat or other forms of grain are milled to make flour or pulses because there are some bugs in grain all the time. Now, you could spray insecticides on crops to kill the bugs, but you are killing them nonetheless.

• We know that some bugs are attracted to light, and thousands of them die when they come too close to light. **Does anyone ever shut off lights to save bugs?**

• We trample over thousands of earth worms, white-lined brown worms (called ghumiars or potters), plant worms, butterflies, and so on, everyday while walking or driving vehicles. I know thousands of lobsters get killed on roads near the ocean in Australia during their migration, and thousands of snakes get killed on roads in Manitoba, Canada, during their mating season. Despite the best efforts of humans to save the accidental killing of these animals, thousands still get killed.

- We also kill zillions of bacteria and other harmful blood suckers everyday to rid ourselves and our pets or domesticated animals of any disease. We kill mosquitoes, flies, wasps, yellow-jackets, mice, lice, ticks, snakes etc. everyday.
- Do vegetarians and people who oppose eating meat very strongly realize that their favorite foods, yogurt, butter and cheese are made by billions of living bacteria. If there were no bacteria in the culture used to make yogurt, they will not have these rich and delicious foods to enjoy. In other words, we are killing thousands of living organisms and still claim ourselves to be vegetarians.

Abusing Living Beings in Many Other Ways

If we preach kindness to animals, then kindness should

also mean not to abuse, mistreat, or do injustice to animals. But do we follow that? Let's examine that too.

- We put oxen, horses, donkeys, camels, elephants and yaks etc to extreme hard work. They do tough labour for us including hard farm work, and as means of transportation. Not only that, many horses, elephants and camels used as vehicles, got killed in battles. Reindeer and dogs are still being used by the Eskimos to pull their sleds.
- The domesticated milch-cattle like buffaloes, cows and goats produce milk for their young ones, and not for us, but who uses them? Us of course! Is this justice?
- Bees do not make honey for us, and silk worms do not spin silk for us. Do we let these insects enjoy their product which they make with hard labour?
- We use the wool of sheep for our own comfort.
- Some people abuse exotic animals like snakes, monkeys, bears, lions, elephants and the like to earn their living.
- Animals are also used as guinea pigs to carry out research to improve the medical facilities for man. How many of you would support putting an end to this practice?
- There are billions of friendly bacteria in our body which protect us from the attacks by harmful bacteria. While protecting us, they get killed by the enemy bacteria which outnumber the friendly bacteria. This is how the immune system of human body works. So, there are billions of living organisms which sacrifice their lives to protect us. Waheguru Himself has arranged this to protect us against diseases". Bhai Dalip Singh Ji explained the special status of man in relation to the other life forms. Everybody was listening very carefully.

Man the Master on This Planet

"It is because of all of the above facts that Guru Arjun Dev Ji has called man the master of this planet , and other life forms are subservient to him. **(Assa M:5. 374).**

He reiterates the same fact again when He says that the man is superior to all the life forms in the world **(Ramkali M:5, Ashatpadian. 913).**

This is not to say that humans should torture the animals for their shear enjoyment. It simply means that humans can use animals and their products to meet their needs. Guru Nanak Dev Ji describes the **planet Earth as Dharamshaal - the place to realize Waheguru** through high living and by worshiping Him. Now that's possible only in human form. So, basically earth is a place for man to live and to realize Waheguru **(Jap Ji, M:1).** This fact has also been reiterated several times by Guru Amar Das Ji when He writes that human body is the dwelling place of Waheguru. **(Ramkali ki Vaar, M:3. Parbhati M:3, Sloak M:3, Over and above the vaars).**

That puts all other life forms to be subservient to man. In fact, Guru Nanak Sahib has ridiculed the extreme practice of trying to avoid killing of small insects and bugs even by accident followed by the Jains.

- The Jainis are completely misguided by the Will of Waheguru HImself. They have no concept of Waheguru and His laws, and they are so obsessed with the idea of mercy for the animals that they cover their mouths with cloth to avoid inhaling any living beings. They pull their hair so they won't get lice; they do not bathe for a long, long time so that they do not kill organisms in water. When they travel, they do so in lines, and the leader has a whisk in his hand to dispel any insects or bugs out of the way. They even spread out their excrement so that organism may not be born in there. They are always depressed and find no joy in life because of their such restrictive faith. **(Malhar ki Vaar, M:1, Pauri, 1258)**

Any questions so far?" Bhai Dalip Singh asked the audience.

"May be later. We're enjoying your lecture very much." A few voices could be heard from the audience.

History of Eating Meat

"Okay. In that case let's now discuss the history of meat eating". Bhai Dalip Singh continued. "Man has been known to eat meat for as long as the recorded history. The Vedas mention eating of meat even by the gods. Lord Indra is described to have been eating a whole buffalo in his meals. And, Lord Rama must have been a hunter otherwise he would not have chased the golden deer at the demand of his consort, Seeta. There have been *yaggas* in our country in which animals were killed for eating purposes. Ashavmedh *yaggas* were very popular. Ashav means horse and ashavmedh means killing a horse for sacrificial purposes. Of course after the sacrifice, the meat was eaten. Guru Nanak Sahib testifies that meat was served in yaggas and at marriage ceremonies. **(Malhar ki Vaar, Sloak M:1, 1289)**

Not only in yaggas and in marriages, meat was served even at the *janeyoo* ceremonies. Guru Nanak Sahib writes that goats were killed and cooked at *janeyoo* ceremonies and their meat was served to complete the ceremony **(Asa ki Vaar, Sloak M:1, 471)**

Since Guru Nanak Sahib's father, Mehta Kalu Ji, was a rich man, and the custom to serve goat meat was there, **there is every reason to believe that Mehta Ji got goat meat prepared for the guests at the aborted janeyoo ceremony of Guru Nanak Sahib.**

With the exception of a very few peoples, the whole world eats meat. Not only the Muslims eat meat, but, their belief in eating meat is so strong that they also offer sacrifice of animals to Allah after the Hajj. Eskimos, who live within the Arctic Circle, cannot survive without meat because of the climatic conditions. They can grow very little vegetables, if at all, because most of the ground is permanently frozen. They eat seal meat, burn its fat to cook and to light, and use its skin to cover themselves. Europeans are the biggest consumers of meat, and probably cannot survive without it - again because of the harsh climatic conditions. Things are changing somewhat now because of the new technology whereby vegetables and fruits can be stored for a much longer period, but meat is still consumed in large proportions.

The first humans to inhabit earth must have been carnivores besides being fruit eaters because they must have learned eating from wild animals which are both carnivores and plant eaters. It must have taken thousands of years for humans to develop farming skills and to produce grain for cooking purposes.

Sikh history (Bhai Vir Singh) mentions that Guru Nanak Sahib cooked a deer brought by a young rajah at Kurukshetra when Guru Ji visited the place during a solar eclipse. According to Hindu beliefs, let alone cooking meat, even fire building is not permitted during solar eclipses . When angry Brahmans led by Pandit Nanoo came to question Guru Ji about building fire and cooking meat, Guru Ji explained to them the whole philosophy of human life, and how Waheguru can be pleased. Guru Ji explained that eating meat is not a sin, and not eating meat is not a virtue by itself unless one's mind is clean. The Brahmans were completely satisfied and bowed to Guru Ji several times." Bhai Dalip Singh paused for a few moments.

"Guru Har Gobind Sahib, and Guru Gobind Singh Ji, both enjoyed hunting, and did so whenever they found some time from their very busy schedules. Again, the Sikh history

(Bhai Vir Singh) describes that Guru Gobind Singh Ji killed some of Baba Banda Singh Bahadur's goats for meal when He went to see the latter at Nader, Maha Rashtra. When some of the Sikhs were reluctant to eat meat because of the Brahmani influence, the leading Sikhs began to call meat "mahaparshad" (greatfood) so that the reluctant Sikhs would not feel bad about eating meat. In Punjab, goat meat is still called mahaparshad.

Also in Sikh Rehit Maryadas (The Code of Sikh Practices), most of which have been written by the well known Sikhs like Bhai Desa Singh, Bhai Chaupa Singh and Bhai Prehlad Singh etc. who were contemporary to Guru Gobind Singh Ji, there is no restriction on eating meat. The only restriction is on eating "halal" meat which is prepared by Islamic practices. 'Halal' is prepared by killing the animal slowly so that it bleeds to death. At the same time they also read some couplets from the Quran with the belief that the killed animal goes to paradise.

This is some of the history of eating meat. Are there any questions now?" Bhai Dalip Singh asked.

Meat Eating and Gurbani

"Yes, Bhai Sahib, I've a question now." Bhai Piyara Singh said, " You've shared some very interesting history and convincing facts about eating meat; but, we are eager to know the verdict of Guru Granth Sahib on the subject? Does it allow eating meat or not?" Bhai Piyara Singh seemed very eager to know.

"I was coming to that Bhai Sahib. As discussed earlier, there are only two Great souls who have written on the subject - Guru Nanak Sahib, and Bhagat Kabir Ji. Let's first discuss the verdict of Guru Nanak Dev Ji." Bhai Dalip Singh cleared his throat.

"There are two holy shabads of Guru Nanak Dev Ji which are devoted only to this issue. One covers the subject more extensively than the other. So, we'll discuss that shabad only. In this sacred sloak Guru Ji addresses a Brahman who is opposed to eating meat. The Brahman pretends to disapprove eating meat so much so that he does not want even to touch it. I will translate the whole shabad in its entirety:

- Only a foolish person devoid of any knowledge of Divinity, will debate the subject of eating meat. It is not even possible to clearly categorize vegetation and meat (animals). [Some sea animals look like plants, and some plants are carnivores. But, even plants have life.] So, how can we decide whether it is sin to eat one or the other. The Vedas and other religious books mention that people killed rhinoceros to perform *heavns* and *yaggas* to please gods. People who suck blood of humans at night (rob them of their wealth and dignity) pretend to be very pious and pinch their noses at the sight of meat to show their disdain, have no knowledge of union with God, and fake their actions only as a show off to the people. They are like a blind man who is unable to follow directions. By 'blind' I do not mean a person who is blind of eyesight, I mean a person who is bereft of intelligence, and who does evil things. Everybody is born from the blood and flesh of their parents, but refuse to eat fish or meat. When a man and a woman get together at night, they use meat to make love. All of us grow in meat, are born out of meat, and are made of meat (the idea is that we abuse the bodies of others to survive) but the Brahman who has neither knowledge nor any concept of union with God, calls himself smart. Why is it acceptable to use the meat at home (your wife's body), but not the meat from outside (a chicken or a goat etc.) Pundit Ji? All living beings are born out of meat, and the soul also resides in bodies made of flesh. (If you can abuse the bodies of others, what rationale is there not to eat meat?) People who are led by blind (incapable) gurus do not eat the well-deserving food, but will relish the food belonging to others. We all develop in meat, are born out of meat and are made of meat, but the Brahman who has no knowledge or concept of union with God, considers himself smart. Eating of meat has been approved by the Puranas (Hindu religious books) and by the Western religious books (The Bible, The Torah and the Quran), and meat was used in all the four Yugas. Meat was also used at the festive occasions of yaggas and weddings. All men and women including the kings and the emperors are born out of meat. According to the Brahmanical philosophy, meat-eating people go to Hell and the non-eaters go to Paradise. In that case Brahmans should accept no charities from the meat-eating people. What a tyrannical situation that people who give in charities go to Hell and Brahmans who accept their donations gô to Paradise! You think you are very smart to teach others what you don't know yourself hey Pundit! You don't even know where meat comes from, hey Pundit. The root of all life is water. All grain, sugarcane, cotton and all life in the universe are dependent upon water. Therefore, water does a lot of noble deeds because it supports life in many different ways. Hence, Nanak professes an important thought that if a person really wants to claim to be non-violent, he should quit indulging in the tastes of all vegetation because it too is supported by water. **(Malhar ki Vaar, Sloak M:1, 1289)**

As is crystal clear from this holy shabad, Guru Nanak Sahib is not opposed to eating meat even though He is not promoting it. He has stated all the facts on the subject, but has left the choice to the individuals. Another important underlying idea of this holy shabad is that we rationalize our own choices to suit our needs. Addressing a Pundit, Guru Ji has highlighted the evil practice of manipulation of human beings by some clever leaders. We abuse others (or other life forms) in many ways and completely justify the abuse. If we can live without some of the things, we call their use sinful, and impose our choices on others. We do not try to understand Waheguru's Laws and ignore them to suit our choices". Bhai Dalip Singh paused for a while, and solicited further questions.

"This wonderful shabad is very enlightening, Bhai Sahib, but, I'm still not clear on a few things about the holy shabad. Would you mind expanding on some of its parts?" Bhai Gurdip Singh asked.

"Gladly, Bhai Sahib". Bhai Dalip Singh was very pleasant.

"When we are growing in our mother's womb, and when we are breast fed, we are definitely using meat in some form, but, it is Waheguru's law for reproduction of human beings and other mammals. But is not killing animals for their meat much, much different from the use of our mother's body?" Bhai Gurdip Singh seemed confused.

"I'm glad that you asked that question, Bhai Sahib." Bhai Dalip Singh said smilingly. "You understood Waheguru's Law about reproduction clearly, but, you also need to understand some other laws of Waheguru which may not be very evident to us, and we need some guru, like Sri Guru Nanak Dev Ji, to clarify those for us. For better understanding of the subject, let's divide it into two parts - killing an animal, and eating its meat. **Life and death are the most fundamental laws of Waheguru**. **Everything that is born must die someday**. As all of us know from our everyday experience, and as discussed earlier, one life form is food for other life forms. As an example, herons feast on fish and toads, while hawks and eagles relish herons. This fact or Law of Waheguru has been articulated very well by Guru Angad Dev Ji when He says that the provider, Waheguru, has created the world in such a way that one life form is food for other life forms. **(Ramkali ki Vaar, Sloak M:2, 955).**

Whether an animal is devoured by another animal, or is killed by a human being, it does not make any difference because death is inevitable in either case. If Waheguru had not intended the killing of animals, He would not have created carnivores. However, torturing of any animal, and hurting the feelings of human beings is strictly prohibited in Gurmat. As we've discussed several times now, Waheguru can be realized in the human form only, and not in any other life form. So, hurting feelings of humans is strictly prohibited. As far as animals are concerned, barring pregnant females, most adult animals have no family ties. If they are killed, there is no one to mourn their death, and their loss goes unnoticed. For example who feels the pain when a male adult chicken or a male goat suddenly disappears? Most adults in jungle roam about independently, and don't seem to have any family ties. So, if they are killed, nobody would miss them. The important thing is that they should be killed instantly, and not tortured. In fact instant killing is a better death for them than being eaten alive by carnivores. According to Gurmat, soul is immortal; so when an animal is killed, its soul is not killed. It is reborn again to enjoy life. **Actually, by passing through different life forms quickly, it advances to human form faster.**

Vegetation has Life Too

But more importantly, as Sahib Sri Guru Nanak Dev Ji has explained in the holy Sloak discussed a earlier, all vegetation has life. Very recently scientists have proved that like animals, not only plants have life, they have feelings too. I watched a

TV show in which scientists demonstrated that plants showed feelings of joy and of fear. By connecting electrodes to the plants and to an oscilloscope, the scientists showed electrical signals produced by plants just like the ones produced by human beings displaying feelings of joy and fear. In fact, the scientists showed how a particular plant produced signals expressing fear when a murderer was brought in front of the plant. This murderer had committed a murder earlier in the presence of this plant. Scientists are working on using plants as witnesses for such crimes in the future. **More recently, I watched another show on the 'Discovery' channel in which they showed that when a giraffe approached a tree to eat its leaves in Kenya, it sent signals to its neighboring trees warning them of the attack. The neighboring trees quickly injected poison in their leaves making them unfit for consumption by giraffes. When a giraffe approached a neighboring tree, he found a change in color of the leaves. On smelling them, he must have found something unappealing about them because he left without eating them. These new amazing discoveries are making vegetation more and more like animals. So, how can we justify killing grains and vegetables which have life, for our food, and label the killing of other life forms as sin?**

Now coming to eating meat, when an animal is killed, it makes no difference to the dead animal whether its body is eaten or is left to decay. A dead body is just like a vegetable. As long as you do not become a slave to eating meat, it is no more a sin than eating vegetables. If you become slave to eating sweets or other tasty foods, you are no better than people who eat meat on availability only. When you become slave to some habit, you could commit sinful or even criminal acts to satisfy your habit. For this reason, *Gurmat* strongly disapproves slavery to any habit or pleasure.

Now coming to your question in which you wondered how the growth of a child in the womb of his mother and the use of breast milk to feed the baby was related to eating meat, the answer should be clear to you. Abusing or misusing others is also a sin. As discussed at the beginning, we abuse animals badly when we use them for hard work for us, when we use products made by them which were intended for their own use, and when we take a big share of their mother's milk, and so on. We've also shown that killing animals is no more sin than killing vegetation. Now Guru Sahib asks this question to awaken us that if abusing the body of your mother (or wife) which is made of meat is not considered sin by you, why should eating of meat be a sin because eating of plants which also have life, is not considered sin. In other words Guru Ji is saying that obey the laws (command or will) of Waheguru, and don't try to be more clever than Him.

Fundamental Principle of Food

Guru Nanak Dev Ji's philosophy about food is very simple. He does not place any restriction on foods which you can eat and which you cannot eat. But, He does put a requirement of a different kind while consuming foods - praising Waheguru. According to Him you can eat anything and everything as long as you honestly sing the praise of Waheguru. **When you sing Waheguru's praise, you will not eat anything that will create a gap between you and Him.** In other words you will not eat food which is not earned by honest means, and which produces guilt in you because eating it generates evil feelings. By the same token, foods which are eaten without singing the praise of Waheguru will cause bodily pain and arouse evil sensual desires. **(Siri Raag, M:1, 16)**. Because when you exclude Waheguru from your life, you will indulge in eating, and to satisfy your burning desire of tastes, you will eat foods that do cause stomach problems and arouse evil desires. This principle of including Waheguru applies to all activities in life and not just to food. **Guru Arjun Dev Ji** also says something similar about wearing fancy clothes. He says, 'burn all those fancy clothes if they are worn without singing the praise of Waheguru.' So, as long as we sing the praise of Waheguru honestly, we are allowed to eat any food, including meat." Bhai Dalip Singh took a pause again to solicit further questions.

"Bhai Sahib, we are very thankful to you for enlightening us about eating meat, but is there any restriction on eating beef (cow's meat) because cow is considered a sacred animal in Indian culture?" Bhai Bachan Singh asked.

"Good question, Bhai Sahib. But animals are still animals. They could be more or less useful, but they cannot be sacred. As we discussed earlier, all other life forms are subservient to man. Are all men sacred? if not - and I'm positive that most of them are not -'how can an animal - a lower form of life - be sacred? If they were sacred, they will be one with Waheguru, and will not be suffering as an animal. Both, Guru Nanak Sahib, and Guru Arjun Dev Ji, have made it very clear that cow is no more sacred than any other animal.

- A cow which does not produce milk is like a bird without wings, or like a crop which has not been watered. All of them are useless.' **(Assa M:1, 354-55)**
- A cow which does not produce milk is good for nothing else.
  (Majh M:5, Bara Mah, 133)

So, why should a cow be considered sacred?. Mind you, I'm not promoting eating of beef, I'm simply saying that if you eat meat, beef is no different than any other meat. The choice is still yours." Bhai Dalip Singh clarified.

"The reason I asked that question, Bhai Sahib, was the interpretation of a sloak of Guru Amar Das Ji which is recorded on page 1413 of Sri Guru Granth Sahib. Some scholars maintain that in the Sloak, Guru Amar Das Ji says that killing of a cow is a sin. Would you please, clarify the meaning of that holy Sloak?" Bhai Bachan Singh clarified.

"That's the sad part about explaining Gurmat. Many preachers or missionaries either don't understand the meaning of holy Gurbani, or purposely distort the meanings to suit their own positions on certain issues. I know the holy sloak you are talking about, and I quoted it earlier in a slightly different context. The meaning of the Sloak is definitely NOT what you have heard from some Sikh preacher. In the Sloak, Guru Sahib says the killing of Brahmans, young girls, and cows is **considered** sinful in Hindu holy books. Another condemnable act is to accept donations from an immoral person. But, even more despicable is the person who does not sing the praise of Waheguru. Such a person is many million times more sinful than the sin of all the above four acts combined, and more.**(Sloak M:3. 1413)**

Let me make it very clear that Guru Sahib is not saying that the killing of a cow is sinful. If that were the intent of the holy sloak, then killing of a Brahman should also be a sin according to Guru Sahib. But we all know that caste by birth has no significance in Gurmat. So, why would Guru Sahib choose only Brahmans from among all other castes and declare the killing of a Brahman sinful? He is simply saying that **people consider** the killing of a Brahman sinful. Nowhere in Guru Granth Sahib has it been written that killing of a cow is a sin. Of course, needless killing or the torture of any animal is disapproved. So, to answer your question, no, Guru Sahib does not say that the killing of a cow is a sin." Bhai Dalip Singh clarified.

Bhagat Kabir ji and Bhai Gurdas Ji

"Bhai Sahib, the proponents of vegetarianism quote sloaks or shabads from the writings of Kabir Sahib and of Bhai Gurdas Ji in support of their position. Those holy writings do seem to disapprove eating of meat. I don't remember all the sloaks or even a single sloak in full, but I do remember one line of a sloak which says 'why did you kill a chicken'. Would you kindly explain the meanings of that and other similar sloaks of Kabir Ji and Bhai Gurdas Ji?" Bhai Chanan Singh asked.

"I know exactly what you're saying Bhai Sahib. That's the most quoted shabad of Kabir Sahib - albeit incorrectly - by the proponents of vegetarianism. Kabir Sahib addresses the Hajjis in that holy shabad to point out to their misplaced belief of pleasing Allah by offering sacrifice of some animal after the Hajj. **The shabad has nothing to do with eating or not eating meat**. Let me recite the holy shabad first, and then we will discuss the meaning.

- Do not desecrate each other's religious books like the Vedas and the Quran by calling them a bunch of lies (oh my Hindu and Muslim brothers). In fact, liar is the person who does not analyze them. Let me ask you this question, dear mullah: On one hand, you proclaim that Allah is present in every living being, but on the other, you sacrifice an animal in Allah's name to please Him. How do you justify that? How can you please Allah by killing an animal in which Allah resides Himself (according to your own beliefs)? You teach the justice of Allah to others, but you are still unenlightened, oh mullah!. You catch an animal (a chicken, a goat or a lamb etc) and kill it. Its body is destroyed and you sacrificed the dirt of the dead body in the name of Allah. But, Allah, which is pure light and is immortal was also present in the dead animal. So, explain to me what did you offer to Allah, because whatever you offered was already His as His light was also present in the sacrificial animal?

What is the use of offering any nivaj (Muslim prayer) or going on hajj to Qaba if you are dishonest, or your mind is unclean? What is the use of the ritual of washing your hands and your face? What good is it for you to kneel in the mosque? Hey mullah! you have been unable to uncover the secrets of the sacred Allah because your mind is unclean. Kabir says that because of your dishonesty, and because of your inability to understand Allah, you have missed the opportunity to go to Paradise, and you must be satisfied with Hell now." **(Parbhati Kabir Ji, 1350)**.

Bhai Dalip Singh finished the recitation of the shabad.

"There is hardly any doubt about the meaning or the intent of the shabad. But, you will understand the meaning even better when we discuss another shabad by Kabir Sahib in which He addresses an idol worshiper who picks flowers to offer to the idol.

- The idol worshiper picks leaves (and flowers) of plants for the idol. But, the poor worshiper does not realize that the idol is lifeless whereas each leaf is full of life. The ignorant worshiper makes this serious mistake and does not understand that God is alive. If we go by the religious beliefs of the Hindu worshiper, by plucking leaves and flowers, (s)he has picked (killed) all the three gods because Brahma was born out of the leaves of the lotus flower, Vishnu resides in the stem (which grew out of his navel) and Shiva resides in flowers. So, which god is (s)he worshiping because she has killed all three? While carving the idol out of the rock, the sculptor set his foot on the chest of the idol thereby insulting him. If the idol had any power, why did not he kill the sculptor artist for that insult? Obviously, the idol is lifeless. ————**(Assa Kabir Ji, 479)**.

As is crystal clear from this holy shabad, Kabir Sahib is educating the ignorant idol worshiper about the fallacy of their worship on two fronts. First, the idol is lifeless, and second, even if the worshiper has faith in the lifeless idol, (s)he is defeating the purpose because as discussed just now, by picking leaves and flowers, the worshiper has killed all the three gods.

By comparing the two holy shabads, you can see the similarity of the ideas. In the first shabad, Kabir Sahib educates the mullah about his ignorance of the way he chooses to please Allah - by sacrificing an animal in the name of Allah. In the second, Kabir Ji similarly educates an ignorant idol worshiper who kills plants to please his gods. The message is clear - if the sacrifice of an animal is unacceptable for Allah, so is the offering of flowers and leaves to a god. So, it is clear beyond any doubt that Kabir Sahib is not preaching against eating meat in the first Shabad because if He were, then He is also preaching against killing vegetation. In that case we won't be able to eat anything at all. Kabir Sahib is simply educating the people about their misplaced beliefs." Bhai Dalip Singh explained the real deep meaning of the Shabads.

"That's so logical and so convincing and makes perfect sense, Bhai Sahib. We are very, very thankful to you for the real meaning of the Shabads. I wonder why some self proclaimed saints misguide people and take them away from holy Gurbani. Would you kindly explain the meaning of one more Sloak by Kabir Sahib which the opponents of meat quote again and again. Superficially, the Sloak seems to mean the same as the opponents claim. The Sloak goes:

- Gruel (a thick multigrain soup) is a wonderful meal which contains a sacred ingredient of salt, oh Kabir! Who would like to have his throat cut for a non-vegetarian meal? **(Sloak Kabir Ji, 1374)**

The opponents of meat eating claim that the meaning of

this Sloak is that gruel is the best meal because people who eat meat will have their throats cut when they are presented before God after death. Please clarify the meaning for us." Bhai Gurdip Singh asked eagerly.

"I know this is the most quoted holy Sloak by the opponents of meat, but, those people either do not know the real meaning of the Sloak or don't want to know. If we go by the literal meaning of the Sloak, then nobody should ever eat anything other than gruel containing salt alone. In that case even butter, milk and sugar are prohibited. Can this be the essence of this Sloak? Let alone masses at large, have even the opponents of meat quit eating everything else? Of course, not! They eat a variety of expensive and rich delicious foods including *pranthas, poories,* different puddings, a variety of vegetable dishes and so on - all to satisfy their taste buds. **And not becoming a slave to the taste buds, is the essence of this Sloak.** Kabir Sahib is simply promoting a simple diet so that you do not become slave to your taste buds or sensual pleasures. To eat meat, you will have to cut the throat (kill) some animal. The sentence ' who would have his throat cut' does not mean that the meat-eater will have his throat cut when he appears before Waheguru. It simply means that it is not easy to find meat, you will have to cut the throat (kill) some animal. When someone becomes a slave to his tastes, he will spend a lot of time to prepare different foods, and in some situations may spend a lot of money to satisfy his habit. That money could otherwise be spent on some worthy cause. The time wasted could have been spent to sing praise of Waheguru. That's the message Kabir Sahib is conveying through this holy Sloak. Also, in a few situations, people may be prompted to do some sinful acts like stealing and lying, to satisfy their sensual pleasures; which is immoral.

Guru Nanak Sahib advises us to be content, and has warned us again and again about becoming slave to our tastes because such slavery leads to unpleasant consequences.

Defining the characteristics of a contented Sikh, Guru Sahib says that the real service to Waheguru is the service rendered by the contented Sikhs who praise Waheguru, and who among others things, eat and drink lightly. **(Assa ki Vaar, M:1)**

There are many more shabads like this by all the Gurus.

To understand the real meaning of this Sloak by Kabir Sahib, let us ponder over a Sloak by Farid Ji.

- My roti is wooden, and my appetite serves for all the other dishes. People who eat rotis coated with butter will suffer immensely. **(Sloak Farid Ji, 1379)**

There is absolutely no mention of meat here. But, according to Farid Sahib, people who even eat rotis coated with butter will suffer. How will the opponents of meat explain this sacred couplet of Farid Sahib? Because of our ignorance, or our vested interests, we misinterpret meanings of the holy writings of Great Souls. First, some people drew the literal meaning of the word wooden used by Farid Ji about His roti. They concluded that Farid Ji really had a roti made of wood. They went so far in their belief that they still display a wooden roti at Pak Pattan (Pakistan) where Farid Sahib had spent most of His life, and claim that that was the roti Farid Sahib used to eat. How disrespectful could one get! Not only eating wooden roti is in total contradiction to the sacred Gurbani, but, Farid Sahib never said that. The second line which says that people who eat roti coated with butter will suffer immensely, makes it perfectly clear that what Farid Ji really means by wooden roti is that his roti is dry and hard like wood because it is uncoated. Otherwise He would have said that those who eat rotis other than wooden, would suffer. If there was any doubt in the meaning of this Sloak, Farid Sahib makes it crystal clear in His next Sloak.

- Live on uncoated (very simple and inexpensive) food, and feel content by drinking cold water, oh

Farid!. Don't show any greed to watch other people eating rotis coated with butter (rich foods). **(Sloak Farid Ji, 1379)**

In this sloak Farid Ji does not say that His roti is made of wood. Here he says very clearly that eat simple and inexpensive food and be content. The whole idea is to eat simple food and not become slave to rich tastes (or food). At the same time one should feel content and be thankful to the Almighty.

Kabir Sahib's sloak discussed earlier has exactly the same message as that of Farid Sahib that do not indulge in tastes, and keep life simple.

If you become slave to some particular food even if it is vegetarian, it is as bad as eating meat. Guru Nanak Sahib has made this important point very clear as follows.

- ——— Human body indulges to enjoy gold, silver, women, perfumes, horses, luxurious beds, elegant houses, sweets and meat. While engrossed in so many pleasures (distractions) how can those hearts be enlightened with Waheguru's Naam? **(Siri Raag M:1, 15).**

The essence of all these holy writings is to lead a simple life by eating simple food and being content. There is absolutely no restriction on eating meat as long as you do not become slave to it." Bhai Dalip Singh clarified the deep meaning of sacred Gurbani very eloquently.

"Beautiful! Bolle So Nihal, Sat Sri Akal! You have really opened our eyes, Bhai Sahib. We're lucky to have you among us." Many voices could be heard from the crowd.

"Now I know for sure that the holy soaks or shabads which I'm going to ask you about, do not mean what we have been told earlier by some self proclaimed saints or holy men, but we still don't know their real meanings. Would you please explain the meaning of another sloak of Kabir Ji which is also quoted frequently by the opponents of meat. The holy Sloak goes like this:

- Kabir says that people who use marijuana, liquor and fish, lose all the credit they earn by pilgrimage, fasting and other religious rituals. **(Sloak Kabir Ji, 1377).**" Bhai Gurdial Singh requested.

"I'll be pleased to do that." Bhai Dalip Singh said in a pleasing tone."But, let's stay focused on the subject of meat for now. As you can see, Kabir Sahib has not **mentioned meat in general.** He has **specifically mentioned fish only** along with marijuana and liquor. The reason for the disapproval of these three substances is the fact that they are known to be sexual stimulants. Normally, people who use these disapproved substances, do not restrict themselves to their use only - which is bad enough as such, and all Guru Sahiban disapprove the use of any kind of intoxicants - but, they use these substances to commit some other immoral acts. They visit prostitutes and also gamble heavily because one bad habit leads to another. Like other Great Souls, the use of such stimulants is highly discouraged by Kabir Sahib too. **Again, Kabir Ji is not preaching against the use of meat in this Sloak. He is also not saying that people eating fish will have their throats slashed. He is simply advising that the use of these substances leads to an immoral life style.** So, people should avoid their use. Individuals with vested interests simply twist the meaning." Bhai Dalip Singh explained.

"One last question, Bhai Sahib. Opponents of meat also quote a shabad by Bhai Gurdas Ji which reads like this:

- The dying goat in the clutches of a lion laughed loudly. The lion was baffled and asked the goat how could she afford to laugh at a time like this when she was going to be killed. (the goat replied)

> We goats eat only wild grass or other vegetation, and still get this cruel and painful death in which our skin is torn mercilessly, and our kids are rendered orphans. I am laughing at you thinking what horrible fate must be waiting for you because you eat flesh of weak and harmless animals, and in the conceit of your strength, you destroy their bodies. You do the immoral deed of eating the inedible. Everyone who is born is bound to die. **(Bhai Gurdas Ji, Vaar 25, Pauri 17)**

Would you please, explain the meaning of this Shabad as well, Bhai Sahib?" Bhai Pritam Singh asked very politely.

"Gladly, Bhai Sahib. This story of the clenched goat appears in the Puranas. Bhai Gurdas Ji has simply narrated the story to advance the **principle of Gurmat in the last line where he says that whoever is born is destined to die**. Otherwise, the whole story is against the principles of Gurmat because as we discussed earlier, it is the Law of Nature that one life form is the food for other life forms. Lions have been created as carnivores by Waheguru. They cannot live on vegetation, and must eat meat. So, how can Bhai Gurdas Ji, a highly respected Sikh scholar, promote something against the principles of Gurmat? We've also discussed that animals do not have that level of awareness where they can teach each other morality or other secrets of Nature. Also, how can it be possible for a goat clenched in the jaws of a lion to laugh and give that kind of sermon? It is impossible, and totally against the principles of Nature. It is a Puranic story of which Bhai Sahib has made fun to educate people that death is inevitable. **Moreover, have lions and other carnivores quit killing goats or other animals since then? If not, what lesson does the story convey? Who is the story intended for? The only lesson that the story conveys is that death is inevitable, so if you eat flesh, it is no sin.**" Bhai Dalip Singh finished his explanation of the shabad.

"We understand fully now that eating or not eating meat is a personal choice, and that Gurmat does not put any restriction on eating meat. But, some self proclaimed saints argue that animals of different sizes have different number of basic elements (building units for bodies) that make them up - the bigger animals have more elements than the smaller, and vegetation has fewer elements than even the smallest animals. So, killing a bigger animal is a bigger sin, and killing vegetation for food is the least sin. How far are they right in their logic? Would you mind shedding some light on this, Bhai Sahib?" Bhai Kashmir Singh asked another question.

"It is an interesting question. As we discussed earlier on, these self-proclaimed saints have to preach something different to keep their shops running. If they preached exactly the same principles as holy Guru Granth Sahib, nobody will go to them. So, they have to say something different. They know full well that eating meat is not prohibited in *Gurmat*, but, they preach otherwise any way. Now, to justify their distorted preaching, they have to say something in their defense. So, they have coined this new idea that the number of elements is different in different animals, and in vegetation. What they really are saying is that killing is acceptable as long as you kill life with fewer elements. What a pitiable argument! They are not concerned about life, they are concerned about the number of elements which are completely lifeless.

Let us go by their logic and apply the test of elements to living beings. According to Hindu religious books, all living beings are made of the following five, so called elements: air, water, earth(mattter), fire (heat energy) and sky (brain or intelligence). All living things, including small animals and vegetation, are made of matter, water and air. They all have energy otherwise they cannot even move around. They all have some feelings, and therefore, intelligence. We discussed earlier that even plants have feelings including fear, so much so that they can even recognize a criminal. Scientists have also proved that plants grow more with appreciation and with music. That clearly means that they have intelligence too. So, which element is missing in any of them?

Recently, scientists have demonstrated that humans share about 99% of their genes with mice! The proclaimers of different number of basic elements are desperate to justify their opposition to eating meat. No statement on their part to defend their position on meat can withstand the test of logic even, let alone the laws of Nature as clarified by our Great Guru Sahiban. The self-proclaimed saints have nothing to do with the spiritual aspect of human life. They are interested only in their business. The sad thing is that they use holy Gurbani to attract innocent people and then twist Gurbani to advance their own interests. The Sikh religious body, the Shromani Gurduara Parbandhak Committee should take some solid steps to curb the abuse of Gurbani by some unscrupulous people." Bhai Dalip Singh showed some disgust at misinterpretation of Gurbani as he continued his explanations. Everybody seemed to be mesmerized with his knowledge.

Some Ill Deeds Much Worse than Eating Meat

"In fact, Guru Sahiban, and even Bhai Gurdas Ji have proclaimed some of the ill-deeds as being much worse than eating meat - if meat eating is bad according to some people." Bhai Dalip Singh said after a short pause to reenergize himself. He was reminded of Guru Sahibans' position on some other ill-deeds.

"Listen to this carefully." Bhai Sahib said.

- To usurp someone else's belongings, or to encroach upon others' rights is equivalent to eating beef (cow's meat) for a Hindu, and eating pork (pig's meat) for a Muslim. (Guru) Nanak says that the Guru will support only those who do not lay claim on something which is not rightfully theirs. **(Sloak M:1,Vaar Majh, 140)**

Now, as all of us know that Hindus consider it a big sin to eat beef, and so is eating of pork by Muslims. **But, Guru Nanak Dev Ji says beyond any doubt that usurping others' rights is even worse than that**. It is very important to note here that Guru Sahib is not using eating of any kind of meat for comparison, He is using the kind of meat strictly prohibited in the two religions. Which means usurping of others' rights is much more sinful than just eating meat. Guru Nanak Dev Ji is even more vociferous in Assa Ki Vaar. **He calls people man eaters and slaughterers who feed on others by usurping their rights through bribery or through force.** Just listen to this:

- Man eaters are offering nivajes (Muslim prayers) to look religious, and people with big knives in their hands (slaughterers) are wearing *janeyoo* (the Hindu religious thread).......To pretend to be highly religious, the butcher of the world wears a tikka (a religious mark on the forehead), and a scarlet colored dhoti (a piece of cloth which is wrapped around the waist). To be acceptable to the Muslim rulers, he then presents himself in blue attire before them. **(Assa Ki Vaar, M:1, 471)**

Clearly, according to Guru Ji, it is much more sinful to feed off others, or to encroach upon the rights of others than eating meat.

Consider another holy hymn by Guru Nanak Dev Ji in which He says that a person is educated only if he helps others selflessly.

- ———Likewise, a naked holy man can be considered holy only if he has kindness at heart and has controlled all his sensual pleasures. **Only that person is really nonviolent (does not kill others) who has controlled all his sensual pleasures. (Assa M:1, 356).**

Again, Guru Sahib is attaching much more importance to controlling sensual pleasures than killing animals. It will be of great interest to you to listen to the following shabad.

- A prostitute had cooked dog's meat in alcohol and was carrying it in a human skull. She had covered the meat with a blood-soaked cloth. When someone asked her why she had covered the meat, she replied that she does not want some thankless person to cast sight on the meat and thus jinx it. **(Bhai Gurdas Ji. Vaar 35, Pauri, 8)**

Now you can decide what is worse - eating meat or a thankless person?". Bhai Sahib concluded the long session. He could have gone into more detail, but he stopped it there. He seemed quite tired.

Bhai Kashmir Singh richly thanked Bhai Dalip Singh for his deep explanation of Gurbani which had dispelled some serious misgivings about eating meat. The session was adjourned with the traditional Sikh Slogan: Bolle So Nihal, Sat Sri Akal. Lungar was served as always.

11

Guru Sahiban: Some Less Known Facts

"Waheguru Ji ka Khalsa, Waheguru Ji ki Fateh." Bhai Dalip Singh appeared on the stage. The lawn of Bhai Kashmir Singh's farm house was overflowing with an enthusiastic crowd. People had started to come from distant villages to listen to the well articulated and highly informative discourses of Bhai Dalip Singh. The congregation responded with a loud and warm voice.

"Are there any questions before I start?" Bhai Sahib asked his usual question.

" I have a question that has been baffling me for some time, Bhai Sahib. Would you mind if I ask that now?" Harkerat Singh, a young man asked.

"No, not at all! Please do so." Bhai Dalip Singh encouraged the young man.

" I've been wondering about the name changes for the Second and the Fourth Gurus. When the Gurmat disapproves superstitions of all kinds, names could not be good or bad. So why were their names changed? Would you, please, shed some light on that?" Bhai Harkerat Singh's curiosity was obvious.

"It is an excellent question. And to tell you the truth, young man, the issue had never crossed my mind. I'm proud to say that our reverence for Guru Sahiban is so deep, and our faith so strong, that we accept everything done, or required by them gladly, as our duty. So, I had never thought about it. I've never read anything on this issue either. So, I don't know the real reasons. Only the Perfect Gurus - Sahiban Sri Guru Nanak Dev Ji and Sri Guru Amar Das Ji - would know the exact reasons when they changed the names of the Second and the Fourth Guru respectively. I know one thing for sure - the name changes had absolutely nothing to do with superstitions associated with particular names. Both, the Second and the Fourth, Gurus were Great Souls and they had attained the level of spiritual awareness needed for them to be the Gurus when they were still known by their original names. So, names were not changed for any superstitious reasons. Why were they changed then? I can only speculate. **At least my speculations will generate some discussion among the scholars.**

Let 's first discuss the Second Guru - Sri Angad Dev Ji. There could be three possible reasons for the name change.

(a) The reason that is most commonly believed is that when Guru Nanak Dev Ji transferred the Divine Light (Knowledge) to Bhai Lehna Ji (Guru Angad Dev Ji's former name), Guru Nanak Dev Ji advised all the Sikhs that Bhai Lehna Ji had become His own "ang" (body part), and therefore should be known as **Guru Angad** (or Angad Dev Ji). This seems plausible because there was a great resistance on the part of Sri Chand Ji and Lakhmi Das Ji, the two sons of Guru Nanak Dev Ji, to accept Bhai Lehna Ji as the Second Guru. The sons, especially the older one, wanted the Guruship to be bestowed on him. But, Guru Nanak Dev Ji did not consider Sri Chand Ji worthy of guruship. By calling Bhai Lehna Ji (Guru Angad Dev Ji) a part of His own body, Guru Nanak Dev Ji proclaimed that spiritually there was no difference between the two, and all Sikhs should accept Bhai Lehna Ji their Guru as a spiritual personification of Guru Nanak Dev Ji. They should have the same faith in Him, and should accord Him the same level of reverence as for Guru Nanak Dev Ji Himself.

Even though this explanation sounds very logical, there is a minor problem with that logic. Every time, the Divine Light was passed on to the next Guru, the latter became an 'ang' of the former Guru. So, each succeeding Guru should have been called the 'Ang' of the former. Which is not the case. So, this logic has some drawback.

(b) The second, and probably the more logical reason for the name change was the fact that angad or agad is the Punjabi form of the Persian word, akad, for marriage. Remember the holy hymn in which Guru Nanak Sahib makes the prophecy of Baabar's attack on Emnabad, to Bhai Lallo. Describing the destructive and the gloomy situation of the predicted attack, Guru Sahib said:

Let alone the Brahmans and the Qazies, agad (marriages) will be performed by rogues. (**Tilung M: 1, 722**)

Before I continue, I may add here that adding 'n' to some Punjabi words does not change their meanings. For example nirakar (formless) is more commonly written as nirankar, sehas (thousand) is also written as sehans, Alakh (undescribable) as alankh and dit (given) as dint. There are many more such examples. So agad and angad mean the same, but angad sounds better.

Now, as all of you know, in Gurbani, all human beings are referred to as brides.

Only Waheguru is the groom. A lucky individual who attains Divine Knowledge is said to have been married to Wahegru as the Groom. When holy Bhai Lehna Ji got enlightened by Guru Nanak Dev Ji, the former got spiritually married (agad) to Waheguru. Guru Nanak Sahib proclaimed to His Sikhs that Bhai Lehna Ji had become agad (married to Waheguru, and had attained the high spiritual level to become the next Guru) so, He should be known as Guru Angad Dev Ji from there on. The significance in the name change was the same as discussed shortly before, i.e. to let people know that Bhai Lehna Ji was fully qualified - and the best choice to be Guru Nanak Dev Ji's successor - and should be revered as such.

(c) Humility is an important aspect of Gurmat (Sikhism). Even though as discussed earlier, the names are neither good nor bad per se, yet, some of them carry meanings which may not be best suited for the position of an individual. In Punjabi, 'lehna' means to receive back things that a person is owed by others. When Bhai Lehna Ji came to Guru Nanak Dev Ji's shelter at Kartar Pur, and on being asked, Bhai Lehna Ji told his name, Guru Nanak Dev Ji commented: If you are the creditor because you are owed, I'm the indebitor (payer). Being a receiver (creditor) was okay as long as Bhai Lehna Ji was a Sikh, but, when He became the Guru, He had only to give (Divine Knowledge and blessings) to His Sikhs, and NOT to receive. So the name 'Lehna' was not appropriate for the Great Soul as judged by the Great Guru - Nanak Sahib - whom Bhai Lehna Ji was to succeed. So, the name was changed. And what other name could be more suitable than Angad (Wedded to Waheguru)?

I must add that what I have said so far is only my personal conclusion. The reason(s) for the name change could be very different, and only the Great Guru - Nanak Sahib -

would know. **However, the logic of 'humility' used here can also explain the name change for the Fourth Guru.**

- The original name of the Fourth Guru was Jetha Ji which means elder (holding a position of respect), higher or great, in Punjabi. It also implies the first-born child. Since, all the meanings of 'jetha' have some degree of highness attached to it, Guru Amar Das Ji might not have been comfortable with the name 'Jetha' for the Guru to succeed Him. The name Ram Das means 'servant of Waheguru' which represents humility of the highest order. Guru Ram Das Ji was known for His humility and dedication. So, Guru Amar Das Ji gave Him the name 'Ram Das' which best reflected the personality of the Fourth Guru and was perfectly suitable for His spiritual position to reflect humility.
- I may also add here that the Second and the Fourth Gurus were not the only 'Sikhs' whose names were changed by their respective Gurus (predecessors). Guru Tegh Bahadur's name was changed from His childhood name, Tiyag Mal, to Tegh Bahadur Ji, by His Father, Guru Har Gobind Sahib, to reflect Sri Tiyag Mal's chivalrous character. Tiyagh Mal Ji, while still in his early teens, displayed a great bravery in the battle of Kartar Pur when Guru Har Gobind Sahib was attacked by enemy forces on His way to Kirat Pur Sahib.

  Similarly, Guru Gobind Singh Ji changed the name of His dedicated Sikh, Madho Das *Bairagi,* to Banda Singh Bahadur before the latter left Nanded for Punjab to punish the evil rulers in Punjab and to end their rule. The reason behind the name change was similar to the reasons discussed shortly before. With a *bairagi* character, Banda Singh could not have punished the evil rulers. The name was changed to reflect his new role as a warrior. **Not**

> **only that, Guru Gobind Singh Ji, also changed His own name from Gobind Rai to Gobind Singh, and also the name of His successor - the Khalsa - for the same reason so that His Sikhs would live up to their name - Singh.**

So, the logic discussed above for the name changes of the two Guru Sahiban seems plausible.

This is my humble view on the subject. I want to apologize for anything which may have been said by me resulting in any unintended disrespect for our revered Guru Sahiban." Bhai Dalip Singh was not sure if his conclusions were right.

"Are there any other questions?" Bhai Sahib asked .

The Sodhi Dynasty as Gurus

"I've a related question, Bhai Sahib. Excuse my irreverence, but, why did all the respected Gurus after the Third Guru, belong to the same family (dynasty) - Sodhi? Was it because of some benediction to Bibi Bhani by Guru Amar Das Ji, as some people claim? Bhai Gurterath Singh asked.

"This is an interesting question, Bhai Sahib, and I know full well that your only objective is to seek truth. This question has been raised many times before at similar gatherings where it sounded more like an objection than a question. But, the funny thing is, nobody has ever objected to (or questioned) the fact that all the members of Guru Gobind Singh Ji's family laid down their lives for righteousness and became martyrs. Likewise, nobody has ever questioned why all the members of S. Bhagat Singh's family were patriots. I can quote many more families like Bhai Mani Singh Martyr's, where a majority of the members laid down their lives for noble causes, but, nobody ever mentions that. The point is, people are so engrossed in haumein that they always try to find some shortcomings in things which are great. People have stooped so low that they are not even ashamed of levying the charge of neglect of family on the Great World Guru - Nanak Dev Ji. Anyway, this logic is not going to satisfy anyone, and it will seem as if I evaded the question. So, let's start with the story of Bibi Bhani first.

There is a story in the book titled ' Gur Bilas Patshahi Sixth' that Bibi Bhani, a daughter of Guru Amar Das Ji, and wife of Guru Ram Das Ji, used to give bath to her father, Guru Amar Das Ji. One day, one of the legs of the low wooden stool on which Guru Sahib used to sit while bathing, became loose. Bibi Bhani quickly put her foot under the stool to provide support so as to prevent Guru Ji from tipping over. When Guru Ji finished His bath, He saw blood gushing out of His daughter's foot. After He took care of her bleeding foot, Guru Sahib greatly appreciated the sacrifice that the Bibi made to save Guru Sahib from being hurt, and asked His daughter to ask for anything at all she wanted, and Guru Ji would grant her wish gladly. Bibi Bhani Ji asked her father to bless her so that the Guruship would stay in her family (her husband's family) - who were Sodhis. Guru Ji had to grant her the wish. That's why all the Gurus following Guru Amar Das Ji were from the same family - the Sodhis.

This ridiculous story is rife with flaws to the degree that it is unlikely to be true. It seems to have been influenced by a similar story in 'Ramayana' according to which Kaikayee, a stepmother of Lord Rama, also got a similar benediction from her husband. Kaikayee, used her arm as the axle to prevent a loose wheel of the chariot in which her husband, King Dashrath, was fighting against his enemy. I'm not going to discuss that story here. It is sufficient to point out the similarity in the two stories. We'll continue with Bibi Bhani Ji's story.

First of all, the wooden stool that was used for bathing purposes by Guru Ji, was probably regularly checked. Even if it wasn't, it is barely 7 or 8 cm (about three inches) high, and loosening of one leg should not have caused any serious danger to Guru Ji. (If it could be supported by Bibi Bhani Ji's foot, how high could it be?). Second, at what point during Guru Ji's bath did Bibi Ji notice that a leg had become loose? Was she focussing on putting water on Guru Ji, or on the leg which she somehow expected would get loose? If the leg was still in place, how did she put her foot under the table? And if the leg had already fallen off, and that side of the table was already touching the floor, it would be very difficult, if not impossible, to put her foot under the table while Guru Ji was sitting on it. Moreover, if that side of the table was already touching the floor, and Guru Sahib did not tip over, then no support was needed.

But, let's focus on some of the more serious implications of this story. Let me mention here that the book, which had the blessings of all the top members of the Shromani Gurduara Parbandhic Committee and the chiefs of the Takhats, has been disapproved and withdrawn by the very same members, primarily because of the objections raised by S. Gurbakhsh Singh Kala Afghana against the authenticity of the contents of the book.

- The story implies that Bibi Bhani, a highly respected GurSikh, was not selfless in her services, and had a hidden agenda while serving her father, Guru Amar Das Ji. This kind of a suggestion is very disrespectful to Bibi Bhani Ji.
- Even more serious is the accusation against the revered Guru amar Das Ji Who passed on the Guruship to Bhai Jetha Ji (the former name of Guru Ram Das Ji) shortly before His death. Guru Amar Das Ji put Bhai Jetha Ji through many tests before passing on the Guruship to him. The most well known of those was the repeated building and demolition of a platform before it was finally approved by Guru Amar Das Ji. If Guru Amar Das Ji had already made the commitment to Bibi

Bhani Ji, then the whole idea of testing becomes a sham, and we are extremely guilty of accusing our revered Guru of dishonesty. Can that be possible ? Are we willing to do that?

- Also, the story implies that Guru Ram Das Ji did not deserve Guruship - it was simply given to him. How unjust! How ignorant! How stupid can we be! My body begins to shiver even at the idea. Clearly, the story is all nonsense. Someone tried to promote his own agenda. There is a shabad in Sri Guru Granth Sahib by the respected Bhatts which says that Guru Ram Das Ji was vigorously tested by Guru Amar Das Ji before passing on the Guruship to Ram Das Ji, and the Guruship was passed only after Guru Amar Das Ji was completely satisfied with Bhai Jetha Ji's spiritual ability. That fact is testified in the following Savvayyeah.
- ———Next, Guru Amar Das Ji radiated His light as the Guru after He was touched by (enlightened) by Guru Angad Dev Ji. ———Guru Amar Das Ji passed on the Guruship to Guru Ram Das Ji only after He was completely satisfied with the latter (His high level of enlightenment). Guru Amar Das was very pleased with Sri Ram Das Ji, and He bestowed the throne of worldly glory and of spirituality on Sri Ram Das Ji. **(Savvayye of the Fourth Guru, 1399)**

The Bhatts reaffirm the high spiritual level attained by Guru Ram Das Ji to the complete satisfaction of Guru Amar Das Ji, before Sri Ram Das Ji was given the Guruship.

- The Guru (Ram Das Ji) who attained the highest spiritual level by following the Teachings of the Guru, and who did not leave Guru Amar Das Ji unattended while serving Him, radiated the sparkling Divine Knowledge which dispelled the darkness of all misery and discomforts. **(Savvayye of the Fourth Guru, 1405)**

There is also a holy shabad Guru Amar Das Ji Himself which is supposed to have been uttered by Him at the time of (or shortly before) passing on the Guruship to Sri Ram Das Ji. The holy Sloak reads like this:

- Why should not the property of someone else held by you in trust be passed on to the rightful owner? You feel relieved only when it has been delivered. **The Divine Knowledge stays only with the real Guru, it does not enlighten anyone else. (Sarang ki Vaar, Sloak M: 3, 1249)**

What the holy Sloak means is that Gurus are determined by Waheguru. This holy Sloak has a very deep implication in the present case. If Guru Ram Das Ji was not the right man for Guruship - and was only appointed because of the said benediction - the Divine Knowledge would not have stayed with Him, and He would not have survived as the Guru. But did anyone notice anything lacking in Guru Ram Das Ji? He was the spiritual incarnation of Guru Nanak Dev Ji in every possible way. The Bhatts have written full 10 pages in praise of Guru Ram Das Ji - much more than for any other Guru.

- The same argument applies to all other Gurus. If Gurus were not predetermined by Waheguru, Guru Nanak Dev Ji could have passed the Guruship to one of His sons who fought hard for their right as sons. But they were not deserving of the great responsibility. Only Guru Angad Dev Ji was qualified to be the next Guru. History reveals that when Guru Nanak Dev Ji saw Bhai Lehna Ji approaching Him at Kartar Pur for the first time, Guru Nanak Dev Ji commented, 'My successor has arrived'. Guru Nanak Dev Ji knew full well who the arriving holy man was. Guru Angad Dev

Ji too, could also have passed on the Guruship to one of His sons, but He did not do for the same reason.

- Could you expect anything more from a non-Sodhi Guru than Guru Arjun Dev Ji, Who has written more Gurbani than all the other Gurus combined, and edited Sri Guru Granth Sahib? He also built Harmander Sahib, and many other gurduaras, including the one at Taran Taran, and founded many cities. But most importantly, gave His life gladly and willingly while suffering inhuman torture for the cause of Truth and Justice. Nobody else could have done anything like that.
- And who could have matched the supreme sacrifices of Guru Tegh Bahadur Sahib, and Guru Gobind Singh Sahib? The Tenth Guru sacrificed all His four sons fighting against oppression, and for righteousness.
- Guru Sahiban were not opposed to passing on the Divine Knowledge to a non-Sodhi, provided someone deserved it. Guru Har Gobind Sahib once publically offered to pass the Guruship on to anyone who could recite the holy Jap Ji Sahib with full concentration. A highly respected Sikh, Bhai Gopal, accepted the offer and began to recite the holy Gurbani. He was quite close to completing the recitation - and Guru Sahib had begun to recede from His throne to offer Guruship to Bhai Gopal Ji - when Bhai Sahib lost his concentration. He began to think of the expensive items that he would own after Guruship was passed on to him. Thus he lost the chance to become Guru. So, it is not true that others were not given chances, they simply had not attained that spiritual level required of the Guru.
- Another important historical fact is worth

considering at this point. When the time came for Guru Har Gobind Sahib to pass on the Torch to the next Guru, He did not give it to His son, Sri Tegh Bahadur Ji. He rather gave it to His grandson, Sri Har Rai Ji, who became the Seventh Guru. The reason? Guru Har Gobind Ji said that Sri Tegh Bahadur Ji wasn't ready yet, he would have to wait. Tegh Bahadur Ji had to practice self-discipline, and worship Waheguru for 21 years before He attained the required spiritual level to become the Ninth Guru. This fact again reiterates the point that as stated by Guru Amar Das Ji, Divine Knowledge does not stay with an undeserving person. **So, all the Gurus following guru Amar Das Ji were Great Souls and were determined by Waheguru to be the Gurus, at appropriate times. It just happened that all of them were born in the same dynasty, which is not unusual.** The genes and the environment produce children who inherit many traits of their parents. You must have noticed that in many cases the children of artists are artists, those of warriors are warriors, and so on. Maharaja Ranjit Singh's father and his grandfather were both great warriors. I know a family in America where all the five brothers are medical doctors, and most of their children are also are either doctors are on their way to become doctors. I recently watched on TV that there is a doctor in Chandigarh whose name plate reads: Dr so and so - One of the twenty three doctors in the family.

Nobody ever questions that. **The funny thing is that Bachittar Natak, a booklet in the Dasam Granth, describes the transfer of Guruship to the Sodhi Dynasty in a very different way which is also highly illogical, and seems baseless. But, two very different rationales provided for the**

same event clearly imply that none of them is correct." Bhai Dalip Singh said in a very confident tone.

"Your arguments are penetrating, and very convincing, but is there a possibility that people got so scared of the Mogul rule after the supreme sacrifice of Guru Arjun Dev Ji that no body had the heart to become the Guru? Bhai Tripinder Singh Asked.

"There is no question that most of the people felt unsafe to be in the lime light. In fact, there was so much fear that some of the Sikhs even 'advised' Guru Har Gobind Sahib not to do anything that could displease the rulers. They wanted Guru Sahib to compromise with them. But that is exactly contrary to the Principles and Teachings of Guru Sahiban. They came to teach us to be *nirbhau* (fearless). To teach that the Guru has to be *NIRBHAU* Himself. **If an individual has not attained the spiritual level of being fearless, he does not deserve to be the Guru.** So, all Sikhs are expected to be fearless. If you are not fearless, how can you fight for justice and against oppression? There are hundreds of holy shabads in Guru Granth Sahib that advise the Sikhs to be fearless. Consider, for example, the following

- Only that person can be considered to have Divine Knowledge who neither intimidates others nor gets intimidated, oh Nanak! **(Sloak M: 9, 1428)**
- Only the person who fights for the noble principles (or for the rights of the helpless) and does not run away from the battle field even if he is cut piece by piece, is truly deserving of being a hero. **(Sloak Kabir Ji, 1105)**
- I will infuse such a spirit among my Sikhs that each one of them will have the courage to fight an army of one and a quarter hundred thousand soldiers.———— **(Guru Gobind Singh Ji)**

If people were intimidated by the Mogul rulers themselves, how could they infuse fearlessness among the people, and deserve to be the Gurus? So, whether they wanted to be the Guru or not, that is beside the point. The point is, if they were intimidated, they did not DESERVE to be the Gurus. When Guru Har Krishan Ji, who was less than eight years old at the time, was invited by the emperor, Aurangzeb, to meet him in Delhi, Guru Ji did go to Delhi, but did not yield to the Emperor's tactics, and refused to see the sly tyrant. At that young age, Guru Har Krishan Ji demonstrated that a Great Soul that houses the Divine Knowledge, is kind to all human beings, but, is not intimidated by worldly powers. That's the kind of fearlessness needed in the Guru, and the choice that each Guru Sahib made to appoint His successor, was perfect. Each Guru had already been decided by Waheguru, and it was NOT a family favour kind of thing. Who could question Guru Har Krishan Ji's Divine Knowledge Who empowered a mute and illiterate water-carrier, Bhai Chhajju, to verbally translate Geeta at Panjokhara, near Ambala, on His way to Delhi?" Bhai Sahib concluded. His face had a faint glow. There was a complete silence for a few moments. Everybody seemed to be mesmerized.

"Is there any other question?" Bhai Sahib asked.

"I don't have a question, Bhai Sahib, but, I do have some comments. You have clarified such important issues tonight that the cloud of some irreverence for respected Bibi Bhani, which had been caused by some unscrupulous people, has completely been dispelled, and we owe you a million thanks for the clarification. Bhai Gurterath Singh was very thankful.

There were no further questions. Bhai Kashmir Singh thanked Bhai Dalip Singh richly on behalf of the whole Sangat.

The congregation ended with a loud Sikh slogan of "Waheguru Ji ka Khalsa, Waheguru JI ki Fateh". Lungar was waiting for the congregation.

12

Supernatural Powers: Miracles

A large number of enthusiastic people have gathered again today at Bhai Kashmir Singh's farmhouse. Bhai Dalip Singh's informative discourses based purely on Gurbani were attracting more and more people everyday. Bhai Sahib was talking to a small group of people in a corner, but, he soon left them to appear on the stage, and greeted the congregation with a loud and warm, 'Waheguru Ji ka Khalsa, Waheguru Ji ki Fateh'. The congregation's response was even louder and warmer. People rushed to suit themselves on the carpet.

"A lot of people have asked me if Guru Sahiban ever performed miracles in Their lives. So, I want to address this important issue this afternoon, if you permit." Bhai Dalip Singh said politely.

"Sure. We would love to hear that." A number of voices were heard.

"Thank you very much. Now, before we discuss whether Guru Sahiban ever performed miracles, let's first define what miracles are, and whether the Holy Gurbani acknowledges supernatural powers by which miracles can be performed.

A miracle is an unusual act or happening which amazes most people. But a simple amazement may not be a miracle for everybody. Many magicians perform tricks which may seem like miracles to some people. For example, I've watched David Copperfield, a well known American magician, on TV to fly over the Grand Canyon while in a sitting position with his legs crossed, and apparently with no support underneath him. Now, this was a miracle to some people, while some others thought that it was only a trick of some kind.

Some people do have the ability to control your mind and make you do or see things that they want you to do or see. This is called hypnosis, and is a recognized branch of science. A hypnotist requires a lot of training and a lot of practice to be effective. Sidh yogis were widely known to possess magical powers with which they impressed people and made them their followers. Such powers had their roots mostly in hypnosis, known as mesmerism at that time. Noor Shah, a widely known magician near Dhaka in Bangla Desh, was a powerful hypnotist. If you know the story, she was the one who was able to hypnotize even Bhai Mardana Ji, and make him produce sounds like a sheep. Some Sidh yogis had acquired even greater powers, and they were able to turn themselves into animals or birds and fly in air. Gurbani does acknowledge supernatural powers. They come from strengthening your mind. Let's first pay attention to some holy shabads (hymns) from Sri Guru Granth Sahib in which **supernatural powers have been acknowledged.**

- ———People usually make fun of the poverty of others. At one time, I was also so poor that everybody poked fun at me. But, **all the eighteen supernatural powers play at the palm of my hand (are my slaves) now**. It is all because of Your kind grace, oh my Lord, Waheguru! ——— **(Bilawal Ravi Das Ji, 858)**
- All kinds of supernatural powers follow an individual (are his slaves) who has realized Waheguru's Naam in his heart **(Sorith ki Vaar, Sloak M:3, 649).**
- Waheguru's Naam is the source of all comforts and all bliss, oh my friend! You Realize Naam

only in the company of holy men who have already realized Waheguru. By taking refuge at the feet of the Guru, you acquire the gift of Waheguru's Naam which is the source of Divine Knowledge, **all supernatural powers,** and truthful living. Also you **sever** the bonds of attachment with *maya* through Waheguru's Naam. ——— **(Ramkali M:1, Ashatpadian, 906)**

- The angel of death cannot even look at, and the fear of death does not come even close to your saints, oh Waheguru!. The only thing occupying their hearts is Your Naam and they find salvation through Your Naam. **All kinds of supernatural powers are their slaves simply because of their (saints) love for the Guru.———(Sorith M:3, Ashatpadian, 637)**
- The saints of Waheguru (the noble people who have realized Waheguru) feel blissful all the time. Waheguru is their shield everywhere - inside and outside the home. Saints find Waheguru to be omnipresent. **All the treasures of the earth and all supernatural powers are at their command. (Dhanasari M:5, 679)**
- There is lotus flower in the right hand of Guru Amar Das Ji, and perfection is right in front of Him. **Supernatural powers** reside on the left side of Guru Ji which are charming all the three worlds. **(Savvayye M:3, 1393)**
- Guru Ram Das Ji has emancipated the world from the bonds of maya which acts as an intoxicant. He has kindly given the all-powerful gift of the Naam-Amrit to the people. Guru Ram Das Ji is the source of all comforts, wealth and glory. **Supernatural powers don't ever leave His company. (Savvayye M:4, 1404)**

- Listen to Naam and sing the praise of the undescribable Waheguru, oh my mind! Waheguru's Naam is the source of all comforts and all bliss, but, you realize it only in the company of the holy men. ———— Follow the Teachings of the Guru and worship Waheguru, oh my mind!. By doing so, you will acquire all the wealth you need, great wisdom, **all the supernatural powers**, and all comforts of life. ————**(Bairari M:4, 719)**
- People who sing Waheguru's praise with His grace, are bestowed with such a Divine gift which includes all the treasures of the earth, **all supernatural powers,** and never loses its might, oh my friend! ———— **(Suhi Chhant M:5, 783)**
- Sing praise of Waheguru Who is the **source of all supernatural powers**, oh my friend! Everybody wishes well of the devotees of Waheguru. ————

  (Bilawal M:5, 818)
- People, who are imbued in the Perfect Guru's Shabad and are focussed on Waheguru's Naam acquire noble character and are unaffected by *maya*. A few lucky people who come to the Guru's shelter, get the gift of **all supernatural powers** and Divine Knowledge from the Guru who connects them with Waheguru. ————**(Maru Solhe M:1, 1037)**
- Why don't you leave the useless talk aside and recite Waheguru's Naam with your tongue all the time, oh pundit ji! Waheguru is the source of all comforts, the five trees of paradise, and the *Chintaman* and *Kaamdhen* cows. **The eight great supernatural powers,** the nine treasures, and the four great gifts - dharma, wealth, salvation and luxuries - reside on the palms of His hands. So, why don't you worship Him?————**(Maru Ravi Das Ji, 1106)**

Note: According to the Hindu holy books, Chintaman and Kaamdhen are cows with magical powers that reside in Paradise.

As we can clearly see from these holy shabads (hymns), Gurbani does acknowledge the existence of supernatural powers. They can be acquired by strengthening (controlling) your mind or determination. Human mind (soul) is a source of unlimited power because it is a tiny part of the Supreme Soul - Waheguru. So, everybody is capable of achieving these powers. But controlling the mind is not an easy task because human mind is very capricious. Some people spend years and years practising how to control their minds. They do achieve some success. **But holy men, who are in unison with Waheguru, have their minds under complete control, and they are gifted with all the supernatural powers for which they don't have to put in any effort.** People who acquire supernatural powers use them to impress common masses to gain popularity or to show their superiority. Such people waste all the years of hard work because they do not gain any advancement in the spiritual world. They rather fall behind because of their conceit or ego which is a big obstacle in the union with Waheguru. **So, the spiritual greatness of an individual is NOT determined by his ability to show miracles.** Actually, a person who shows miracles to boost his conceit or ego, has a very low spiritual level. Conceit or ego is an aspect of haumein (focus on self). Guru Sahiban have made it very clear that Waheguru does not enlighten the heart which harbours *haumein.*

- Haumein and Waheguru's Naam are mutually exclusive, and both cannot exist together. A person with haumein cannot serve Waheguru, and thus cannot improve his mind spiritually. ——— **Wadhans M:3, 560)**
- You cannot realize Waheguru as long as you are guided by haumein. You will attain the immortal

status (realize Waheguru) only after you have gotten rid of your haumein. ———**(Gauri M:1, Ashatpadian, 226-27)**

- The knowledge contained in the Vedas simply defines virtuous and sinful deeds. ———But, Amrit-like Gurbani on the other hand, provides Divine Knowledge which teaches us that Waheguru has created the whole world with His Huqam and looks after it with His Huqam too. By reciting Gurbani and acting upon it, **one can rid himself of haumein - a prerequisite to be acceptable in Waheguru's Court. (Sarang ki Vaar, Sloak M:2, 1243)**

Also, people with supernatural powers have to continue practising their mind control regularly otherwise they lose their power. Now, mind control requires a lot of energy input; so people get tired soon, become irritant and lose any good quality they have had. Because of these reasons too, Guru Sahiban had been against the display of supernatural powers - particularly when they are intended to boost one's ego. Guru Sahiban always advised the Sidh Yogis against the use of such powers." Bhai Dalip Singh paused for a short moment.

"Does anyone have any questions so far?" Bhai Sahib asked.

"I'm just eager to know if any of the Guru Sahiban ever displayed a supernatural power?" Inder Bir Singh, a young man asked.

"I'm coming to that in a few minutes. But, let's be clear on another important point first. Most of the actions are neither good nor bad **per se** - the important thing is the objective underlying them which could be noble or evil. For example, killing a human being is considered a sin and a crime under normal circumstances. But, you may have to kill a tyrant or a cruel aggressor to save a large number of helpless and innocent people. Guru Gobind Singh Ji sent Prince Ajit Singh Ji to punish the Pathan chief of Bassi in Hoshiar Pur District who had robbed a young Hindu groom of his newly-wed bride. The Pathan was killed and the bride recovered. Would you call the attack on the Pathan a sin? Similarly, thousands of soldiers were killed in battles between the Sixth and the Tenth Guru Sahiban on one hand, and the unjust and evil enemy forces on the other. Again, would you call the killing of the evil forces in the battle fields a sin?

Guru Nanak Sahib was not opposed to wearing janeyoo (the cotton thread that the Brahmans and the Khattris wear around their necks) or the pilgrimages. Guru Nanak Sahib could not care less if people wore thousands of janeyoos or went on pilgrimages everyday. He was opposed to the fact that Brahmans were misguiding and robbing innocent people by the total false claims that wearing janeyoos and undertaking pilgrimages wash away the sins of people. Guru Nanak Sahib visited hundreds of so called holy places Himself, and so did Guru Amar Das Ji and Guru Tegh Bahadur Sahib. But their purpose was entirely different. They went there to enlighten people and not to wash away their sins! **So, it is the purpose underlying an action that determines the good or bad nature of the action. The only bad deed by itself is not to worship Waheguru.**

I can give you hundreds of examples on actions which are neither good nor bad. The objective underlying them determines their nature. There are quite a few holy shabads (hymns) in Guru Granth Sahib that clarify this point.

- Killing of a Brahman, a cow or an infant female (infanticide), and accepting donations from an immoral person are considered despicable and sinful acts in Hindu holy books. But, the act of forgetting Waheguru is million times more despicable and sinful than all the four combined.

(Sloak M:3, 1413)

Note: Some people used to kill their daughters at birth.

- The noble and the bad characteristics among people have been created by Waheguru Himself (according to their deeds in previous incarnations). But, If an individual with bad characteristics contemplates Guru's Shabad, and obeys Waheguru's Huqam, **his bad characteristics are equally good as those of another person with so called noble characteristics (if he does not sing Waheguru's praise). (Maru ki Vaar, Sloak M:3, 1092)**
{For example, robbing someone is a bad deed, but robbing a robber and returning the belongings to the rightful victims is NOT a bad deed}
- All the belongings like big houses, temples, mansions, inns, horses, and other valuables of the people who are imbued in Waheguru's Naam, are all pious whereby beloveds of Waheguru can take comfort. Their use of wealth, their eating and their wearing are all pious if they sing Waheguru's praise.

(Sorith ki Vaar, M:4, Pauri, 648)

- It is impossible to describe the Greatness of Waheguru, my friends! We should not complain if we are in bad circumstances in our judgement; we should rather be happy in whatever circumstances He provides for us. Sometimes He provides so much that the person does not enjoy even very rich foods like milk pudding, sugar and butter oil, while some other times He forces the same people to go from door to door to beg for food. Sometimes He provides high quality horses to ride while at another time there are even no shoes to wear. ————

(Bhairon Naam Dev Ji, 1164)

The last Shabad by Naam Dev Ji implies that comforts or discomforts by themselves are neither good nor bad, and we can be happy in either circumstances provided we accept the Will of Waheguru. Likewise, no act is good or bad by itself as long as the underlying cause is noble. Thus, there is no doubt left that most actions are neutral - the motive behind their use is the determining factor.

With this principle in mind, now let's turn to the discussion whether Guru Sahiban displayed any miracles. **Let me first admit proudly that yes, Guru Nanak Sahib performed miracles! And the most outstanding of all of them is His enlightening the whole world with Divine Knowledge and showering it with affection.** He travelled for twenty three years through dense forests, huge deserts, and a world full of risks to His life at every step. He went without food and water for days disseminating Waheguru's Word and teaching love and harmony to millions of ignorant people. **Yes, that was a great miracle!** But that is not the kind of miracles you folks are wondering about.

History provides solid evidence that there have been many amazing incidents which people would call miracles. There are scores of such incidents associated with Guru Nanak Sahib. For example the very popular event of Punja Sahib where Guru Nanak Dev Ji stopped a huge rock pushed down the hill by a Muslim ascetic, Wali Kandhari, with the intent to crush Guru Ji; and revolving of the Kaaba in Mecca. As also the emancipation of Bhai Mardana from the confinement of Noor Shah, and causing all the water sources to go dry in Ruhelkhand to stop the evil practice of slavery by the Pathans there. The list could go on and on, but in none of these situations did Guru Sahib perform miracles to boost His ego or to impress people so that they would become His followers. **They were performed either to demonstrate Waheguru's supremacy when the other party refused to be convinced by reason, or in situations where there was no other**

alternative for survival. For example, Kaaba was moved simply to demonstrate the omnipresence of Waheguru because our Muslim brothers believed that Allah resides in Kaaba. And if Guru Sahib had not stopped the rock pushed down the hill by Wali Kandhari, that could have crushed Guru Sahib and Bhai Mardana. Likewise, Guru Ji made the water sources go dry in Ruhelkhand only after the local Pathans refused to stop the practice of slavery. **So, the objectives behind all those miracles were noble. They were not performed for a show off.**

The holy Shabad of the Fourth Guru Ji just discussed a few minutes ago in which He says that all the wealth, the houses, the mansions, the horses and the like, of Waheguru's saints are all pious, applies perfectly well in all those situations. We also acknowledge generally that ends justify the means - particularly when the ends are noble. Let me emphasize one important thing before I continue that **Guru Nanak's greatness did not lie in the fact that He was able to perform miracles. He was Great because He listened to people's problems with empathy, showered them with affection, lessened their misery, awakened them from ignorance, and enlightened them with the Divine Knowledge.**

Some people do not want to believe that Guru Sahiban performed any miracles. Their rationale for this claim is based on the disapproval of miracles by Guru Sahiban. I tend to agree with them fully, but, they will have a very hard time to negate all the miracles attributed to Guru Nanak Sahib in history books. Even though none of the above miracles has been discussed in Sri Guru Granth Sahib, the highly respected GurSikh, Bhai Gurdas Ji, has discussed the miracles attributed to Guru Nanak Sahib in quite a detail in his books. Some people may claim that history has been distorted somehow, and Guru Nanak Dev Ji or any other Guru Sahib, or even any Bhagat for that matter, did not perform any miracle. However, there are many holy hymns in Sri Guru Granth Sahib that make mention of some miracles associated with Bhagat Kabir Ji, Bhagat Naam Dev Ji, and to a small degree with Guru Arjun Dev Ji as well." Bhai Dalip Singh paused for a few moments. He took a few sips of water.

"Are there any questions so far?" Bhai Sahib asked.

"You are doing a wonderful job at clarifying things for us. Thank you very much for that, Bhai Sahib. But, we are eager to listen to those holy shabads in your simple language. So, please, continue." A number of voices were heard.

"Okay, I will. Thank you too for being a wonderful audience." Bhai Sahib was really thankful.

"I'll discuss the miracles associated with Bhagat Naam Dev Ji first which he wrote with his own pious hands, and which are recorded in the holy Guru Granth Sahib. There are four of them, but, I'll discuss only two. In the first, Bhagat Ji describes his confinement by the then king of India - Muhammad Tughlak - who also threatened to kill Bhagat Ji if he failed to revive the king's dead cow. The King gave Bhagat Ji twenty four hours to revive the cow, or to embrace Islam, otherwise he would be killed. The following autobiographical Shabad describes the incident.

- The King arrested Naama (Naam Dev Ji) and asked him to show the power of his Beethul (Waheguru). Revive the dead cow, otherwise I will kill you on the spot! (The king ordered). **(Naam Dev Ji explained) How can that be possible, your majesty! The dead cannot be revived. It is not in my hands. Whatever happens, happens at the Will of the Almighty.**

  The King got enraged. He ordered that Naam Dev Ji be trampled over by an elephant. Naam Dev Ji's mother began to wail and implored him to recite Allah (as desired by the king) rather than his

Beethul. Naam Dev Ji did not like the suggestion and told his mother that neither she was his mother nor he was her son. He would worship his Beethul (Waheguru) alone even if he had to die. The elephant attacked Naam Dev Ji with his trunk, but Naam Dev Ji was saved by the Almighty. ——— — Naama was in shackles and in handcuffs, but he kept singing praise of his Beethual. Even if the Ganges and the Jamuna began to flow in the reverse direction, Naama would still sing his Lord's praise (and will not lose faith in Him). ——— Waheguru appeared shortly before the deadline to protect His devotee. Waheguru assured Naam Dev Ji that He would do anything at all for him. ——— The dead cow came back to life, and was milked. (The king was convinced of the faith of Naam Dev Ji in his Beethul) and released him. The king also tendered his apology and begged to be forgiven. ——— **(Bhairon Naam Dev Ji, 1166)**

This holy Shabad clearly describes a miracle for Naam Dev Ji where a dead cow had been brought back to life by Waheguru. **I want you to pay attention to the part of the holy hymn where Naam Dev Ji expresses his inability to revive the cow. Naam Dev Ji does not want to show any miracle, but the King is NOT convinced by Naam Dev Ji's logic.** The reason this holy hymn has been included in Sri Guru Granth Sahib by the Revered Fifth Guru is that it glorifies the omnipresence of Waheguru and His Grace to shield His devotees in all circumstances. Again, there are many holy shabads in Guru Granth Sahib in which Waheguru's commitment to protect His devotees and to enhance their dignity has been described. I'll quote only one of them.

- Waheguru forces the whole world to surrender and to kneel to His devotee whom He wants to glorify. The devotee does not need to be embarrassed by this special respect for him, because

it is Waheguru Who is displaying His power (to glorify His devotees). ———— Waheguru protects His devotees in all circumstances, and brings disgrace to the malevolent. ————
(Gauri ki Vaar, Sloak M:4, 308)

The second shabad is about a visit to a temple by Naam Dev Ji where only upper class people - Brahmans and Khattris - could go. The upper class people showed contempt for Naam Dev Ji who was a low-class washerman, and pushed and shoved him out of the temple. Naam Dev Ji went to the back of the temple and began to sing Lord's praise. The temple rotated so that it faced Naam Dev Ji. Naam Dev Ji describes the whole episode as follows, which Guru Arjun Dev Ji kindly included to be a part of the Holy Guru Granth Sahib.

- Why was I born as a washerman, oh Waheguru! People consider me a low caste (and treat me poorly). I went enthusiastically to salute You at the Temple, but, the upper-class people kicked me out of the temple during my prayer. I took my blanket and turned around to sit at the back of the temple. As I was singing Your praise, the temple was turning towards me. ———— **(Bhairon Naam Dev Ji, 1163)**

It is again a big miracle shown by Waheguru to honour His devotee. Naam Dev Ji did not intend to show any miracle. As Bhagat Ji says, it was Waheguru who did that. When Naam Dev Ji was being shoved away, **he must have tried to convince the upper-class people that he was there to worship Waheguru like anybody else, but, obviously they refused to be convinced.** So, like He does it all the time, Waheguru recognized His devotee's dedication, and established his superiority among the conceited 'worshippers'. Now it is a recorded incident in Sri Guru Granth Sahib, so nobody can doubt that miracles have happened for the beloveds of Waheguru.

A couple of very important observations follow from this episode.

(a) Some people - particularly, bigoted, prejudiced and egoistic - are almost impossible to convince. If they could be convinced, we will have no problem in the world. There will be no Israel - Palestine conflict, no trouble in Ireland, and no apartheid based on race or beliefs. But, as all of us know, there has been no period in history when there was complete peace in the world. The law courts are overflowing with people. Why? Because some people are irrational and they will never allow logic to change their minds. **Was someone able to convince the Talibans not to dismantle the historic statues of Buddha in Afghanistan! Was the Nawab of Malerkotla able to convince the Nawab of Sirhand not to kill the two innocent younger Princes of the Tenth Master mercilessly! Was Aurangzeb convinced that he should not kill the holy Ninth Master because His only fault was to enlighten the ignorant masses!**

The conclusion is that not everybody can be convinced. Even Guru Sahiban have said that although they tried every possible way, they could not convince the mean-spirited people to refrain from talking ill of others.

- All ills can be cured, but there is no cure for a mean-spirited person who talks (and thinks) ill of others. Such people have been misguided by Waheguru Himself and are born again and again (because of their mean spirit). **(Sloak M: 5, 314)**
- ———The foolish people who bear enmity with holy men never find comfort and suffer from the agony of their ego. But they are helpless because such unlucky people are born with those qualities (for there evil deeds in previous incarnation) **and**

they will not improve. ——————(Gauri ki Vaar, M: 4, Pauri, 306)

- A money-minded individual is always engrossed in maya, and is blind and deaf (to the Teachings of the Guru). Such an individual pays no attention to Guru's Shabad (Teachings), but loves to hear the noise of *maya* (loves to hear any discussion about monetary issues no matter how meaningless that might be).——————**(Sloak M:3, Gauri ki Vaar, 313-14)**

That 's why the Tenth Master justified the use of weapons to settle some problems where all other peaceful means fail. That clearly means that some people are so irrational that they will not listen to reason.

(b) Since the temple where Naam Dev Ji went to worship was rotated by Waheguru for Naam Dev Ji, why could not Kaaba revolve for Guru Nanak Dev Ji! Guru Nanak Dev Ji was teaching the fundamentalist Muslims that Allah (Waheguru) was everywhere and not just in Kaaba. But, it was hard to convince them. Waheguru performed that miracle for His beloved, Guru Nanak Dev Ji to enlighten the bigots.

"Are there any questions so far?" Bhai Sahib paused for a short break. It was also his style to ask questions at appropriate times to make certain that the audience understood what he was saying.

"Everything you've said so far is very convincing Bhai Sahib. But let me play the devil and ask if there is a possibility that the two episodes described by Naam Dev Ji are only the height of poetic beauty rather than the actual happenings, and Bhagat Ji simply expressed his love and faith for Waheguru using his wonderful imagination?" Bhai Aman Bir Singh, another young student, asked.

"It is a very good and a very plausible question, but the possibility of mere poetic beauty is not likely in this case for at least two reasons.

(a) Even though Bhagat Ji has gone on a wonderful poetic flight when he describes the arrival of his Beethul (Wahguru) on Garur (a mythical bird used by Lord Vishnu for his travels) to revive the dead cow in the first episode, there is hardly anything imaginary about the whole episode. The description is definitely that of a real story. Bhagat Ji has addressed his Lord as 'Allah' many times in his writings, then why would he refuse to call his Beethul 'Allah' this time? There is also a clear description of some Hindus going to the Bhagat and expressing their happiness at the revival of the dead cow. Such stories are not required to be reported to praise Waheguru. There is the highest type of poetic beauty in many holy hymns in Sri Guru Granth Sahib used to praise Waheguru, but not to describe some events like this.

For example, Guru Nanak Sahib writes:

- ————(Guess what I will offer if someone talked to me about You, oh Waheguru! I will cut my head off to offer the messenger, and serve him headless. ——— **(Wadhans M: 1, 557)**
- ———— You have beautiful eyes, teeth, nose and beautiful long hair. Your body seems to be made of gold, oh Waheguru! —————You have very attractive gait, and melodious voice. ——— **(Wadhans M: 1, Chhant, 566)**
- If wings were on sale, I would buy them paying an equivalent amount of my flesh. I will attach them to my body and fly in search of my dear Waheguru! **(Sloak M: 5, 1426)**

These beautiful pieces of poetry are parts of three of the many holy shabads that Guru Sahiban have written about

Their love for Waheguru. Everybody knows that Waheguru is formless and has no specific place to live. But the picture of Waheguru painted above by Guru Nanak Dev Ji in the second Shabad is an expression of poetic beauty of His love for Waheguru. There are many more pieces of poetic beauty in Sri Guru Granth Sahib, but unlike the holy hymns just discussed, the two holy writings of Naam Dev Ji's are clear descriptions of real stories.

(b) **Guru Ram Das Ji testifies Naam Dev Ji's story of the rotation of the temple - not just once - but twice.** If that were only a poetic beauty, Guru Ji would not have mentioned that let alone repeating that.

- ———People referred to Naam Dev Ji as washerman, but he became a beloved of Waheguru so much so that Waheguru turned His back (rotated the temple) on the upper-class Brahmans and Khattris and turned His face to Naam Dev (Ji).

  ————**(Suhi M: 4, 733)**
- Waheguru has created His bhagats (highly dedicated devotees) in every era, and has not only protected them, but also enhanced their prestige. He killed the evil Harnakash and protected his son, Prehlad. Waheguru turned His back on the egoists and ill-willed people and turned His face towards Naam Dev (embraced him). ————— **(Assa M:4, Chhant, 450)**

Naam Dev Ji has also described the same event again in **Malhar Raag on page 1292** of Guru Granth Sahib. So, clearly, rotation of the temple (as also the revival of the dead cow) was not just a poetic flight of Naam Dev Ji. They are true stories.

Kabir Sahib also writes his own story when the ruler of his time became very unhappy with him because Kabir Sahib was 'enlightening' people. First the king ordered Kabir Ji trampled over by an elephant - a common way of punishment in those days. That having failed, the king handcuffed and shackled Kabir Ji and threw him in the Ganges. Listen to Kabir Sahib's own account:

- They tied my arms and my body to make a bale and threw me before the elephant. The mahout hit the elephant on the head to move him with the intent to trample me over. But the elephant ran away screaming as if he was saying that he would sacrifice his life for this beautiful man (Kabir Ji). The *qazi* (religious judge) was shouting at the mahout to move the elephant, but I had full faith in You, oh Waheguru! The qazi was screaming at the mahout asking him to whip the elephant to move him (to trample over Kabir Ji) otherwise he would kill the mahout. The elephant would not move and seemed to be meditating as if Waheguru had appeared in his heart. ———— The elephant saluted Kabir Sahib in the bale. ————**(Goand Kabir Ji, 870)**

They tried three times but the elephant did not hurt Kabir Ji at all. Kabir Sahib describes the incident of being thrown in the Ganges next:

- A man whose mind stays connected with the beautiful feet of Waheguru, never panics in trouble nor shows any weakness. No one can gain anything by hurting his body. Those people chained my body and took me to drown in the deep and mighty river whom they call mother Ganges. But rather than being drowned, the waves in the River broke my chains loose, and I was floating on the surface as if I was sitting on a deerskin. Kabir (Sahib) says where friends or relatives fail to help you,

Waheguru is always appears to protect you.
(Bhairon Kabir Ji, 1162)

Now, as you can see, this is another true story indicative of a miracle was again shown for Kabir Ji. There is poetic beauty in the description, but the story is true and not just imagination. Kabir Sahib has written many stories from his life in which his mother or his wife complains to him about some financial hardships. They are not just imaginations. They are true stories, and so are the stories of the elephant and the Ganges.

So, the conclusion of the whole discussion is that yes, there have been miracles where Waheguru enhanced the prestige of His devotees or saved them in trouble.

There are also some incidents in the life of Guru Arjun Dev Ji where Waheguru helped Guru Sahib when He or His family were attacked by some evil people. In one incident, a Brahman at the instigation of Pirthi Chand, the elder brother of Guru Sahib, tried to administer poison to Guru Ji's only child, Sri Har Gobind Ji, when he was still an infant. The Brahman died of severe stomachache before he could do any harm to Har Gobind Ji. Guru Sahib describes the incident in His own holy writing as follows:

- Waheguru protects His devotees all the time, folks! The sinner died himself with Guru's radiance. Because of Waheguru's Grace, no harm was done (to the child) while the unfaithful and evil Brahman died of severe stomachache.———— Waheguru listened to the prayer of His devotee and the mean and evil sinner died without achieving his goal (of killing Sri Har Gobind Ji). **(Bhairon M: 5, 1137)**

Guru Sahib has mentioned the same incident again in the same Raag, (Bhairon) on the next page, 1138.

Yet, there was another incident in which an army commander, Sulhi Khan from Lahore, was on his way to attack Guru Arjun Dev Ji. Again it was Pirthi Chand, Guru Sahib's elder brother, who bribed Sulhi Khan to attack Guru Sahib. When some Sikhs came to know of the impending attack, they expressed concern to Guru Sahib and advised Him to either send some mediators or write a letter for compromise. But, Guru Sahib showed no concern. He had full faith in Waheguru that He would protect Guru Ji. On his way to attack Guru Ji, Sulhi Khan went to assess the bricks at the brickkiln owned by Guru Arjun Dev Ji, where bricks were being baked to be used at Harimander Sahib (Golden Temple). Sulhi Khan had planned to use the bricks for a mosque being built in Lahore. Somehow Sulhi's horse was startled and jumped into the kiln, burning Sulhi Khan to death. Guru Sahib describes this incident as follows:

- My only prayer to You was to protect me from Sulhi Khan so that his evil hands would not reach me, oh Waheguru! You were very kind to me and the evil Sulhi died an unholy death. He had very sinister plans, but was burned by the Creator. The Lord cut off his head and Sulhi was a pile of ash in a moment.

  ———I am very thankful to you my Lord for answering my prayer.

  (Bilawal M: 5, 825)

As you can see from this holy shabad, the death of Sulhi Khan, as described by Guru Arjun Dev Ji, was clearly a miracle for Him.

Finally, there is a holy hymn in which Guru Nanak Dev Ji discloses His knowledge of a future attack on Emnabad by Baabar to Bhai Lallo. The description of the last part of the holy shabad is in the future tense, but, I want to draw your attention to one sentence in particular where Guru Sahib forecasts not only the impending attack but also the defeat of the Mughals. Both the predicted dates turned out to be completely true.

- I am going to share some Divine Knowledge with you as I receive it, Bhai Lallo. Baabar will attack (Emnabad) from Kabul with his evil forces and will force people to offer him (cash, jewellery, and even women). ——— The fabric of bodies will be cut into pieces. The Mughals will attack in 1521 and will be driven away in 1540 when some other chivalrous fighter will rise (to defeat them). —— ————— **(Tilung M: 1, 722-3)**

The whole forecast turned out to be true word for word. But some people claim the Shabad was not a forecast, it described the events after they happened. However there are two problems with that.

(a) If the holy Shabad describes events after they had taken place, they would be known to everybody, then why would Guru Sahib start with the sentence 'I am going to share some Divine Knowledge—— ———'? He could have simply written the episode the same way as He has written a few others on the same subject.

(b) The future date of the defeat of Mughals is clearly a forecast which turned out to be exactly true. How can people deny that? Since the forecast turned out to be true, it was a miracle.

So, did miracles happen with Guru Sahiban and the Bhagats? I will leave the conclusion to you.

There are many holy shabads (hymns) in Guru Granth Sahib in which the protection of His devotees by Waheguru has been emphasized as Waheguru's everlasting commitment. I will just quote one of those holy Shabads.

- The loving Waheguru is pleased on His own with His devotees, and He Himself initiates the bond between Himself and His devotees. He bestows the real 'kingdom' on His devotees with royal canopy on their heads. Following the Teachings of the Guru, the devotees are always holy and blissful. The rulers who fight battles and are killed to be born again and again are not the real Kings. Without Waheguru's Naam even the earthly kings get no respect anywhere. **(Wadhans ki Vaar, Sloak M: 3, 590)**

It is clear from this holy hymn and many others like this that Waheguru never lets His devotees down. He rather enhances their prestige. While doing so, miracles may happen. Let me also mention here that performance of miracles had not been restricted to Guru Sahiban and the Bhagats alone. Jesus Christ is also known to have performed many." Bhai Dalip Singh concluded.

"Are there some further questions?" Bhai Sahib asked after a brief pause.

Stories of the Heroes

"There is a trend these days to dissociate Guru Sahiban from miracles. Some scholars believe that Guru Sahiban never performed any miracles, and all the stories involving miracles by Guru Sahiban are untrue. They claim that such stories have been written by people out of jealousy to discredit Guru Sahiban. They claim further that such stories do not guide us in any way in our spiritual journey. But, a few overzealous people have gone so far as to claim that not only Guru Sahiban did not perform any miracles, **they were incapable of doing that.** According to their belief, nobody - not even Guru Sahiban - has the ability to perform miracles. They preach that the Sikhs should follow Sri Guru Granth Sahib only, and should not even listen to any other story. I would like you to comment on this emerging trend, Bhai Sahib." Bhai Nirmal Jit Singh asked. He seemed to be a little disturbed.

"Who can deny the advice to follow the Teachings of Guru Granth Sahib, Bhai Sahib? Guru Granth Sahib is the beacon for spiritual life of the Sikhs. Without Guru Granth Sahib, there's no existence of Sikhism. But, stories of our heroes have their own importance in inspiring, and thus shaping, the character of the coming generations. Guru Amar Das Ji has highlighted the importance of such stories when He writes: **Stories of the heroes convert sons into good sons (heroes)**. There aren't too many stories in Sri Guru Granth Sahib to share with our children and to inspire them. There is no direct mention of the dedication and devotion of Bhai Lehna Ji, of Baba Amar Das Ji, or of Bhai Jetha Ji towards their respective Gurus. There is no mention of the supreme martyrdom of the Fifth and the Ninth Gurus. There is no mention of the unparallel sacrifice of the Tenth Guru and His young Princes. Nothing else can inspire our children more than the stories of the undaunted younger Princes of The Tenth Guru who, at the tender ages of six and eight, boldly rejected the rich offers of the Muslim ruler, and gladly accepted to be walled alive in concrete rather than embracing Islam. There are hundreds of stories about Guru Nanak Dev Ji Who showered the downtrodden and the helpless with His unlimited love, and Who challenged the tyrants to end their injustice. Then, there are stories of thousands of Sikhs who laid down their lives fighting against oppression. The list could go on and on. None of those stories are part of Sri Guru Granth Sahib. Without such stories how can we inspire our children to develop faith in Guru Sahiban, and follow the foot steps of our heroes? You cannot expect a young child to develop love for Waheguru or for Guru Sahiban simply by listening to the holy Gurbani!

Now some of those stories may not be 100% accurate,

but not all of them are imaginary stories written by our adversaries. To reject all of them without any valid reason will be the biggest disservice to all of us. If there is some concern about the authenticity of some of the stories, they can be evaluated using the principles of Sri Guru Granth Sahib. Some Sikhs have raised genuine concerns about the authenticity of some of the books, like Gur Bilas Sixth Patshahi, and the Dasam Granth, and they should be evaluated without any reservation because there are some glaring contradictions with the Divine Principles of Guru Granth Sahib. But to reject our entire invaluable heritage of history is like throwing the baby with the bathtub. If scholars propose to reject the stories because some of them deal with supernatural powers, they are then following their hearts and not the philosophy of Sri Guru Granth Sahib. They have not either studied Guru Granth Sahib carefully, or have not studied It with open mind, and are drawing conclusions based on their biased views. **Earlier in our discussion, we clearly demonstrated that supernatural powers are acknowledged in Sri Guru Granth Sahib. A few of the many scores of holy shabads were quoted to highlight the observation.**

People, who are in favour of rejecting all Sikh history, are a product of evolution who want to be politically correct. Look what's happening around us. A vast majority of our youth (some sources put the number at 90%) have cut their hair and many of them are on drugs. Young girls are smoking, drinking alcohol, and are dating freely. They are embracing Western values at an alarming rate. Speaking Punjabi even in Punjab has become embarrassing for them. They take pride in eating western food and listening to English music. Why is all of this happening? The answer is not very difficult to find. **We are NOT telling our youth the stories of our heroes, and of our glorious past.** They don't have any icon to follow. Why would they grow hair if we don't tell them the importance of hair for the Sikhs, and if we don't inspire them by telling stories of Bhai Taru Singh, Bhai Mani Singh, Bhai Shubeg

Singh and Shahbaz Singh, and many others who laid down their lives gladly to keep the principles of Sikhism alive? There is no shabad in Sri Guru Granth Sahib which stresses the requirement to grow hair. So, it is very important that we keep the stories of our heroes fresh in the minds of our youth if we want them to lead a life of a true Sikh.

Our leaders are too busy to save their chairs, and have no time for our precious national treasure - our youth. It is a matter of shame for all of us that we are not doing anything to educate our youth. If we start campaigning to focus on Guru Granth Sahib alone without teaching our extremely rich history, we will be forcing more youth to turn away from Sikhism.

Also, people need faith in some superpower to solve their day to day problems. If they are bluntly told that our Guru Sahiban are incapable of helping them, what will stop them from turning to the self-proclaimed saints or even to Christianity or other faiths for help? They must be educated about the fact that our Gurus are fully capable of helping them, but they must follow their Teachings and must worship Waheguru as advised by Guru Nanak Sahib.

Political pressure of democracy and the desire for cheap popularity is forcing the leaders and the governments to allow even certain immoral issues to be legally acceptable. Legalization of gay marriages is just one of them. Women in the Western world are also fighting now to go topless in public. I don't know where all this degeneration will stop. It is very scary. If we want to preserve our rich heritage and want our youth to lead their lives according to the golden principles of Sikhism, **we must inspire them by telling the stories of our heroes in addition to teaching them Gurbani.** In fact, we must use modern technology like videos, TV serials, and audio tapes to educate our youth of our glorious past. I see no other way to keep our youth from turning away from Sikhism." Bhai Dalip Singh concluded. There were signs of concern on his face.

"I hope, I've answered your question, Bhai Sahib?" Bhai Dalip Singh addressed Bhai Nirmal Jit Singh.

"You, sure have, Bhai Sahib." Bhai Nirmal Jit Singh nodded.

"Are there any other questions?" Bhai Dalip Singh asked.

There were no further questions. Everybody seemed spellbound.

Bhai Kashmir Singh thanked Bhai Dalip Singh profusely and also the holy congregation for being wonderful listeners. They chanted the traditional Sikh slogan in a loud voice, and everybody headed to the kitchen to partake in the Lungar.

13

Amrit (The Liquid of Immortality) and the Five K's

It is again time for the daily gathering at Bhai Kashmir Singh's farm house. The number of people coming to listen to his discourses has been growing steadily over the last three weeks or so, but, the number was particularly large today because the topic for tonight was very important to some people in the gathering. Bhai Dalip Singh was going to speak on Amrit and the five K's.

People welcomed him with the traditional salutation of "Waheguru Ji Ka Khalsa, Waheguru Ji Ki Fateh", and gave him a standing ovation when Bhai Dalip Singh appeared on the stage. Bhai Sahib thanked them all, and welcomed them. Everybody sat on the floor as usual, and began to wait eagerly for Bhai Dalip Singh to start his informative and pleasant lecture.

"Dear congregation, I am gong to talk about a very important topic today viz. Amrit and the five K's. I will start with the mythical amrit, and then discuss Amrit in terms of Gurbani.

The Mythical Amrit

"Ever since the dawn of history, man has been searching for two main things - amrit, and touchstone. Amrit is supposedly a liquid or a concoction that when taken internally makes a man immortal. The touchstone is supposedly some metal or a stone which turns all the base metals into gold when they are touched by it. It is said that one of the objectives of Alexander the Great was to find amrit when he set out to conquer the world. Well, after thousands of years of search, man has not been successful in either of these two areas yet. And he is not expected to find them either because both are imaginary concepts against the law of Nature. However, there is a story in the Vedas that when the gods and the demons had been fighting for thousands of years, they agreed to churn the ocean together to get 'gems' (precious items) ,which were supposedly there in the deep waters of the ocean. They used forest as the agitator and Bashak Naag (a huge snake) as the string to spin the agitator. Lord Vishnu incarnated as a turtle to provide base for the agitator. When they finished churning the ocean, they found 14 'gems' including amrit. The other gems included a goddess, the moon, a physician, a cow, a horse, an elephant, a conch, a special tree, and alcohol. I wonder how the moon was immersed in the ocean which has a maximum depth of about 11 km while the diameter of the moon is about 3500 km! (Harvey White). And how the amrit and the alcohol existed together! Oh, well, that is a story - albeit quite fascinating.

We will not talk about touchstone because attachment to worldly objects or riches is not an objective in Gurmat. So, we'll keep our focus only on Amrit.

Gurbani and Amrit (The Liquid of Immortality)

Gurbani does not believe in any liquid of immortality because nothing - absolutely nothing - is everlasting in this universe. Everything has to come to an end sooner or later including the sun, the moon and our earth. Likewise, all living things must also die; that's the law of Nature. No liquid is capable of making a living being immortal. Listen to the following holy shabads (hymns).

- ——How can we consider this world a permanent

residence for anyone? —— The whole world is destructible. Only Waheguru is everlasting. The sun and the day, the moon and the night, and all the millions of stars in the sky will vanish. The only everlasting thing is Waheguru.**(Siri Raag M:1, 64)**

- No leader, no ruler and no subjects will live for ever. All shops, all bazaars and all cities will vanish. Only a fool may consider the cemented and beautiful homes as his own. Lockers full of wealth may become empty in no time. ————(Majh ki Vaar, Pauri, M:1. 141)
- Human life is as temporary here in this world as the stay of cattle in seasonal pastures, oh man! So, what is the sense in multiplying your wealth? When your time is up, you will have to leave this world, but, you're still contemplating possessions and property. ——— Why are you so involved with your family which is also short-lived like a garden of flowers? Your stay here is just like a guest who is here for the night and will leave in the morning. —— **(Siri Raag M:5, 50)**
- Don't you feel ashamed of yourself when you say that this is **your** house, oh man! How can it be yours for ever when nothing will be yours when you leave this world? Man takes birth, grows, and finally dies. Just like many who have died before, you will watch the whole world dying one by one with your eyes. ———— **(Gauri Kabir Ji, 325)**

You could go on and on. There are hundreds of holy shabads to support this idea of everything in the universe coming to an end. So, there is no way that some amrit (liquid of immortality) would exist in nature which would make a man immortal. Let's now discuss what Gurbani has to say about Amrit.

Gurbani maintains that sure a person can become immortal, but, only by being one with the Immortal - Waheguru. There's absolutely no other way to become immortal. So, the real Amrit is the Naam of Waheguru, and that is the only Amrit that can make a person immortal. You have to recite the Naam of Waheguru with dedication while following the teachings of the Guru, and you will be one with Waheguru and become immortal. There are hundreds of shabads that unequivocally proclaim this principle. I'll quote only a few.

- Those who sing the praise of Waheguru, are imbued in His Naam. (Guru) Nanak says that there is only one Amrit (the Naam of Waheguru), and nothing else could be Amrit. (Guru) Nanak further says that the Amrit (Naam of Waheguru) is always there in human body, but can be realized only by Guru's grace which is available only to those who did good deeds in their previous incarnations and were destined for such grace. Such individuals drink the **Naam Amrit** and are always connected to Waheguru. **(Saarang ki Vaar, Sloak M:2, 1238)**
- It is always raining of Amrit, but, only those come to realize who have attained that level of spirituality. ——— **Amrit is the Naam of Waheguru** and it rains of Amrit because of His kindness. (Guru) Nanak says that it can be realized only through the grace of the Guru when you envision Waheguru. **(Malhar ki Vaar, Sloak M:3, 1281)**
- Amrit is the Naam of Waheguru which is realizable only through the grace of the Guru, oh my soul! Personal ego, selfishness, and other forms of maya are poison whose effect can be washed away with the **Naam Amrit**. ——— **(Bihagra M:4, 538 - 39)**
- If you wait for some appropriate time to worship

Waheguru, then there will be no time to do so (because there will always be some excuse not to do it). —— Guru's **shabad is Amrit** and all types of your thirst can be quenched by it.
(Siri Raag M:3, 22)

- Lucky are the people who spend their time in the company of holy men singing the praise of Waheguru. Your mind is enlightened by concentrating on the **Amrit (life sustaining) Naam of Waheguru**. By doing so, you will be spared the pain of the life and birth cycle (which would be broken), and you will not be subjected to the scrutiny of the angel of death. However, only those people are able to realize Waheguru who are liked by Him (because of their noble deeds and because they sing the praise of Waheguru). **(Bilawal M:5, 802)**
- The true Guru is source of Naam Amrit. His utterings are Amrit (because they are in the praise of Waheguru), and He makes His Sikhs recite the Amrit - Gurbani. Because it is uttered by the Guru, the Naam is unblemished (sacred). Everybody should recite Guru's sacred Gurbani. Guru's Amrit Gurbani is a manifestation of Waheguru, and through Guru's grace, it finds home in a Sikh's heart. **(Sloak M:4, 1423-4)**
- Listen to the Amrit Gurbani in praise of Waheguru, hey lucky person! It (the Gurbani) resides in the hearts of the people who earn the kindness of Waheguru. **(Bihagara M:5, 545)**
- The Amrit Gurbani of the Guru is very sweet, but very few people enjoy it through the grace of the Guru. Those individuals have been enlightened and they enjoy its great taste by singing Waheguru's praise at His door steps. **(Majh M:3, 113)**

- Come and sing the everlasting Gurbani, oh beloved Sikhs of the Guru! Recite the Bani (hymns) of the Guru only, because this is supreme among all other baanis (hymns). The Bani resides in the hearts of people upon whom Waheguru bestows His kindness. Worship Waheguru, and drink the Naam Amrit while you stay connected with Him. **(Ramkali M:3, Anand, 920).**

From the few holy shabads just quoted - and there are hundreds more - it is perfectly clear that **Waheguru's Naam or Gurbani is the only Amrit.** By singing the praise of Waheguru by reciting Gurbani, one can rid himself of all the sins and impious qualities. Thereby he acquires the qualities of Waheguru, and thus becomes one with Him. When an individual becomes one with Waheguru, he can live for ever as part of Waheguru. **In that sense, Gurbani is the only Amrit.** So, if a person wants to live for ever, he should drink Naam Amrit." Bhai Dalip Singh explained. The whole congregation was spell bound.

"Having discussed that, let me also share with you that some items of good qualities have also been called amrit in Guru Granth Sahib. Listen to the following holy shabads." Bhai Sahib continued.

Some Delicious Foods and Comforts of life also Called Amrit

Let us listen to the following holy shabads.

- .... Milch-cattle win our praise because they consume vegetation and give us amrit (milk) in return. ———**Gujri M:1, (489)**
- Hey man, always remember Waheguru because of Whose grace you enjoy 36 kinds of amrit (varieties of food). ———**Gauri Sukhmani M:5, (269)**
- Gruel is wonderful food because it contains salt-

amrit, hey Kabir! ———**Sloak Kabir Ji (1374)**

- A crow will not be satisfied with a food containing amrit-juice (delicious for humans). It will rather enjoy filth like feces and cow dung for food. —— —— **Gujri M:4 (492)**
- Living in the clean water of a clean pool, you do not enjoy the water or the lotus flower growing in it, oh ignorant frog! You are like a tick on the tits of a cow who sucks blood rather than enjoying the amrit (milk) in the tits which is sweet like sugar or honey. ———**(Maru M:1, 990)**

These are only a few of the many holy shabads in Sri Guru Granth Sahib in which the word 'amrit' has been used for rich foods.

Amrit has also been used a few times synonymously with comforts of life. Consider the following holy Shabad, for example:

- **Parbhati Bibhas M:1 (1328).** A person who accepts amrit (comforts) and poison (discomforts) at par in life, is honoured in Waheguru's Court, and has his wishes granted.

Not only rich foods and comforts of life, even sweet or polite language has also been called amrit.

- ———It is because of Waheguru's Grace that you have 'amrit' on your tongue, (you have politeness and sweetness in your speech) and it is because of His grace that you have peace of mind. So, how can you ignore such a kind Waheguru and indulge in other things, oh man! **(Sukhmani, M:5, Ashatpadi, 6)**

"Are there any questions so far?" Bhai Sahib asked.

"Your explanation of Amrit was very detailed and convincing as it was well supported by Gurbani, and we are very impressed. But, I'm afraid, that raises a question in my mind. If Waheguru's Naam is the only Amrit, then what is the importance of the bowl-and-the dagger Amrit? Why did the Tenth Master administer that Amrit to His Sikhs? Would you, please, clarify that? Bhai Param Jit Singh asked curiously.

"That's a wonderful question, and I was going to address it later. But now that you've asked, I'll respond to this as soon as I finish this glass of water." Bhai Dalip Singh said smilingly. He was holding a glass of water in his hand.

The Bowl-and-Dagger Amrit

"Waheguru has created the world in such a way that it appeals to all living beings, but more so to human beings. There is breathtaking beauty in nature, countless tasty foods, beautiful precious stones for ornaments, and a variety of animals to ride and to provide milk and other products for human beings. And then of course, members of opposite sex for closest company. There is enough of everything for everybody if we could learn to share. But, all living beings want to control as much of all natural resources as possible. Not only that, they also want to control and rule over other living beings - particularly the members of their own species. This tendency is more prevalent among humans because they want to be respected and be feared by their fellow humans. All these natural attractions, and therefore the tendencies to control them, are collectively called **'maya'**. Maya gives birth to tendencies of selfishness and ego, called **'haumein'**. According to Gurbani, haumein is the most powerful disease-like tendency from which all humanity suffers. It can be overcome only by singing the praise of Waheguru through the recitation of Gurbani. In fact, haumein and its control is a big topic in itself which has already been discussed. As long as an individual is a victim of haumein, he cannot realize Waheguru. Guru Nanak Dev Ji and His other nine spiritual incarnations worked very hard for 239 years to teach humanity how to control haumein, and thus become good human beings. Their hard work and unprecedented sacrifices resulted in producing high quality Sikhs who were dedicated devotees of Waheguru, and who were willing to lay down their lives for noble deeds like fighting for justice and against oppression. They routinely displayed these noble qualities. They fought four successful battles against injustice and high handedness of the Mogul rulers at the time of Guru Har Gobind Sahib, and many of them laid down their lives gladly to defend the freedom of other religion (Hinduism) during the time of Guru Tegh Bahadur Sahib while suffering unprecedented torture. They were sawed off alive from top to the bottom, and were boiled to death. Finally, they offered to be beheaded gladly when Guru Gobind Singh Ji challenged them in Anand Pur Sahib on the Vaisakhi day in 1699. By their deeds of selflessness, the Sikhs demonstrated that they had acquired the qualities of perfect human beings for which Guru Nanak Dev Ji had laid the foundation and the other nine Gurus had preached hard and made all sorts of supreme sacrifices. The Tenth Master was very pleased to see those good qualities in His Sikhs, and He wanted to ensure that they did not lose them. He was concerned that with time, the Sikhs may be absorbed by the main stream religions - Hinduism and Islam. As you know, Buddhism and Jainism are almost nonexistent in India - the country of their origin - and have been assimilated in the main stream religion.

Also, haumein is a powerful force of nature that can overpower all of us any time if we are not careful, and not connected with Waheguru. **So, to ensure that the Sikhs are not assimilated by other religions, and they do not become victims of haumein, the farsighted Tenth Master decided to give the Sikhs a distinct identity and get a commitment from them to remain devoted to the high moral values of Sikhism.** To achieve these objectives, the Tenth Mastered administered the bowl-and-dagger amrit to His Sikhs. The amrit is sweet water prepared by five Sikhs, one of whom moves a double-edged steel dagger constantly in the water taken in a steel bowl and sweetened by patasas (light weight bubbly sugar cakes which dissolve readily in water) while all five of them recite Gurbani with full concentration. **The administration of bowl-and-dagger amrit had multi-faceted functions and importance as follows:**

- By taking this amrit, the Sikh takes a sacred oath that he will be the devotee of only one power - Waeguru, Who is the creator of the whole universe - and will never worship any other god or goddess. And the Gurbani (Guru Granth Sahib) will be his only Guru.
- The Sikh also takes the oath that he will lead a life of high moral values as preached by the ten Gurus, **which includes equality among all human beings without any discrimination based on caste, colour or gender;** an honest living; and fighting against all evils even if his life is at risk:
- Taking of this amrit fosters solidarity among the members who start feeling strong bonds of brotherhood among themselves because of the common goal. **Because amrit is administered from the same bowl, it also demolishes the highly undesirable walls of caste system thereby raising the morale of the so considered low castes, and the hollow conceit of the upper classes.**
- The real Amrit - Waheguru's Naam - resides covertly in all human hearts without them realizing it. This amrit initiates a connection with the real Amrit, and with the efforts of the Sikh, and the grace of the Guru, the real Naam-Amrit appears in the heart of the Sikh. **That is why the bowl-and dagger amrit is called pahul (the primer).** Just as

we apply primer before the real paint to impart fastness and shine to the item being painted, the amrit serves as the primer for the Naam Amrit to appear in the Sikh's mind.

- The Guru showers His affection on the Sikh and guides him in his efforts to lead a noble life as long as the latter obeys Guru's Teachings. There are many holy shabads that testify to this affection of the Guru for His Sikhs, but I'll quote only a couple of lines:

  The True Guru is always kind to His Sikhs, and He nurtures them. ..... The Guru ensures that His Sikhs succeed in both the worlds - here in this life, and after death. ..... Nanak says that the Guru cares about His Sikhs just the way He cares about His own life **(Gauri Sukhmani, M:5, 288).**
- In the absence of the living guru, the bowl-and-dagger amrit serves to establish a bond between the Guru and the Sikh. The Sikh makes the commitment to the Guru to mold his life as per the Teachings of the Guru, and the Guru bestows His grace on the Sikh.

Last Names, and the Five K's

Having administered this oath, The Tenth Master ordered His Sikhs to wear the following five items (kesh, kangha, kutchhehra, kirpan, and karra) - called the five K's - all the time as constant reminders of their responsibilities in everyday life which include high living as required by the Teachings of Guru Granth Sahib, and singing praise of Waheguru. He also made it a requirement that all Sikh males must have 'Singh' (meaning a lion) as their last name, and all Sikh women must have 'Kaur' (meaning a princess) as their last name. The significance of these last names was two fold. Firstly, there is a valid expectation that people strive to live up to their names. Singhs are expected to be fearless. India's slavery for centuries had demoralized its natives. By comparing them to lions, Guru Sahib infused a new life in them and challenged His Sikhs to fight for freedom. The recitation of Gurbani with dedication would keep them from becoming tyrants.

Women were conventionally treated as inferior to men, if not slaves. The last name 'Kaur' was supposed to infuse high self-esteem among them.

Secondly, conventional last names reveal the castes of the individuals which had a very damaging effect on the morale of the low castes, and on the progress of the fledgling Sikh religion. **By giving the same last names to all Sikhs, Guru Ji was hitting the poisonous snake of caste system on the head. Guru Sahib also changed His name from Gobind Rai to Gobind Singh on that day.**

The importance of the five K's is as follows:

(1) Kesh (Hair): All Sikhs are forbidden to cut hair from any part of their body. Hair must be allowed their natural growth. This requirement is very significant for the following reasons.

(a) Sikhs believe very strongly in the will of Waheguru. The growth of hair on body is a natural process, and human body is incomplete without it. Since the growth of body hair is natural (will of Waheguru), the Sikh is expected to show respect for it. Then the question for the Sikh is not why to grow hair, but why to cut it. All the prophets and saints wore uncut long hair no matter what their religion was.

(b) Uncut long hair imparts saintly look to individuals. A person who wears uncut hair for his saintly beliefs is more likely to behave in a saintly manner. Just as a policeman in uniform is less likely to commit crime, a saintly looking person is less likely to commit sin. The Sikhs grow their hair for this reason as well.

(c) The hair grows for very good reasons. Firstly, the facial hair creates a visible distinction between males and females - which is very essential. Facial hair also gives impressive looks to males. Even though many men shave their beards, the growth of hair still shows on their faces. Imagine a male without beard!
Secondly, the body hair enhances human beauty. Imagine a person without eyelashes or eyebrows! Some women apply false eyelashes to look more beautiful - and they do.

(d) Body hair protects the loss of many vital nutrients in the body, and also protects against heat or cold, and improves electrical signals.

(e) Lastly, but very importantly, the growth of hair gives the Sikhs a very unique identity which makes it difficult for them to be assimilated in any other religion - which was a big concern of the Tenth Master. They can be recognized among thousands of other individuals and cannot hide easily to do something against the Teachings of the Gurus, including assimilation in other religions.

(2) Kangha (Comb): The Sikh is required to keep a small comb in his hair all the time. The reason for this requirement is very clear. Guru Sahib did not want His Sikhs to show any negligence in their personal hygiene. Since they are required to grow hair, they could not be allowed to have tangles in their hair, or let their hair get dirty. So, Guru Sahib made it mandatory for the Sikhs to keep a comb in their hair so that they won't have any excuse not to comb their hair, and thus keep their hair neat and clean.

(3) Kutchhehra (Long Underwear): All Sikhs are required to wear underwears as a reminder of high moral character. If a Sikh makes the mistake of undressing in front of people other than his own spouse, the underwear reminds him of his oath of high moral values to the Guru. The underwear must be long enough that, if the need be, it can be worn alone in public and still look decent.

(4) Kirpan (Sword): The Kirpan is another important item required of all Sikhs. But, the Kirpan and the steel bracelet (discussed next) are probably the least understood of the five K's of the Sikhs. Most people think that kirpan is just a weapon which should be used for defense, but can also be used in offense, if need be. If defense (or offense) were the only reason to wear kirpan, then it will have no relevance in the modern world in which kirpan is no match for the ultramodern hand guns or the laser guns. Do we think that the farsighted Tenth Master was not aware of this? It is a big sin even to let that idea flash through our mind. Of course kirpan is a weapon, but obviously, it must have some other deeper significance. The word 'sword' has been used in Sri Guru Granth Sahib quite frequently. Let's find out the sense in which this word has been used in Guru Granth Sahib. Consider the following holy shabads which are only a few of the hundreds in which the word 'sword' has been used.

- I have realized the **sword-like powerful Knowledge** from the Guru which has decimated the fort of my misgivings of worldly attachment, greed and conceit (or ego). Now, Waheguru's Naam has appeared in my heart as I contemplated Guru's Shabad. ————**(Maru ki Vaar, M:3, Pauri, 1087)**
- ————If a person fights against his mind using the **sword of Knowledge,** all his desires can be overpowered by his own mind, and he can kill (control) the evil forces of lust, rage, and conceit. He can destroy the fiverobbers of (lust, rage, greed,

attachment, and conceit) following Guru's Shabad. **(Maru Solhe, M:1, 1022)**

- You can become very lucky if you worship Waheguru's Naam, oh my young camel-like mind. The Guru has taken the **sword of Knowledge** in His hand and has killed the angel of (moral) death.————————**(Gauri M:4, Ashatpadian, 220)**
- The Guru is like a touchstone who converts base metals (sinners) into a touchstone (holy men), oh my Waheguru! ————The sandal tree (good qualities) is surrounded by snakes (maya - worldly attractions), how can one have access to the tree to get some wood? (Waheguru says) take the powerful **sword of Knowledge** from the Guru, and cut the snakes into pieces and sip the juice (the sandal wood - good qualities) slowly to enjoy it, oh man! **(Kalyan M:4, Ashatpadian, 1324)**
- Worship the unaccessible and the endless Waheguru, oh my mind!———— The wave of greed is just like a mad dog which has infected everybody with madness by biting them. This (disturbing) news has reached the Court of my Waheguru, and the Guru has killed the mad dog with the **sword of Knowledge.**
(Raag Nut, Ashatpadian, M:4, 983)
- Singing the praise of Waheguru is the best form of wealth with you, oh my mind! Waheguru's Naam is like having the support of hundreds of thousands of people. The Guru has kindly given the **sword of Knowledge** with which I have attacked and killed all the demons (lust, rage, greed, attachment, and ego). **(Maru Solhe, M:5, 1072)**

It is perfectly clear from the above holy shabads that kirpan (sword) represents Divine Knowledge in the same way as poison is representative of 'maya', or the crow of a sinner, as used in Sri Guru Granth Sahib. Sword also represents power. The rajahs and the maharajahs always used to carry a sword in their hands to symbolize power. For the Sikh, the ultimate power is Waheguru. So, when the Sikhs wear a kirpan, they are constantly reminded of the presence of the supreme power, Waheguru, Whom they should never forget. So, the prime objective of wearing kirpan is to remember Waheguru all the time. If there is still some doubt left in this interpretation of wearing kirpan, pay attention to the following holy Shabad:

- ———Bhai Lehna Ji succeeded Guru Nanak Dev Ji to the throne of Guruship. He earned this privilege because He had been drinking Naam Amrit by singing the praise of Waheguru. Guru Nanak Dev Ji passed on His Divine Light to Bhai Lehna Ji and injected Him with a new life of high morality using the **kirpan (sword) of Divine Power. Ramkali ki Vaar, Satta and Balwand (966)**

This holy hymn leaves absolutely no doubt about the meaning of kirpan and the implication of Sikhs wearing it. **Kirpan represents Divine power, and its wearing serves as a constant reminder of the omnipresence of Waheguru and for the Sikh to worship Him.** There is a strong evidence that **each of the Guru Sahiban wore kirpan for exactly the same reason as discussed here, and the kirpan was passed on to the succeeding Guru as He acquired Guruship.** As all of you know, Guru Har Gobind Sahib wore two kirpans - one symbolizing saintliness, and the other political power. He was the first among the Gurus to wear the second kirpan. So, obviously, the previous Gurus must have been wearing a kirpan symbolizing saintliness.

We also pray to Guru Granth Sahib for Guru's approval before serving langar (food) and krah parshad (the traditional pudding) at the Gurdwaras and other religious congregations, and then touch the langar and parshad with kirpan. Why do we do that? The significance is clear. **Kirpan represents the Guru, or in other words, Divine Knowledge.**

Of corse, the kirpan is also a weapon, but, it is to be used only against oppression or in self defense. **It is NOT to be used as a weapon of offense.** By wearing a kirpan, the Sikh also takes the oath of fighting oppression, no matter who the victim of the aggression is. Fighting oppression does not have to involve the use of force. It could be fought by peaceful means. **When Guru Arjun Dev Ji and Guru Tegh Bahadur Sahib laid down their lives in exemplary peaceful manner, They were also fighting oppression**. And in the case of Guru Tegh Bahadur, the oppression was against Sikhs, it was against a select group of people from Kashmir.

History testifies that when Karam Chand, a son of Chandu Lall (the evil assassin of Guru Arjun Dev Ji) attacked Guru Har Gobind Sahib with the help of the Nawab of Jallandhar, he came face to face with Guru Sahib. During the duel, Karam Chand's sword broke into two pieces, and he was left with no weapon on him. The high-moral Guru Sahib did not attack the unarmed Karam Chand, and gave him His own kirpan (sword) to fight. Now Guru Ji was left with no weapon other than the kirpan He was wearing as a symbol of saintliness. Guru Sahib did not use that kirpan, and fought empty-handed with Karam Chand whom He killed in a matter of minutes.

So, the struggle against oppression can be absolutely peaceful. Kirpan only reminds the Sikh of his responsibility. Guru Gobind Singh Ji had clearly professed that kirpan as a weapon (force) was to be used only when all other avenues of achieving justice have been fully exhausted.

(5) Karra (Bracelet): A karra is the fifth important item to be worn by the Sikh. This is another item not very well understood. The karra must be made of steel so that every one can afford it, and that it does not become a symbol of riches. The word karra is synonymous with kerri (hand cuff) and its implication is exactly the same. A karra reminds the Sikh never to do an immoral act or never to use kirpan for oppressive purposes. Because most of us use our right hand to do most of the tasks, the karra is required to be worn on the right arm as a reminder of the restrictions placed on us by Guru Sahiban.

Now let me clarify a few things about the five K's because the administrators of amrit do not clarify their implications. They simply advise the recipients of amrit to wear them. **These are not the items of worship**. They are strong reminders of our moral values. The five demons (lust, rage, greed, attachment to worldly things or possessiveness, and conceit or ego) are the big obstruction in the union of man with Waheguru. These K's are simply reminders of our oath with the Guru for certain do's and don'ts. As explained earlier, the five K's help us control the five demons, and thus unite us with Waheguru. **To earn Guru's grace, and lead a life of high moral values, every Sikh must take amrit as soon in his life as he is able to understand its importance."** Bhai Dalip Singh concluded his detailed explanation of Amrit and the five K's.

Everyone was listening with full attention and was amazed at the deep meanings of the symbols. The impressed congregation began to chant slogans of 'Bolle So Nihal, Sat Sri Akal' to express their thanks for the wonderful explanation put forward by Bhai Dalip Singh.

"Are there any questions?" Bhai Sahib asked as he drank another glass of water. It was getting late in the evening, and everybody seemed to be a little tired.

At this point, Bhai Kashmir Singh whispered something to Bhai Dalip Singh who nodded with a smile, and retreated a little.

"I don't want to disrupt a wonderful and an extremely important session, but it is getting a little too late. I'm sure there are still some important questions left for Bhai Sahib to analyze deeply. If we continued, we may not get the depth that we want because Bhai Sahib also seems to be tired now. So, if you permit, I would like to adjourn the session now, and continue with this important topic tomorrow." Bhai Kashmir Singh sought the approval of the congregation.

"That's a good idea." A number of people liked the suggestion.

Bhai Kashmir Singh thanked Bhai Dalip Singh tremendously as also the congregation. The session was adjourned with the traditional Slogan: Bolle So Nihal, Sat Sri Akal.

Were Patasas (Bubbly Sugar Cakes) Available at the Time of Amrit?

The session resumed the following afternoon. After mutual exchange of greetings, Bhai Kulbir Singh started the session with his remarks,

"Your explanations were amazingly informative, and extremely well supported by Gurbani. You've really opened our eyes, Bhai Sahib. We did not know most of the things about amrit before. May I ask a question that is related to the process when the Tenth Master prepared amrit? Bhai Kulbir Singh asked hesitatingly.

"I encourage the holy gathering to ask questions. So, please don't hesitate and go ahead". Bhai Dalip Singh said assuringly.

At this point, Bhai Kashmir Singh

"I am just curious to know if patasas (bubbly sugar cakes) were available at the time when the Tenth Master administered amrit?" Bhai Kulbir Singh asked reluctantly.

"I am not in a position to say 'yes' or 'no' at the moment. However, there is clearly mention of sugar and mishri (big hard crystals of sugar) apart from the brown sugar, in Sri Guru Granth Sahib. I'll quote only a few holy writings.

- No worldly possessions like Turkish horses, gold, silver, and expensive clothes accompany a man when he dies, oh Nanak!. All such possessions are left behind, oh foolish man! I have also tasted the best kind of **mishri** and all sorts of fruit, but only Waheguru's Naam is the real Amrit. **(Gauri Cheti M:1,154-55)**
- ——— Just like you cannot describe the taste of a drink of **mishri** - only the drinker enjoys the real taste - similarly, no one can describe the bliss that one enjoys when he is one with God. The person in that state can only enjoy the bliss. **(Gauri Bairagan Kabir Ji, 333)**
- Brown sugar, sugar, nivat **(mishri)**, honey, and buffalo's milk are all very sweet items, oh Farid! But, none of them could come even close to the sweetness of waheguru's Naam. **(Sloak Farid Ji, 1379)**

Clearly, sugar and even mishri (which cannot be prepared from brown sugar) were available long before amrit was prepared in 1699. I don't recall the mention of bubbly sugar cakes in Sri Guru Granth Sahib, but, if sugar and mishri were being used in the thirteenth century (Baba Farid's time), I see no reason why patasas (buubly sugar cakes) won't be available in the late seventeenth century. There has been a well known humourous poet, named Sutthra, at the time of Guru Har Gobind Sahib. There are some popular cliches associated with his name, and one of them mentions patasas:

- **I couldn't care less if someone lived or died, Sutthra will just enjoy a drink of patasas.**

Now, this clearly proves that patasas were being used at the time of Sutthra and hence, Guru Har Gobind Sahib, in the early seventeenth century.

"Thank you very much Bhai Sahib. One more question if you don't mind. Mata (Mother) Jeeto (Guru Gobind Singh Ji's wife) is mentioned in the history to have brought patasas and added to the bowl when the amrit was being prepared for the first time by the Tenth Master HImself in Anand Pur Sahib. Did Mata Jeeto Ji do anything wrong, or was there any disrespect for the Tenth Master when Mata Ji added patasas?" Bhai Kulbir Singh asked.

"I'm not clear yet about the direction you are taking me in by asking these questions, Bhai Sahib, because the focus of my response will depend very much on your interest. However, I 'll respect your position of not disclosing your interest at this point, and will try to respond objectively. Whether there was anything wrong or whether any disrespect was shown by that act depends upon what exactly happened. I cannot imagine for a moment that Mata Ji would do any thing in this world to show any disrespect for her Guru-husband. I'm fully convinced that the things were prearranged that way with the approval of the Tenth Master, otherwise Mata Ji would not have known about the precise time of preparing the amrit.

But let's suppose for a moment that Mata Ji brought the patasas on her own without the Tenth Master knowing that. I still do not believe that there was any disrespect for the Tenth Master. Respect and disrespect all depend upon the objective behind an act. Perfect Sikhs, like Mata Ji, were loved and held in high esteem by the Gurus. There are many incidents in history where, not only Guru Sahiban approved the selfless acts of Sikhs for which they had no preapproval of the Guru, but also recognized and praised those acts. A few examples come to my mind.

- Guru Angad Dev Ji (the second Guru) loved and respected Guru Nanak Dev Ji tremendously. So, soon after Guru Nanak Dev Ji had left this world, Guru Angad Dev Ji felt strong pangs of separation. He went into hiding and locked Himself in a secret room at Khadur Sahib and sat there for a few months, connected to Guru Nanak Dev Ji. The Sikhs felt His absence badly and were feeling like a fish out of water. They searched for Him hard, but could not trace Him. Finally, Baba Buddha Ji, a highly devoted Sikh of Guru Nanak Dev Ji, sensed where Guru Sahib could be. He approached that room, uncovered the hidden door, pried it open, and found Guru Sahib in deep meditation. When Guru Ji opened His eyes and saw Baba Buddha Ji. Guru Ji was not offended by Baba Buddha Ji's prying open the door, He rather welcomed Baba Ji, and hugged him. Now clearly, Baba Ji had violated Guru Ji's wish to stay in hiding for some time, in a way. But, Guru Ji did not mind that because it was an act of selflessness performed by a great Sikh.
- Until only about sixty years or so ago, all matrimonial relations were arranged by the Brahmans. A Brahman fixed the matrimonial relation of the daughter of Chandu Lall, a resident of Lahore, and a high official in Emperor Jehangeer's privy council in Delhi, with Guru Arjun Dev Ji's son, Har Gobind Sahib. When the Brahman told Chandu Lall where he had fixed the relation, the latter felt very insulted went through the roof. Not only he reprimanded the Brahman, he also said many derogatory things about Guru Sahib, implying that the match was highly unfair - Chandu Lall was much much higher in social status than Guru Sahib. When the Sikhs of Delhi came to know

that Chandu Lall had said some mean and evil things about their revered Guru, they could not tolerate that and decided not to accept the matrimonial proposal. They then rushed to Amritsar to share their feelings with Guru Arjun Dev Ji. Guru Ji listened to them patiently, and even though Guru Ji was not in favour of declining the proposal because it was considered unethical to reject a girl who had been accepted once, He honoured their decision, and said 'no' to the new relation. Guru Ji did that despite the fact that rejection of the relation could have very negative repercussions. Again, as you can see, Guru Ji did not get angry with the Sikhs of Delhi. On the other hand, He honoured their view point.

- At one time, the bards (musicians) of Guru Arjun Dev Ji - Satta and Balwand - became unhappy with Guru Sahib, albeit due to their own greed. They quit coming to Guru Ji's court, and refused to show up come even after Guru Ji had sent a few prominent Sikhs a few times to persuade them to come back. Finally, Guru Ji went Himself to ask them to come back. However, they were so conceited that not only they refused to go back, they made some derogatory remarks in Guru Sahib's honour, which Guru Ji ignored. But they did not terminate their comments just there, they went so far as to say a few unflattering things even against Guru Nanak Dev Ji, including that Guru Nanak Dev Ji was Guru only because of their (Satta and Balwand's) ancestors. Guru Ji could not tolerate anything against the honour of His revered Guru Nanak. He left their place, and announced publically that He will never forgive Satta and Balwand for the disrespect they had shown for the Great Guru Nanak. Not only that,

Guru Ji further announced that He would black paint the face of any individual who approached Him for their forgiveness.

The two cousins (Satta and Balwand) were completely ignored by the Sikhs, and they began to starve. They asked many prominent Sikhs to seek Guru Ji's forgiveness for them, but nobody agreed because of the disrespect they had shown for Guru Sahiban. Eventually, Bhai Laddha, a very kind Sikh, agreed to plead their case even though he was aware of Guru Ji's announcement. So as not to show any disrespect for Guru Ji's orders, Bhai Laddha painted his own face black, and went to Guru Ji to ask for forgiveness for the cousins. Guru Ji hugged the kind and selfless Sikh, and forgave the cousins. Now you can see again that Guru Ji did not get offended by this act of kindness on the part of Bhai Laddha even though he had violated Guru Ji's wishes.

- Bhai Kanhayya was a highly devoted Sikh of Guru Gobind Singh Ji, and was a very kind hearted Sikh. He would go to battles with Guru Sahib, not to fight, but to serve water to the wounded - friend and foe alike. **(In a way, Bhai sahib was the first person to start the services of the Red-Cross).** He served water tirelessly without any discrimination while reciting Gurbani. Some Sikhs did not approve Bhai Sahib serving water to the enemy even though the latter was only giving a practical shape to the Teachings of Guru Nanak and His nine Spiritual Incarnations. They advised him to discontinue the noble service, and also threatened him with a complaint to Guru Sahib. When Bhai Ji did not stop, the Sikhs complained to Guru Sahib. When Guru Sahib asked Bhai Ji with a smile to explain his action, the latter said, "I don't see any enemy there in the battlefield, my Lord; I only see Your Divine face in every wounded soldier." Guru Ji hugged Bhai Ji tightly, and also gave him some ointment to dress the wounds of the soldiers - the friends and the foe alike. As you can imagine, Bhai Ji had not sought approval of the Guru for the noble cause.

These are just a few examples of incidents in which Guru Sahiban praised the noble initiatives of the Sikhs rather than blaming them of any disrespect. I'm sure I can recall some more, but these are enough to clarify the point in response to your question, Bhai Sahib. I hope it answers your question." Bhai Dalip Singh concluded.

"This was wonderful Bhai Sahib, and I'm highly thankful to you for a very convincing explanation based on historical facts, but some people doubt if patasas were available at the time of Guru Gobind Singh Ji. They are also of the view that holy Mata Jeeto Ji did not accept the will of the Tenth Master when she brought patasas and added them to the amrit being prepared. But I'm very thankful to you for clarifying the issues." Bhai Kulbir Singh seemed really thankful.

"Are there some other questions?" Bhai Dalip Singh asked.

Amrit a Ritual?

"I feel very uncomfortable asking this question, and my humble apology in advance if I hurt anybody's feelings because that's not the objective of my question. It is purely for reasons of clarification. Some people argue that taking of amrit is nothing more than a ritual which is against the Principles of Guru Granth Sahib. Could you please share your thoughts on the subject? I once again apologize for this irreverent question." Bhai Ajit Singh showed a great reluctance in asking the question.

"You don't need to be that apologetic for the question,

Bhai Sahib. I strongly believe that the intent behind any question or act, determines its nature. You seem to be very candid about your question, and don't seem to have any ill will, so I'll try to answer your question as best as I can." Bhai Dalip Singh allayed any concerns of disrespect on the part of Bhai Ajit Singh.

"Before I attempt my response, let us define what a ritual is in religious context. A ritual is an act purported to be religious which people perform with the belief or expectation that it would bring them some spiritual gain. For example, our Hindu brothers believe that pilgrimage and/or donations dispel their sins. Some rituals, like fasting by married women on some special days, are also performed for worldly gains. Here the belief or the expectation is that such fasting prolongs the lives of their husbands. Our Hindu brothers believe in many rituals. Whether a ritual is intended for a spiritual gain, a worldly gain, or merely for happy occasions, it is usually an **act performed over a short period of time.** A ritual may also be quite torturous and demanding. Most of the times the ritual is based purely on faith and has no sound logical basis. Also, once the act of a ritual is over, the individual is not obligated to sing praise of Waheguru on regular basis, or perform some acts of high morality. The whole emphasis is on the performance of the ritual.

In the case of administration of the **dagger-and-bowl 'amrit'**, there was never an expectation attached to it by the Tenth Master that the recipient would gain anything spiritually or worldly by simply taking the 'amrit'. **The act is not over soon after the administration of 'amrit', it actually starts from that point on.** In fact, as discussed earlier, by taking the 'amrit', the recipient takes vows to follow the Teachings of Guru Granth Sahib to lead his life. Many restrictions in the form of do's and don'ts are placed on the recipient who is expected to remodel his life according to the tenets of Gurbani. **He is required to sing the praise of Waheguru on regular**

basis and remember Him all the time. The five K's remind him constantly of his obligations. Guru Gobind Singh Ji made it perfectly clear to His Sikhs that by simply wearing the five K's, an individual does not become a real Sikh. The important thing was to lead a model life as per the Teachings of Gurbani. In fact, He cautioned that an individual wearing the five K's but not leading the life of a true Sikh is a big cheat like a wolf in a sheep's garb, and such an individual will be held guilty in Waheguru's Court. Many *Rehatnamas* (Sikh codes of discipline) by the contemporary Sikhs of Guru Gobind Singh Ji testify to such requirements by Guru Sahib. They are all in the name of the Tenth Master. I will quote a few.

- Only the individual who leads his life as per the Teachings of the Guru, will be my Sikh. In fact, such a Sikh will deserve my respect as though he was my guru. An individual will not be considered a Sikh if he does not lead a disciplined life. Such an individual will be punished in the Court of Waheguru.**(Bhai Desa Singh)**
- Every Sikh is required to rise early in the morning and sing praise of Waheguru. He should recite Jap Ji Sahib and Jap Sahib in the morning, and Rehras Sahib in the evening. ———He should consider all humanity the creation of the same Waheguru, and therefore, must treat all individuals the same. He should not inflict any harm on anyone, or treat them maliciously. Waheguru is not pleased when you hurt His creation in any way. **(Bhai Nand Lall)**
- A Sikh should earn his livelihood by honest means, and must donate one-tenth of his income for noble and worthy causes. **(Bhai Desa Singh)**
- A Sikh is expected to treat other women as his daughters, sisters, or his mother (depending upon

their ages), and love only his wife. **(Bhai Desa Singh)**

There are many more Sikh codes of discipline by other prominent Sikhs, but I am sure you've got the idea.

Finally, as discussed yesterday under the importance of Kirpan, Guru Hargobind Sahib wore two kirpans. How will the people who profess 'amrit, as a ritual only, **defend the two swords worn by the Sixth Guru? Will they call them a ritual too?**

Also, it is well documented in history that Guru Amar Das Ji had made it a requirement that whoever went to see Him, must have meals in the Lungar before seeing Him. What was the significance of that practice? If that practice was not a ritual (and it was not) how can administration of 'amrit' be a ritual? I will be shocked to hear someone actually saying that." Bhai Sahib was a little emotional.

"Are there further questions?." Bhai Sahib asked with his usual politeness.

Baanies and 'Amrit'

"I know you must be very tired now, Bhai Sahib, but, I cannot afford not to seek clarification on one more question. Three of the five baanies (holy compositions) recited during the preparation of amrit are not part of Sri Guru Granth Sahib, and are from the "Dasam Granth" the authenticity of which is being seriously challenged. Would you, please, comment on that?" Bhai Ajit Singh asked very candidly.

"That is a question of great significance, and I'm very glad that you asked that. There is no unanimity among the contemporary scholars about the actual *baanies* recited by the Tenth Master when He prepared the amrit for the first time. Three of the baanies which have been reported consistently are: Jap Ji Sahib, Anand Sahib, and Jaap Sahib. The other two

- "Savvayiye" and "Chaupai" - are not mentioned consistently. Some people may be displeased to hear this, but, I myself have grave doubts about the authenticity of the entire Dasam Granth. The Shromani Gurduara Parbandhak Committee (SGPC) should appoint a committee of five unbiased Sikh scholars immediately to look into the matter, and clarify the issue once and for all. The indecision on the status of Dasam Granth is hurting the Sikh cause. However, the indecision about the baanies does not undermine the importance of the bowl-and-dagger amrit." Bhai Dalip Singh expressed some disappointment about the reluctance of the SGPC to seek solution on the status of the Dasam Granth.

"Are there further questions?" Bhai Sahib asked.

Hearing no further question, Bhai Kashmir Singh thanked Bhai Dalip Singh profusely before concluding the session with the traditional Slogan.

The whole gathering gave a standing ovation to Bhai Dalip Singh who had enriched the spiritual lives of thousands of people in the area for about a month or so.

14

Controlling the Five Demons

"Waheguru Ji ka Khalsa, Waheguru Ji ki Fateh." Bhai Dalip Singh greeted the large congregation with a big smile.

"Does anyone have any question before we start?" Bhai Sahib asked.

"I may have a question, Bhai Sahib." Bhai Sundeep Singh, a young man availed himself of the opportunity.

"Go ahead, please." Bhai Sahib said in a welcoming gesture.

"I've heard some scholars saying that the so called five demons cannot be controlled under any circumstances. Is that true? Is there no way to control them?" Sundeep Singh seemed unconvinced that the demons cannot be controlled.

"This is a very pertinent question, young man, and a lot of people would like to know the answer. Let's discuss it in detail." Bhai Dalip Singh said encouragingly.

"Guru Granth Sahib has recognized five major emotions - lust, rage, greed, emotional attachment or possessiveness, and conceit or ego. These emotions are very powerful and are very hard to control. Left uncontrolled, they rob people of their virtuous qualities thereby creating an ever growing gap between them and Waheguru. That's why these five emotions are called five demons or robbers. As long as a person is slave to these emotions or is controlled by them, he cannot realize Waheguru. These emotions are manifestations of a bigger urge called *haumein*. The word *'haumein'* is made of two words - haun and mein - both of which mean I or me. In other words haumein means self serving tendencies. All the five demons or emotions result from selfishness or haumein. Guru Granth Sahib maintains that haumein and Waheguru's Naam cannot exist together.

- Haumein and Waheguru's Naam are mutually exclusive. The two cannot coexist at the same place (heart). One cannot worship Waheguru if his mind harbours haumein. Such a mind remains completely devoid of Waheguru's Naam. ———**-(Wadhans M: 3, 560)**
- A man who harbours *haumein* cannot find peace of mind and his whole life is spent without peace. Haumein is a serious sickness and a man suffering from haumein cannot break the cycle of death and rebirth (so cannot be one with Waheguru). **(Wadhans ki Vaar, Sloak M: 3, 592)**
- Man comes into this world possessed by haumein (ego and self-centeredness) and leaves the world in haumein. All his activities of donations, accepting gifts, earning livelihood, losing wealth, being truthful and dishonest, and so on are all guided by his haumein. In fact, he is born because of his haumein (and as long as he is possessed by haumein, he cannot realize Waheguru). He gets enlightened about Waheguru only when he recognizes (and gets rid of) his haumein. ———— **(Assa ki Vaar, Sloak M:1, 466)**

These holy Shabads clarify the point. As we discussed earlier, the five demons or the robbers are manifestations of haumein, and they cause an ever widening gap between Waheguru and the person gripped by them. Listen to the following holy Shabads:

• I am helpless, oh my Lord! My mind has become a slave of *maya* (haumein).——The five demons have corrupted my mind and I am getting farther and farther away from You every moment.————**(Jaitsari, Ravi Das Ji, 710)**

• ———There are five robbers - lust, rage, greed, emotional attachment and ego - residing in the human body. They rob people of Waheguru's Naam and there is nobody around to help. The manmukh (people who follow their mind) is unaware of the consequences. ————**(Sorith M: 3, 600)**

Demons Hard to Control

As is perfectly clear from the above holy hymns, one cannot realize Waheguru as long as he is possessed by the five demons. So, to be one with Waheguru, one must control the demons. But, as we will discuss next, the demons are almost impossible to control by traditional methods. The following holy hymns tell us how difficult it is to control them.

- I am alone and there are five of them (the demons). How can I guard my door and my house (heart and mind) from them? They attack and rob me of my noble qualities all the time, and there is nobody I can call upon for help. ————The five demons are robbing everybody of their good qualities, and the ignorant human beings are enjoying themselves unaware of the consequences————
(Gauri Cheti M: 1, 155)
- Save me, oh my Father, Waheguru! I am without any noble quality while You are the Master of all the noble qualities. There is only single helpless of me, but, there are five demons attacking me. They cause a lot of uneasiness in me and force me to do evil things. I have tried every which way to get rid of them, but, they do not leave me alone. I am

tired of them and have come to Your shelter. Please, please protect me! ———**(Gauri M: 5, 205-6)**

- ———There are five robbers who rob the unprotected houses (human body and mind). All the senses are busy in enjoying themselves and nobody is aware of the damage being done when their noble qualities are robbed. The robbers (demons) are so powerful that nobody - father, mother, friend or brother - can save from their attack. ——— **(Gauri Guareri M: 5, 182)**
- Authority, wealth, beauty, upper class (status) and youthfulness are five big robbers. They have robbed the whole world and nobody has been able to save their dignity. ———**(Malhar ki Vaar, Sloak M: 1, 1288)**
- The sinner mind is harbouring lust. Because of that the capricious mind is beyond control. The lust is so powerful that even the so called holy men like yogis, jangams (a sect of yogis) and sages, are caught in its web. ———**(Basant M: 9, 1186)**
- You are responsible for people going to hell and for their birth again and again in different life forms, oh lust! You have access to the whole world and you rob people of their spiritual qualities, of their self-discipline, and of their high morality with your charm. Nobody can escape from you.— ——**(Sloak Sehskriti, 1358)**
- Because of my fickle mind, now lust has taken residence in my body, and has robbed me of my precious Divine Knowledge, oh my Lord! I am really suffering from this and have become helpless. Who else should I go to for help, oh my Lord! Who has not been a victim of lust? Lust has affected even the gods. Who am I to resist it? ——— **(Basant Kabir Ji, 1194)**
- ———No matter how hard one tries, he cannot

control the feelings of lust. His mind is still capricious and as a result he will go to hell. ——— — **(Ramkali M: 1, Ashatpadian, 905)**

Demons Can Be Controlled

As is clear from these holy hymns, it is almost impossible to control the five demons by traditional methods. People have tried different ways to control them. Some of them left their homes to live in isolated places so that they won't come in contact with other humans and thus their emotions will not be aroused. Some others use yoga exercises to calm down their emotions while some others use self-discipline to control their emotions. But very few, if at all, are able to control their desires. Guru Sahiban have acknowledged that very few individuals are able to control their sexual urges using yoga exercises or self discipline. Listen to the following holy Shabads:

- Worship the Naam of Waheguru alone, oh my mind! The perfect Guru has given me this very treasure. **If someone is able to control his sexual urges using yoga exercises,** and practices the path of yoga, he still cannot get rid of his dirty thoughts and his haumein. ———**-(Wadhans M:3, 558)**
- Some people go to the jungle (isolated places) and meditate hard. They also undertake pilgrimages of holy places. But because of forced control on their bodies, they become very ill-tempered and are never able to search their inner-self. They gain nothing spiritually by renouncing the world. **Some others are able to control their sexual urges through hard self-discipline and call themselves celibates**. But without the real Guru, they too cannot rid themselves of *haumein*, and are born again and again.———**-(Assa M:1, Ashatpadian, 418)**

Even though a few people may be able to control their sexual urges using self discipline and yoga exercises, but as

Guru Sahiban have said, they fail badly in their efforts to control the other demons like, greed and rage etc. without taking Guru's refuge.

Remember, I have been saying that the demons are very difficult to control. But, they are not impossible to control. As Guru Granth Sahib maintains, they can be readily controlled with Guru's Grace.

I don't know what their ulterior motives are, but people who use Shabads like the ones used earlier to profess that the five demons cannot be controlled no matter what, use only those parts of the holy Shabads which state the difficulty of controlling them. **If they read the whole Shabads, they would find clearly that the solution to control the demons is also given somewhere in the same very Shabads. The solution lies in coming to Guru's shelter and worshipping Waheguru Who is the Master of all the noble qualities.** All the holy shabads quoted earlier to point out the difficulty in controlling the demons, also teach us towards their end that they **CAN be controlled** by taking refuge of the Guru and acting upon His Teachings. I'll quote a few more shabads which explain that the demons can indeed be controlled.

- ——— **The whole world is controlled by the five demons, but they are slave to the devotees of Waheguru.** They collect revenue (use people's bodies for their enjoyment) from the world, but, they salute the devotees of Waheguru. They rob those people of their dignity who are disconnected from Waheguru, but, they respectfully wash the feet of the devotees. ————**(Goand M: 5, 865)**
- ————The five demons come under control in the company of the Guru because you are taking in and enjoying the life-sustaining Naam - Amrit in the company of the Guru. ——————— **(Sukhmani, M:5, Ashatpadi 7)**

- There is one fort-like body which is controlled by five robbers (demons) all of whom unjustly demand revenue (their share of my body for enjoyment). It is very difficult for me to make this unjust payment to them (I do not want to pay them) because I haven't done any bad deeds using my body. But the fear of doing bad deeds under their pressure - and then held accountable for them (the bad deeds) in Waheguru's Court - is always haunting me. **I called upon my Guru for help by raising my arm. My Guru kindly protected me.———(Suhi Lalit Kabir Ji, 793)**
- The lucky human heart which has become the home of Waheguru begins to dance with joy, and feels as if all the five kinds of musical instruments are playing in there. All the five demons of that lucky person come under control, and the thorn of dreaded death is destroyed. **———(Anand Sahib, M:3, 917)**
- I run around in every direction seeking my Waheguru and His affection (but, the five demons are in my way). The demons really torture me. How could they be killed (controlled)? (Answer): By taking the refuge of the Perfect Guru. You worship Waheguru by the Grace of the Perfect Guru. **Then the big torturous demons can be killed by the sharp arrows of Waheguru's Naam. (Funhe M: 5, 1363)**
- Those who are imbued with Waheguru's Naam have overpowered their urges of lust, rage and conceit, and have thus become holy. They sing the praise of Waheguru and have His Naam occupying their hearts all the time. ——— **(Siri Raag M:1, Ashatpadian, 57)**
- There is some rare person who can get rid of the sickness of lust, rage, greed and conceit etc. I get

attuned to the Naam and sing the praise of Waheguru in the company of holy men and worship Him day and night to control these demons. **(Assa M: 5, 408)**

- Recite the Naam of Waheguru, oh my mind! Only He can be with you and help you in this world and the next (after death). Keep Him in your mind all the time. ———If you keep reciting Waheguru's Naam to serve Him, you will meet the Guru, and will get rid of lust, rage, and your ego, oh my mind! ———**(Assa M:5, 405)**
- The kind Third Guru made Bhai Jetha Ji (later Guru Ram Das Ji) worship Waheguru with His grace. Because of the recitation of Waheguru's Naam Guru Ram Das Ji has been able to control the five demons. ———**(Savvayye M:4, 1396)**

These holy Shabads make it perfectly clear that the five demons can indeed be controlled by taking refuge of the Guru and worshipping Waheguru's Naam. The Bhatts, and the bards - Satta and Balwand - were so overwhelmed by Guru Sahiban's personalities that they professed that all sorts of diseases including sickness due to the five demons, are eradicated just at the sight of the Guru.

- Worship Guru Angad Dev Ji with affection and dedication oh Tal (Kalsahar)! The suffering of death and birth is eradicated at the sight of the Guru. (Which is possible only if one has controlled the five demons). **(Savvayye M:1, 1392).**

  Note: Tal (Kalsahar) is the name of the Bhatt poet.
- The praise of Waheguru is sung, and lights from the spiritual world are shining in the Court of Guru Angad Dev Ji. The filth of many incarnations due to our evil deeds is washed away at Your gracious sight, oh Guru Angad Dev Ji! **(Satta and Balwand ki Vaar, 966)**

- Worship the Eighth Guru, Har Krishan Ji, oh man! His mere pleasant sight dispels all the illnesses. **(Var Sri Bhagauti Ji Ki, M:10)**

So, there is no doubt that the five demons can be controlled, but one has to labour hard to do that. One must surrender his mind to the Guru and act upon His Teachings." Bhai Dalip Singh concluded.

"Any further questions?" Bhai Sahib asked.

Since no further questions were asked, Bhai Kashmir Singh thanked Bhai Dalip Singh and the entire congregation. The session was adjourned with the traditional salutation: Bolle So Nihal Sat Sri Akal. Lungar was served at the end.

15

Recitation of Selected Baanies

"Waheguru Ji ka Khalsa, Waheguru Ji ki Fateh, dear brothers and sisters." Bhai Dalip Singh welcomed the gathering on another beautiful evening.

"Waheguru Ji ka Khalsa, Waheguru Ji ki Fateh, Bhai Sahib." The gathering responded with a great enthusiasm.

"I've been enjoying your questions very much. So, let us start with questions before I embark on a new topic." Bhai Sahib suggested.

"I have a question, Bhai Sahib. Our most revered Guru Granth Sahib is a treasure of hundreds of invaluable pieces of holy *baanies* or compositions which guide us in our spiritual journey. Then why are we advised to recite only the five chosen Baanies? Could you, please, shed some light on this requirement?" Bibi Gopal Kaur asked.

"I could not agree more with you, Bibi Ji, on this subject. Guru Granth Sahib is indeed a treasure of priceless gems of shabads, and all of them are beacons for spiritual life. However, I'll start by saying that if the edict of reciting the five Baanies - Jap Ji Sahib, Jaap Sahib, Savvayye (Tenth Master), Rehiras Sahib, and Sohila Sahib - came from the Tenth Master, who am I to question? I can only speculate why the Master made that requirement. There could be a few possible reasons as follows.

- There were no printing presses those days. So, the duplication of Guru Granth Sahib was a very tough job and a big undertaking, and could not be done at a speed to make it readily available for everyone. The duplication of short holy Baanies was relatively easy and some dedicated Sikhs brought hundreds of *gutkas* (booklets of short baanies) when they came to pay homage to the Revered Guru Sahiban. It was much easier to have access to the *gutkas* than the entire Guru Granth Sahib.
- Most of the people those days could not read. So, even if copies of Guru Granth Sahib were available, most people could not have benefited. But, many people could memorize short baanies when they listened to their recitation a few times. I remember people going to learned gianies (scholars) or priests and listening to them with full attention when they (the gianies) recited small portions of Jap Ji Sahib or Rehiras Sahib quite a few times for them (the people) to memorize. Then the individuals recited the portions of the holy Baanies repeatedly until they had memorized them well. The process continued until they had memorized the particular Baani in its entirety.
- The Sikhs are advised to recite holy Gurbani as often during the day as possible even when they are doing their daily routine work. That's possible only when people have memorized baanies by heart. It is not possible to memorize the whole Guru Granth Sahib, so they were advised to recite only a few select Baanies which they could memorize easily. Other highly enlightening Baanies like, Sukhmani Sahib, Oankar, Sidh Goshit and many more are long and difficult to memorize.
- Light was also a factor. The most convenient and appropriate times to concentrate on Gurbani for

most people are the early mornings and the late evenings. Both these times of the day required good lamp light to make reading of script possible. Most of the people did not have good lighting system to read. If people had not known Gurbani by heart, they would have had difficulty to read. Thus poor lighting was another reason for people to memorize Gurbani which was possible only if the number of baanies to be recited was kept small.

- Even though all Shabads (or compositions) in Guru Granth Sahib are precious gems which serve as beacons in the spiritual journey of mankind, some holy Shabads focus on a single idea while some others cover either a wide range of ideas or an important unique idea. **Jap Ji Sahib contains the gist of all Divine Knowledge, and therefore is the single most important composition in Guru Granth Sahib.** Likewise, the holy Shabad, 'So Der Tera keha, so Ghar keha' appears three times in Guru Granth Sahib with minor differences. It explains an extremely important idea - Waheguru's Residence. Most people believed (and still believe) that Waheguru (or Allah or God) resides in Heaven, somewhere in the sky. But Guru Nanak Sahib explains that Waheguru resides in the gathering of the holy men where His praise is sung. This is a revolutionary idea. So, Guru Arjun Dev Ji recorded this holy Shabad (which is a part of Rehiras Sahib as well) right after Jap Ji Sahib, in Guru Granth Sahib. Another Shabad - So Purakh Niranjan - with somewhat similar idea is also a part of Rehiras Sahib. Like wise, 'Aarti' in Dhanasari Raag by Guru Nanak Sahib with a non-traditional meaning has been recorded as part of 'Sohila Sahib'. **Holy Shabads with new perspectives on common concepts or ideas have been recorded by Guru**

Arjun Dev Ji in Sri Guru Granth Sahib before the start of holy Baanies based on Ragas. There is a collection of 14 such holy Shabads. The first nine Shabads constitute 'Rehiras Sahib' and the next five 'Sohila Sahib'. Thus, the three Baanis -Jap Ji Sahib, Rehiras Sahib and Sohila Sahib - are sufficient to understand the Principles of Guru Granth Sahib, and to sing the praise of Waheguru. The rest of Guru Granth Sahib is a detailed explanation of these three Baanis. The Khalsa Panth have added a few more holy Shabads to Rehiras Sahib. **It is noteworthy that Rehiras Sahib and Sohila Sahib were recited on regular basis even at the time of Guru Nanak Dev Ji although the number of shabads was smaller than the present in the two Baanies.** Because of the special importance of these 14 holy Shabads constituting Rehiras Sahib and Sohila Sahib, and because of the fact that the recitation of the two Baanies on regular basis had been advised by the First Master and the relative ease with which they can be memorized, The Tenth Master must have advised the Sikhs to recite these Baanies along with Jap Ji Sahib, Jaap Sahib and the Savvayye. Jaap Sahib by The Tenth Master, is holy Baani written purely in the praise of Waheguru and does not espouse any other idea. Since there is so much emphasis on singing the praise of Waheguru in Gurmat, this is an excellent Baani to sing the praise of Waheguru.

But as I said earlier, my thoughts on the subject are speculative at best. Only The Tenth Master would know the real reasons for the requirement. I hope I haven't offended any one by my thoughts." Bhai Dalip Singh concluded.

Meanings of Some Holy Shabads

"That was wonderful Bhai Sahib. Your thoughts on the

subject seem very convincing, and I'm glad that Bibi Ji asked this question. I have another question, if you don't mind. While discussing the subject of pilgrimage a few days ago, you explained its futility based on holy Shabads from Sri Guru Granth Sahib, yet there are a couple of holy Shabads, like 'Ram Das Sarovar nahate, sabh uttrey paap kamate', which promote pilgrimage of Darbar Sahib Amritsar by the Sikhs. Then how is pilgrimage of other holy places different from this? I'm a little confused by this contradiction. Could you, please, clarify that for me?" Bhai Kirpal Singh asked.

"I'm really impressed by the deep thoughts of this holy congregation, and I'm very pleased that you ask probing questions which are so important to all of us. I want to make a minor change to your question with your permission, Bhai Sahib, if you don't mind." Bhai Dalip Singh said in very pleasant tone.

"By all means, Bhai Sahib. We are so ignorant that we don't even know how to word a question." Bhai Kirpal Singh said in a equally pleasant tone.

"I'm terribly sorry if I sent a message of ignorance on your part, Bhai Sahib. You are not ignorant, to say the least. As I said earlier, it is an extremely intelligent and a vital question. I only wanted to say very emphatically that there is absolutely no contradiction in the holy Guru Granth Sahib. Also, the great holy Shabad of which you quoted a part, does NOT promote pilgrimage, it only seems to do so, and that too only because our religious leaders want the Shabad to mean that either because of ignorance or for political reasons." Bhai Dalip Singh clarified.

"Normally, people think that Ram Das Sarovar means the pool of water which was dug in Amritsar by The Fourth Master at the centre of which the holy Harmandir Sahib is now standing majestically. But even though the Sarovar is extremely dear to us and deserves all our respect, the sarovar referred to in the holy Shabad does not mean the Sarovar of the Forth Master. To understand the meaning of this holy Shabad, we need to understand the meaning of the word Ramdas (or Ramjan) which has not been used in reference to the Fourth Master in these holy shabads (hymns). As all of you know, the word 'das' (or jan) means slave or servant, and the word 'Ram' is the most common name of Waheguru used in Sri Guru Granth Sahib. So, the word 'Ramdas' means the slaves of Waheguru - the holy people who are one with Waheguru. The following holy Shabads will clarify the meaning of Ramdas (or Ramjan).

- An individual is called Ramdas if his heart becomes a home for Waheguru. **(Gauri Sukhmani, M:5, 275)**
- An individual who firmly believes that Waheguru is always with him is recognized in the Court of Waheguru. Waheguru Himself kindly enlightens the heart of such a slave. An individual who practices complete detachment from worldly attractions even though he has to deal with them in everyday life, is a real Ramdas (slave of Waheguru). **(Gauri Sukhmani, M:5, 275)**
- ———I really don't know how to worship Waheguru. I simply recite His Naam with the tongue, but people have started to call me 'Ramdas'.——— **(Sorith M:5, 612)**
- Waheguru's feet are the ship to swim across the sea of *maya* in this world.———

  But nobody - not even the yogis, the controllers of all sensual pleasures, the Vaishnavs (followers of Lord Vishnu) or the Ramdases - can find the limit of the immortal Waheguru. ———**(Goand M:5, 867)**
- Even when I tried very carefully, I could not hold on to *maya*. ——— *Maya* has bewitched the

whole universe, but Ramjans have cut it into small pieces (They are completely indifferent to it). ——
——**(Ramkali M:5, 891)**

As is perfectly clear from the above holy Shabads, the word 'Ramdas' or 'Ramjan' means the holy man who has realized Waheguru. Also, most of the times the word has been used in the plural form and not in singular which further removes any doubt about the meaning of the word that it cannot refer to the Fourth Master. Thus the term 'Ramdas Sarovar (pool)' will mean the company of the holy men. There are many shabads in Guru Granth Sahib in which the term 'Ramdas sarovar' appears and means the same - the company of the holy men - where *Naam-Amrit* is produced. With the meaning of the words clear, let us now discuss the meaning of the holy Shabad in question.

- If an individual **ponders the Shabad of the Guru** with full faith, and moulds his life accordingly, he is ferried across the sea of *maya* safely. Waheguru provides all the comforts and bliss to the individual. By taking a dip in the sarovar of Ramdases (pool of *Naam-Amrit* of the holy men), all your sins are washed away. The perfect Guru has given this gift of the holy sarovar (company of the holy men) to mankind. One should clean his mind by taking a dip in this sarovar. **All the mental filth is washed away in the company of the holy men**, and Waheguru becomes your companion. ——**(Sorith M:5, 625-26)**

As is clear from the Shabad, the emphasis is on the shabad of the Guru and the company of the holy men to clean your mind and be one with Waheguru which leaves no doubt that the sarovar used in the Shabad is not the Sarovar of the Fourth Master in Amritsar. There are a few more Shabads in Guru Granth Sahib, that use the term 'Ramdas

Sarover' for 'the company of the holy men', but, as in the case of the above holy Shabad, people draw different meanings. I want to draw your attention to one particular Shabad in which people believe that the Fifth Master refers to Harmandir Sahib (The Golden Temple) when He writes that I have visited many places but none is like you. I will first quote the Shabad as is and then discuss its meaning.

- I have visited all the places but none is as beautiful as you are. You are majestic because Waheguru Himself has founded you. Unmatched in beauty, the city of Ramdas Pur is bustling with dense population. (Guru) Nanak says that all your sins are washed away by taking a dip in the pool of Ramdas. **(Funhe M:5, 1362)**

  As before, the Fifth Master is referring to the company of holy men and not to Harmandir Sahib, or the Sarovar of the Fourth Master.

  The meaning of the holy Shabad is as follows:

  I have visited all the places on earth, but none is as beautiful as the company of the holy men which is very majestic because Waheguru Himself has founded it. Unparallel in beauty, the company of the holy men where Waheguru's praise is sung all the time is densely populated by its members. (Guru) Nanak says that all sins are washed away by listening to the **Naam-Amrit** in the company of the holy men.

If there is still some doubt left in the meaning of the term Ramdas or Ramdas sarovar, the following Shabad will make it perfectly clear.

- Take a dip everyday in the sarovar of Ramdases (congregation of holy men) and drink the Naam-Amrit of Waheguru by mixing it well (enjoy its best taste). Waheguru's Naam is holy water, and a

> dip in it grants you all your wishes. You meet with holy men there and wash away the sins of millions of your incarnations (by listening to their Divine Teachings and acting on them). The holy men worship Waheguru and feel blissful. Waheguru resides in their minds and bodies. (Guru) Nanak says that He will lay down His life for people who have become one with Waheguru. **(Gauri M:5, 198-99)**

The Fifth Master has clearly defined the holy water or the pool of water as Waheguru's Naam. He again clarifies that the sins of an individual are washed away in the company of holy men, and not by a dip taken in some pool of water no matter how much reverence we may have for that. The whole Shabad is about the importance of holy men and their company and not about pilgrimage of any holy sarovar or place. Similarly, the first two Shabads are not about pilgrimage or promotion of pilgrimage, they too are about the importance of the Guru or the holy men." Bhai Dalip Singh explained in detail.

"Are there any further questions?" Bhai Sahib asked.

No further question came forth.

Bhai Kashmir Singh thanked everyone present, and the session was concluded with the traditional religious slogan: Bolle so nihal, Sat Sri Akal. Bhai Kashmir Singh also made an announcement about the departure of Bhai Dalip Singh in about a week or so. Everybody became sad at the unpleasant news.

Lungar was served as usual, but very few people enjoyed that. They had lost their appetite at the news of the departure of Bhai Dalip Singh.

16

Examples and Stories: Are They True?

It is again the same time of another beautiful day - late afternoon—and people are assembling for the daily discourses of Bhai Dalip Singh at Bhai Kashmir Singh's farmhouse. Sweet fragrance is emanating from the basmati (a type of rice) fields making the environment very pleasant. The sugarcane crops are almost ready, and tall sugarcanes are swaying with a light wind. Birds are chirping on the tall trees and seem to be getting ready for retirement in their nests. Even though most people are using gas to cook these days, but, smoke from open fires is still rising from a few houses. People have settled down in their seats for the lecture, and Bhai Dalip Singh is appearing on the stage.

"Waheguru Ji ka Khalsa, Waheguru Ji ki Fateh." Bhai Dalip Singh welcomed the congregation.

"I wonder if anyone has a question before we start?" Bhai Sahib solicited questions as usual.

"I've always wondered if the examples used or the stories mentioned in Sri Guru Granth Sahib are true! Would you mind discussing that subject, Bhai Sahib?" Sharan Jeet, a young woman asked.

"I'll be delighted to. But, would you elaborate on your question a little more? What examples or stories are we talking about here? Bhai Sahib asked.

"For example there is a mention of four yugas (major time eras), 8400000 life forms, stories of Ajamal, and that of the elephant who was caught in the tentacles of an octopus, of many gods and sages (ascetics) etc. etc. I wonder if they all are true?" Sharan Jeet had heard those stories.

"Let's be very clear on one fundamental Principle of Guru Granth Sahib before we discuss some individual stories, Bibi Ji. **Guru Granth Sahib has no room for the praise of any individual or for the promotion of any stories. The Holy Book is all about the praise of Waheguru and the Guru only.** Guru Sahiban and the Bhagats used the popular stories from the Hindu and Muslim religious books to emphasize the Greatness of Waheguru. They were not promoting the stories, and NOT certifying that they were true. As we will discuss soon using holy hymns, gods and the stories associated with them have no importance of their own in Guru Granth Sahib.

Another important thing to keep in mind is that no one can put any numbers to the creation of Waheguru. **Guru Nanak Sahib has made it clear time and again that Waheguru's creation is limitless and it is foolish to associate any numbers with it.** Almost half of Jap Ji Sahib alone, is dedicated to the fact that the expanse of the universe is limitless. Once we keep these two important Principles of Guru Granth Sahib in mind, we will be able to judge right away if the stories or the examples used are real or not. But, even if they were real, the important thing for us to learn from them is how to love Waheguru and His people, and how to lead a noble life - the Principles for which the stories have been used.

Now let's discuss some of the individual examples.

The Yugas (Major Time Eras)

The subject of "Yugas" has been brought up and discussed

many times in Sri Guru Granth Sahib. As for a few examples, listen to the following holy Shabads (hymns). At this point, the meanings of the holy Shabads that I'll quote, are not the issue. The point I'm going to make is that the yugas have been mentioned in Guru Granth Sahib many times. So, if you do not grasp the meaning of the holy shabads at this point, please, don't worry.

- Waheguru has been here since times immemorial. **He was here before the yugas.** He is here right now, and He will be here forever in the future, oh Nanak! **(Sloak M:1, Jap Ji, 1)**
- **——In Satyug,** contentment is the chariot and dharma is the pilot. In **Tretayug,** celibacy is the chariot, and might is the pilot. ——— **(Assa ki Vaar, Sloak M: 1)**
- You say that charity was the predominant noble act in **Satyug,** and *yags* were the main religious act in **Tretayug,** oh Pundit Ji! You say further that worshipping gods was the predominant act in **Duaparyug,** and now Ram's naam is the basis of salvation in **Kalyug.————(Gauri Bairagan, Ravi Das Ji, 346)**
- Can someone tell me the dharma (the religious rituals) of **Kalyug** so that I may practise it and achieve salvation! The only way to swim across the ocean of life is to recite Waheguru's Naam. Naam is your support, and Naam is your boat. **(Dhanasari M:4, 668)**

There are many more holy shabads in which the yugas have been mentioned. The present yuga (era) is considered to be Kalyug according to the Hindu religious books. Satyug is considered to be the best era in which people were not selfish. They were all very just and reasonable. Treta was not as good as Satyug and Duapar was worse than even Treta. Kalyug is considered to be the worst in which people are very selfish and are less moral. Hindu religious books also believe that there is some mysterious living power that affects the minds of people differently in various yugas. In Kalyug, that living power is believed to be destructive in nature, and affects the minds of people in such a way that they are selfish, unjust and immoral (Holy Shabads to follow). Guru Sahiban do not believe that there is some mythical living power that affects the minds of people. They believe that the nature of people has not been much different from one yuga to another. Waheguru created the world in such a way that people would find *'maya'* attractive in every yuga. Man has always enjoyed sensual pleasures, and has done immoral and unjust things in every yuga. So, all the yugas have been very similar in nature - people did good and bad things in every yuga. So, we could not tell the difference in yugas (eras of time) based on human nature which has been fairly consistent. **Guru Sahiban profess that the behaviour of individuals may be called satyugi (as expected in Satyug) or kalyugi (as expected in Kalyug) in any yug. There were kalyugi people even in Satyug - if there was any - and there are satyugi people even today in the period of Kalyug.** Remember, if there was Prehlad - a strong devotee of Waheguru - in Satyug, there was his father, Harnakash too - a supposedly evil person, who tried to kill his own son, Prehlad, several times. Likewise, if there was Lord Rama in Tretayug, there was Ravana too at the same time who was considered to be a demon.

If Guru Sahiban had certified the yugas to be the time periods with their predominant features as described in the Hindu Religious books, then Guru Nanak Sahib would not have questioned the arrival of Kalyug as He did in the following holy hymn.

- Get rid of your selfishness, oh pundit! (Because selfishness is what Kalyug is about). Because of the selfishness, the mighty aggressors encroach upon the rights of the weak, and such aggression is deemed justified. That is what Kalyug means, i.e. where unjust things are deemed justified. Otherwise there is no such thing as Kalyug because it is the same moon, the same stars, and the same sun that is providing warmth to the earth as it did during the other three yugas. It is the same earth, and the same air that is pervading the atmosphere. (You believe that there is some mysterious living power that controls the minds of people in different yugas, and now it is Kalyug which is prevailing). But, he (kalyug) has not been heard to have come in any country, or been sitting by some holy place. He is not found at holy places (to stop) philanthropists from donating, and he is not known to be living in a palace either.——**(Ramkali M: 1, Ashatpadian, 902)**

In fact, Guru Sahiban have praised Kalyug many times in Guṛu Granth Sahib because contrary to what the religious books say, one is assessed on his own deeds only in Kalyug, and not held accountable for the deeds of others (in the Court of Waheguru). According to the Hindu religious books one could be held accountable for the misdeeds of his relatives. Moreover, many holy people are known to be born in Kalyug, including the ten Guru Sahiban, the *Bhagats,* many Sikh saints, The Buddha, Jesus Christ, and Muhammad Sahib. So, how could Kalyug be bad? The following holy Shabads rather glorify Kalyug.

- —— The Guru has washed away the sins of Kalyug (people in the yug) thereby stopping the cycle of death and birth for its people. All those people with dirty and unclean minds and those with low intelligence are all now serving you, oh Waheguru! ———Of all the yugas - Satyug, Treta, Duapar and Kalyug - Kalyug is the best. Only the hand that does something bad is arrested and punished - the other is not held accountable. ————**(Assa M:5, 406)**

- The *Bhagats* have earned the treasure of **Waheguru's Naam in Kalyug** and have attained the high spiritual level: Acting on Guru's Advice, they recited Waheguru's Naam everyday, and thus made their hearts a place for Waheguru to reside.——— **Goojri ki Vaar, Sloak M:3, 513)**

The attraction of people for *maya* in every yuga has to be the same because when Waheguru created the world, He also created attraction for *maya* at the same time making maya the basis of all life. So, there should be no difference in the basic nature of people in any yuga. The following holy Shabads explain the idea.

- You created the world Yourself, and Yourself got it busy too, oh Waheguru! You Yourself misguided the world by **generating attraction for *maya*** among the living beings.————**(Maajh ki Vaar, M: 1, Pauri, 138)**
- ———Making **attachment (or possessiveness) for *maya* the basis for the creation,** The Creator has created the world, and thus Himself has misguided it (got it busy into acquiring maya).———— **(Bhairon M:3,1128)**
- You created the world Yourself for its living beings to play, oh Waheguru! You created *maya* **with its three attributes, and Yourself infused attraction for it** among the living beings.———**(Sorith ki Vaar, M:4, Pauri, 643)**

There are many more shabads like these which make it clear that the attraction for maya is an innate urge among the living beings, and people have been fighting for its control ever since the world came into being. It has been like this all the time (in all the yugas). So, the yugas have no relevance and Guru Sahiban are NOT supporting the concept of yugas. They used the concept of yugas only to praise Waheguru.

Gods and Goddesses

"Returning to the original question where the young Bibi asked about the stories of Ajamal, of the elephant, and many others like that, it will be impossible for me to discuss all those stories individually and then analyse them critically. Let's discuss what the Holy Guru Granth Sahib has to say about the gods and the goddesses in general because most of the stories are related to them. To begin with, we will consider a few holy shabads which reveal that there is not just one Brahma or one Vishnu or one Shiva - there are countless of them - implying that either there is none of them at all, or if they are there, they have no importance in Waheguru's Court because there are millions like them. Next we will discuss that if they do exist at all, they are all victims of *haumein* like anybody else, and have little knowledge about Waheguru let alone being one with Him. So, they are no better than a common man." Bhai Dalip Singh shared his approach for discussion.

NUMBERS

- ———There are countless Krishanas and countless Shivas in Waheguru's creation. There are countless Brahmas who are (said to be) creating a variety of shapes, colours, and dresses. ————There are countless Inderas, countless moons, countless suns and countless galaxies. ————(Jap Ji, M:1, 7)
- How limitless is our Lord? I cannot describe His limitless and vast qualities, oh my friend! He is so vast that He has created millions of Vishnus, and millions of galaxies as places of worship. **He creates millions of Shivas, and then at His sweet will absorbs them back into Himself.** He has assigned

millions of Brahmas to create the world. There are millions of goddesses like Luxmi who are slaves in His house.———There are millions of gods like Inderwho are guards at His door. ————**(Bhairon M: 5, Ashatpadian, 1156)**

- If I need something, I always ask Waheguru for that. I have nothing to do with any other god or goddess (because all gods and goddesses are subservient to Him). There are millions of Shivas and millions of Kailash mountains (the residing place of Lord Shiva) at His door, and millions of Brahmas are reciting the Vedas. —— There are millions of goddesses like Luxmi who are adorning themselves (to serve Waheguru), and millions of Inder-like gods who are serving Waheguru. There are millions like Lord Rama who (is said to have) defeated Ravna, and millions like Lord Krishana who (is said to have) destroyed Darjodhan's (The Kaurav rajah at the time) ego.———— **(Bhairon Kabir Ji, 1162)**

There are many more holy shabads like these which elaborate the extent of gods and goddesses. It is perfectly clear from these holy shabads, that not only are there countless gods and goddesses, but, it is also clear from the second holy Shabad that gods like Shiva are being created and destroyed continuously by Waheguru. What it really means is that there aren't any of them. Now listen to the following holy Shabads about the spiritual level of the gods and the goddesses, if there are any.

Spiritual Level

- Without the worship of Waheguru, no human being has ever been able to elevate his spiritual level; he rather has remained gripped by the fear of death. —— Let alone an ordinary person, even gods like Brahma suffered from spiritual death. With the ego of a god that he was great, he went into the underworld through the stem of the lotus flower from where he was born, to find the ultimate reality of his creator - Waheguru. But, he was completely unsuccessful, and therefore felt ashamed. ——— All gods and goddesses are possessed by the temptation of *maya* which in turn becomes the cause of their spiritual death. ———— **(Gauri M: 1, Ashatpadian, 227)**

NOTE: Lord Brahma - the perceived creator of the world - is said to have been born out of the lotus flower growing out of the navel of Lord Vishnu!

- This whole world is unclean (because of the malice due to *haumein)*. Only the limitless Waheguru is holy and unblemished. Due to haumein, even god Brahma (although he is considered to be the creator of the world) is unclean, and so is god Indra even though he is considered to be the king of all the gods. The gods - sun and the moon - are also unclean. ——Likewise, god Shiva, also known as Shankra and Mahesh, is also unclean———— **Bhairon Kabir Ji, 1158)**
- The mental sickness resulting from haumein (selfishness and ego) is really vicious, oh Nanak! Wherever I look, I find people suffering from haumein. Only those few are immune, who worship Waheguru by reciting Guru's Shabad by His Own Grace. ———Even gods Brahma, Vishnu, and Shiva are suffering from the sickness of haumein, and so is the rest of the world. ——————

  (Bhairon M:1, Ashatpadian, 1153)

So, as we can see from these and many other holy shabads that all gods and goddesses are victims of *haumein* like any one of us, and they have not attained any higher spiritual level. *Bhagat* Naam Dev Ji has gone even further, and has described the gods and goddesses as insignificant, having no importance in the Court of Waheguru even though they are considered omnipotent in the old religious books. Listen to the holy Shabad by Bhagat Ji:

- I have worshipped the Lord who is the protector of the whole universe, has no dynasty, Who is totally unaffected by *maya,* and at Whose door the gods are begging for His Grace to worship Him.— — The Lord is so Great that even though god Brahma is considered to be the creator of the universe, yet in reality, the four-faced god is only like a small potter in His House. God Shiva, who is considered to be the guru and the destroyer of the world, is only a crazy jester in the Court of the Lord. —— The holy Ganges that is considered to have its origin in Paradise, is like the sweat of the nails of the Lord.——— **(Malhar Naam Dev Ji, 1292)**

We could go on and on, but clearly, according to the Holy Guru Granth Sahib, gods and goddesses have no significance. Essentially, the implication of all this discussion in Sri Guru Granth Sahib is that there are no gods and goddesses as described in old religious books. Even if they do exist, they have low spiritual levels and have no significant roles to play in the spiritual world. Now, if the existence of gods and goddesses is questionable, how can the stories related to them be true? For example, there is a mention of the fourteen rattans (valuable gems like amrit, the moon, Kamdhen cow, physician Dhanvantri, goddess Luxmi, Rambha, conch, poison, alcohol, etc. which were retrieved from the ocean when a joint team of the gods and the demons churned it) in Guru Granth Sahib several times. **Now, would you believe that there was no moon in the world before it was retrieved from the ocean! Also, the maximum depth of**

the ocean is about 11 km while the diameter of the spherical moon is about 3500 km. How could the moon sink in the ocean and be invisible? There are many improbabilities in this story alone. So, the stories are not necessarily true, and Guru Sahiban ane NOT certifying them. Yes, Guru Sahiban have used the stories as examples, but, only to emphasize the praise of Waheguru and how He protects His devotees in all circumstances. We also know that some of the things are mythical - and not real. For example, nobody has found the touchstone yet which converts base metals into gold, still, the term has been used again and again in Guru Granth Sahib. Likewise, even though Guru Granth Sahib teaches us again and again that Waheguru is nirnankar (formless) and has no particular place to live, yet, in the state of great reverence for Him, Guru Sahiban have wished to reach Him by attaching wings to the body and flying to Waheguru! There are many such poetic beauties which are not literally true. Let's listen to some of them:

- The company of the holy men treasures the invaluable Naam where you can get it. ——**Just like iron is converted into gold upon touch with the touchstone,** you can acquire Naam in the company of the Perfect Guru, oh Nanak!——— **(Sarang ki Vaar, M: 4, Pauri,1244)**
- Worship the **feet** of Waheguru, oh my mind! The thirst (desire) of His Holy sight has overcome me so much that **I want to fly to Him by attaching wings to my body. (Malhar M: 5, 1269)**
- If wings were for sale, I will sell the equivalent weight of my flesh to buy them. I will attach them to my body and **fly around in search of my beloved Waheguru. (Sloak M:5, 1426)**
- Just like a young bride who is sighing and waiting with tears in her eyes for her husband to come home, I also feel restless to see my Lord. And just

like the bride who is not tired of looking at the way of her husband, I am not discouraged by the wait for my Waheguru-husband. Will you fly and take my message quickly to my Lord, oh black crow! ——————**(Raag Gauri, Kabir Ji, 337-38)**

NOTE: It has been a belief for a long time that if a crow crows on the roof of a house, some guests are expected to visit that house. And if a crow flies away soon after crowing, guests are sure to come. So, in the last Shabad, Kabir Ji is using that belief in a poetic way to show His love and impatience to 'see' Waheguru.

Now, as you can see clearly from these holy Shabads, the ideas used are mythical only and definitely not real. They have been used in a beautiful poetic way by Guru Sahiban and the Bhagat to express the intensity of Their love for Waheguru. Many a time some numbers have been used to emphasize some important point. The correctness of numbers is NOT the issue. For example pay attention to the numbers in the following holy hymns.

- ———When the rulers of Emnabad heard about the impending attack by Baabar, they put **MILLIONS** of peirs (holy men) in confinement to pray for their (Rulers') victory. ————**(Assa M: 1, Ashatpadian, 417)**
- Immediately after being born, you ignored Waheguru, oh man! Waheguru created you from the (insignificant and ugly-looking) semen of your father and the egg of your mother, and protected you in the womb of your mother for **TEN MONTHS.** But, as soon as you were born, you were overcome by maya at once (and ignored Him). ————**(Assa Kabir Ji, 481)**
- ——The mortals left this world with all the unfulfilled desires in their minds. It takes **SIX**

> **MONTHS** to create a human body but only a moment to destroy it. ———— **(Assa Farid Ji, 488)**

The number, millions, of peirs who were detained by the rulers of Emnabad as described by Guru Nanak Sahib in the holy Shabad, is obviously not an exact number. It is used simply to emphasize the large number of the holy men who were detained. In the last two holy hymns, Kabir Sahib and Farid Sahib are using **two very different numbers for the same event.** Is one of the numbers right and the other wrong? It doesn't matter. The issue is not the discussion of numbers, the subject being discussed is the importance of Waheguru's Naam in life. I'm sure, now you understand that the emphasis of Guru Granth Sahib is on the glory of Waheguru and NOT on the examples which have been used only as a vehicle to glorify Waheguru." Bhai Dalip Singh paused for a short while. He took a few sips of water.

Life Forms (Number of Species)

Coming to the number, 8400000, for different life forms on the Earth comes from the Puranas - another set of 18 Hindu religious books. According to the Puranas, there are 8400000 different forms of life (creatures) on earth. This number does not have the approval of Guru Granth Sahib for reasons which we will discuss very shortly. (According to the **World Book Encyclopaedia,** the present estimates of life forms is close to 1,000,000 even though more and more species are being discovered regularly). Like many other examples, Guru Sahiban have used this number many times simply because it has been used repeatedly in early books. But the number has been used only in the context of praise for Waheguru. They have never said that the number is correct. When it comes to the creation of Waheguru, Guru Nanak Sahib has always maintained that it is infinite and that no number can be put on Waheguru's creation. In fact, putting such numbers to the Creation of Waheguru is against the fundamental Principles of Guru Granth Sahib.

- ——There are countless types (gods) of air (gases), water and fire, and countless Krishanas and Shivas. Countless Brahamas are creating bodies, and there are countless appearances, colours and dress codes. ————There are countless Inderas (clouds), moons, suns and galaxies. ———There are countless ways of life reproduction, and countless languages (ways of communication).———— **(Jap Ji, M:1, 7)**

The Hindu religious books profess that there are four different ways of reproduction of life -live birth, eggs, vegetation, and from sweat (bacteria in the air). But, as is clear from the above holy Shabad, Guru Nanak Sahib maintains that there are infinite ways of reproduction of life to which the scientists now agree **(World Book Encyclopaedia).** When you don't even know the number of ways by which life is reproduced, how can you put a number on different life forms? So, to answer your question, Bibi Ji, I'll have to say, no! The number 8400000 for different life forms does not have the stamp of Guru Sahiban's approval." Bhai Dalip Singh concluded. He paused fora short while and took a few sips of water. "Are there further questions?" Bhai Sahib continued.

Bhagat Prehlad

"You've done a wonderful job in enlightening us, and have pulled us out of the ignorance of believing in gods and goddesses. We were not sure whether to believe in them or not because there are repeated references to them in Guru Granth Sahib. I'm really thankful to you for that. But, would you do me a favour, and analyse the story of Bhagat Prehlad. The story is so popular that we celebrate Holi to commemorate

Prehlad's victory, yet it does not sound very convincing." Bibi Puneet Kaur, another young lady, asked. "Like many other stories used in Sri Guru Granth Sahib in the glory of Waheguru, the story of Bhagat Prehlad has also been used a few times in Guru Granth Sahib. According to the Puranas, Prehlad, a small boy, was the son of king Harnakash (Hirnkashyap) of Multan, who had worshipped Lord Vishnu and pleased him. Because of the worship, Harnakash was blessed by the Lord that he would not die during day or night, neither in a room nor in the open, and would not be killed by a human being or by an animal. With the blessing, Harnakash became so conceited that he proclaimed himself God and ordered everybody to worship him. Prehlad was a staunch devotee of Waheguru and would not worship anybody else than Waheguru. Harnakash got upset at his son's refusal to worship him because it was a big challenge to his ego. Hanakash tried many times to persuade Prehlad to quit worshipping Waheguru, and worship him alone, but, the young boy would not listen. Harnakash began to use torturing tactics next, and dropped Prehlad from a hill, tried to drown him in water, and threw him before an elephant, and so on. But, Prehlad was unhurt, and undeterred. Harnakash became so enraged that he drew a sword to kill Prehlad. At this point, Lord Vishnu appeared on the scene in the form of a lion-headed man to protect Prehlad, and tore Harnakash apart with his powerful and sharp claws. So as not to break his commitment of the blessing, the Lord took the form of a lion-headed man so that Harnakash's killer was neither a man nor an animal. Also, while standing on the door-step of a room, the Lord put Harnakash in his lap so that he was neither on the ground nor in the sky. The sun was setting at the time, so it was neither day nor night when the Lord tore Harnakash apart.

Guru Sahiban have used this story to glorify Waheguru and how He protects His devotees everywhere. Even though, it was Lord Vishnu whom Prehlad is said to have worshipped, but, according to all Hindu religious books, the three Lords - Brahma, Vishnu and Shiva -are representatives of Waheguru. So, Guru Sahiban and the Bhagats use this, and other stories, to praise the almighty Waheguru. As you can see, the story has too many weaknesses to be true:

- First and most important, Lord Vishnu's blessing to Harnakash that he would never die was against the fundamental Principles of Guru Granth Sahib according to Which all living beings must die. Listen to the following holy Shabads
  - — No emperor, no common man, and no chief will live for ever. All of them will vanish. Even the strong structures will fall to the ground by His Will. The strongly built storages full of valuables which the ignorant believes belong to him take no time to be emptied at His Will.——————**-(Majh ki Vaar, Pauri, M:1,141)**
  - — Nothing is everlasting. So what should I ask for from Waheguru? I see the whole world dying slowly with my own eyes. Raavan, the king of (Sri) Lanka, who is said to (have confined the angel of death to the frame of his bed) and who is supposed to have one hundred thousand sons and hundred and twenty five thousand grandsons is completely out of memory now.——————**(Assa Kabir Ji, 481)**
- Rather than asking that he not be killed by a man or an animal **(which does not include disease),** inside a room or in the open, on the ground or in the sky, during day or night, why did not Harnakash ask for a single blessing in his benediction that he should never die under any circumstances?
- Why did Harnakash choose a precarious time -

close to sun set - to kill Prehlad when he knew full well that some mighty power was working mysteriously for Prehlad, and a time like that was dangerous for him? Remember, Prehlad had survived some serious fatal attempts on his life like being pushed down from a mountain, attempt to burn him alive, being thrown before an elephant to be trampled over, and so on?

- According to Guru Granth Sahib, Waheguru is infallible. He never makes any mistake or gives away someone something for which He may have to repent.
  - — The Creator is infallible and cannot be misguided by anyone. ———————— **(Majh ki Vaar, M:1, Pauri, 145)**
  - — ————I make mistakes all the time, but, You are infallible, oh my Waheguru! I am unholy, but Your touch makes everything holy. I possess very low qualities, but, You are like a Chandan tree(which has an extremely pleasant and strong fragrance which can mask all foul odours). Please imbue me with Your fragrance as You live alongside me. ————— **(Sarang M:5,1213)**

But, in this story, Lord Vishnu seems to be repenting his blessing to Harnakash so much so that he had to kill him. Why could not the Lord foresee Harnakash's future behaviour which was so easy to predict?

- According to Guru Granth Sahib, Waheguru never takes a life form. But in this case, Lord Vishnu appeared himself in the form of a lion-headed human. So, the story contradicts the philosophy of Guru Granth Sahib.
- Waheguru will never be conceited. He is always

in the same state - blissful. But, Lord Vishnu becomes very conceited after killing Harnakash and stays angry for a long time. Listen to the following holy hymn by Guru Amar Das Ji.

— All the gods praised goddess Luxmi (Lord Vishnu's wife) and requested that she ask the Lord to relinquish his lion-headed form now. But even goddess Luxmi was afraid and would not go near the Lord (who was conceited and angry). ——— **(Bhairon Ashatpadian M:3,1154)**

- When a human being is able to realize Waheguru, he finds the union so blissful that no other worldly possession or comfort comes even close to that. But, in the story, Harnakash, who has realized Lord Vishnu, asks for his long life - a very petty wish -because a person who realizes Waheguru becomes immortal and lives for ever in the company of the Almighty, anyway.

So, the story has many weaknesses, but, as discussed earlier, Guru Sahiban do not focus on the truthfulness of stories. They use any opportunity to praise Waheguru. Since such stories were popular among the masses at the time, Guru Sahiban simply used them to glorify Waheguru." Bhai Dalip Singh concluded. His face was shining. "Does anyone have any further question?" Bhai Sahib asked after a brief pause. There were no further questions. Bhai Kashmir Singh thanked Bhai Dalip Singh and the congregation profusely. The session ended with the traditional Slogan : Bolle so Nihal Sat Sri Akal. Lungar was served as usual.

17

Death: Is It Predetermined Comforts and Discomforts

It is another beautiful Fall day. It is late afternoon and the weather is just comfortable. Even though farmers are busy in preparation of wheat crop seeding, they did not want to miss Bhai Dalip Singh's lectures. They are here even earlier than expected. They are discussing his previous lectures in small groups appreciating his knowledge and his style of delivery. It was hard for them to wait for Bhai Sahib, but they knew that they were their earlier. They did not have to wait much. Bhai Dalip Singh appeared on the stage with his ever smiling face. Everybody took their seats, and Bhai Sahib greeted them a warm "Waheguru Ji ka Khalsa, Waheguru Ji ki Fateh" to which the whole gathering responded with equal enthusiasm.

"So, what's the question of the day?" Bhai Sahib asked smilingly. The congregation had become used to the new style of starting the sessions.

"You talked about Huqam a few days ago, Bhai Sahib. I've a related question which has been baffling me for sometime. I've read many times in Sri Guru Granth Sahib, and have also heard from many, so called saintly people, that all comforts and discomforts in life that a man experiences, and all births and deaths are caused by Waheguru. If that's the case, how can we hold the individuals responsible for the alleged grief that they cause for others?. For example, if an individual is murdered by someone, why should the latter be treated as a criminal because the death of the former took place by the Huqam of Waheguru?" Bibi Surinder Kaur, a young lady asked.

"That's an extremely important question which I've always dreaded. And probably all of you would like to know the answer which is not simple, to say the least. However, I'll try my best to answer. Let me start with Guru Nanak Sahib's invaluable assertion from **Jap Ji Sahib that Waheguru's Huqam is unexplainable.** It is beyond our comprehension how He takes care of His Creation. The only thing that we know for sure is that everything happens with His Huqam or Will. Now, we discussed the other day that His Huqam is simply the set of laws with which He governs His universe. **Nothing - absolutely nothing - falls outside His Huqam.** We also discussed that as Guru Nanak Sahib explains in Assa ki Vaar, after creating the universe, Waheguru is completely carefree and is just watching the universe from His throne. What it means is that He rarely interferes in our everyday affairs and has given us much freedom to make choices - good or bad. He interferes only when a dedicated devotee of Him is in trouble or in need of Him. Once we make choices, we have to reap the rewards - pleasant or unpleasant. That's where we lose our freedom. So, when we say that the comforts or discomforts of life are caused by Waheguru or they are a result of His Huqam, what we are really saying is that **those comforts or discomforts are results of our actions as assessed by Waheguru's justice system.** Remember, Waheguru is nirvair (without prejudice). Being nirvair is one of the few characteristics of Waheguru which are listed at the very beginning of Sri Guru Granth Sahibunder the so called, **Mool Mantra. Since Waheguru is nirvair, all the comforts and discomforts result from our own actions.** Guru Sahiban have made it very clear again and again. For example, consider the following holy Shabads.

- You cannot hold someone else responsible for what

you get in life, oh my mind! I am reaping the rewards of what I had sowed; I cannot blame anyone else for misery. **(Raag Assa, M:1, Wooden board written, 433)**

- Virtues and vices (or sins) are not just in the name, oh man! A full record of your deeds - good or bad - is kept by Waheguru. Whatever you sow, so shall you reap. You will be born again and again (for your deeds) as per Waheguru's Huqam. **(Jap Ji, M:1)**
- Your comforts and discomforts in this life are a result of your deeds in your previous incarnation, oh man! Only the Lord, Waheguru, knows Who gave those to you. Who else can you blame for them? You have to live with them because only you are responsible for them. **(Maru Solhe, M:1,)**
- Why do you curse Waheguru, hey ignorant and unrefined man! The comforts and discomforts are the result of your own deeds. ——————— **(Dhanasari, Trilochan Ji, 695)**
- Do not blame others, folks! You have to accept the results of your deeds. You are caught in the net of your own deeds, and now you will die and be born again and again due to your acts of *maya*. **(Ramkali M:5)**
- ——— Ravi Das says that when the lives of humans are evaluated by Waheguru's Justice System, they reap exactly the rewards of their deeds. **(Malhar, Ravi Das Ji, 1293)**
- Waheguru keeps ongoing records of all human beings. All of them will be evaluated according to their deeds. **(Basant M:1, 1169)**

All the above holy Shabads clearly teach us that we are responsible for our own acts, and now we are suffering their consequences. We cannot blame Waheguru. He is only delivering His justice. Let me clarify this by giving an example from our school system. A teacher does not pass or fail a student. He is assigning an honest mark to the performance of the student. A student who did not do well on the exam, cannot expect to pass, and cannot blame the teacher for his failure. You can say that the student failed as per the orders of the teacher, but, the teacher has only made the evaluation. The same is true about the justice of Waheguru.

Farid Ji says something similar in a beautiful way:

- How can a farmer expect to harvest the popular grapes of Bijaur (an area in Afghanistan) when he sows the seeds of a *kicker* (a tree with sparse leaves but with long sharp thorns)? And how can he expect to wear silk when he had been spinning wool all his life? **(Sloak, Farid Ji, 1378)**

So, if we are facing some problems in life, most of the times, it is the result of our own deeds. How can you expect a good crop, when you did not prepare the field well, and you did not water the crop?

Now the situation is a lot more complex than that. **Sometimes, you could be a victim of circumstances and may suffer because of them and not because of your deeds.** Waheguru's laws are unbreakable. If somehow, you happen to break a natural law with negative consequences, you have a very high probability of suffering. For example, if you are exposed to the bacteria or virus of certain disease, you are highly likely to contract that disease. It is the law of Nature (Waheguru). Remember the historical facts of the holy child Har Gobind Ji, and Gur Har Krishan Ji contracting small pox because they were exposed to the deadly bacteria? Waheguru's laws - even if they seem to be punitive - apply even to His favourite holy men. Guru Nanak Sahib has written a holy hymn about the universal applicability of Waheguru's laws.

- ——Your high caste cannot save you from Waheguru's laws, hey man! You too will die if you taste poison. ——**Maajh ki Vaar, M:1, Pauri, 142)**

By the same token, if treatment is applied, diseases can be cured. Just as Waheguru has given poison the ability to kill, some chemicals are also given healing power by the same Waheguru. Since diseases can be cured, it cannot be the wish of Waheguru for all victims of circumstances to suffer. They just happen to be at the wrong place at the wrong time either by chance or by negligence. Waheguru is not necessarily punishing them, and again some fault could lie with the victims as well.

Remember again, that Gur Har Rai Ji had maintained a comprehensive dispensary where Prince Dara, the eldest son of Emperor Shah Jahan, was cured. Likewise, Guru Gobind Singh Ji gave ointment to Bhai Kanhayya Ji to dress the wounds of all the victims of battles, including the enemy. These examples clearly demonstrate that suffering and **misery can be eliminated, or at least reduced, and it is not always punishment by Waheguru.** This is further proven by the most recent medical and surgical advances by which some deadly and epidemical diseases like small pox and plague have almost been eliminated, and major operations involving organ transplants, separation of joined twins, and reattaching severed limbs are being successfully performed everyday. **Waheguru has given the humans the ability to escape from dangerous situations and use the resources to improve or change their lives.** As a class, humans are completely free to use Nature's abundant resources to change their lives. Having said that, it does not mean that all the trouble in our lives is the result of our own deeds. Fellow humans cause a lot of problems for others, and there's a lot of mention about that in Sri Guru Granth Sahib. But, before we discuss that, are there any questions?" Bhai Sahib asked politely pausing for a few moments.

"What about the natural calamities, like earth quakes, volcano eruptions and fires etc. which cause thousands of deaths and human misery? Such events are beyond the control of man. How can human beings be held responsible for such events of devastation? Isn't that Waheguru's punishment to people?" Bhai Jagir Singh seemed a little agitated.

"Could be, but not necessarily. Don't accuse me of hiding behind this shield, but let's **never forget the most fundamental principle of Guru Nanak Dev Ji that Huqam is undescribable.** So, we are unable to explain everything that takes place in nature. There **are** some natural events by which Waheguru does punish us for our misdeeds unknown to us, but, most of the events are regular occurrences in nature whose consequences could be drastic for human beings if they happen to be there. The situation of natural calamities is no different from the killer diseases that we just discussed a few minutes ago. All such events take place in accordance with Waheguru's laws, and they have been taking place ever since the earth came into existence, and even before life appeared on the Planet. For example, tides, eclipses, earth quakes, hurricanes, and some other powerful natural phenomena have been happening on the planet regularly from times immemorial, and they have resulted in some dramatic changes on the Planet. Scientists have solid proofs that the present continents broke apart from a single mass of land. Such incidents result from Waheguru's everlasting laws. Whenever natural conditions are ripe for a particular event to take place, it will take place. It may result in great destruction, and many lives may be lost, but, these powerful events are nothing new. Scientists know to a great degree what areas are more prone to earth quakes and hurricanes. You probably know that hurricanes attack the same parts of the earth year after year. There are very few hurricanes originating in the Pacific Ocean. Most of them originate in the Carribean Sea or the Indian Ocean. Likewise, there are certain areas on the earth, which are more likely to be hit by earth quakes. So, man has some freedom to protect himself from their devastating effects. Likewise, man may change the environmental conditions to make conditions more favourable for such natural phenomena, and such drastic events may become more frequent and may have more catastrophic results. For example, ever since the Bhakhra and the Pong dams were built, Punjab's climate has changed considerably. Also there's a lot more pollution around Ludhiana than any other city in the Province because of so much industry in Ludhiana. The world as a whole is destroying the natural ecosystem at an alarming rate by cutting down the rain forest, injecting harmful gases in the atmosphere and dumping poisonous chemicals in our waters. We are polluting our rivers, lakes, seas, and air. As a result of this pollution, our health is suffering, and more and more new diseases are springing up. Cancer was very uncommon, and AIDS was unheard of until only a few decades ago, but, now they're among the leading causes of death. And it's all because of our new life style - poor diet, polluted environment, stressful life, and unethical life style. So, can we blame Waheguru for the ill consequences? Aren't we reaping the rewards of our own deeds, and following the path of self-destruction?" Bhai Sahib paused again for a few moments to solicit further questions.

"What you've said so far makes a lot of sense, but, who can we blame for the birth defects, Bhai Sahib? Some people are born blind, lame, deaf, or even without a clear gender. Whose fault is that? Aren't those defects a punishment to the individual by Waheguru for some previous deeds?" Bibi Aman Deep Kaur seemed puzzled.

"May be, may be not. Prenatal defects are no different in causal ways than the health problems we face later in life. A person can be born blind, or may become blind later in life as a result of some accident or disease. In either case, the victim's life becomes a big challenge. The birth defects can be explained in terms of the body chemistry of the mother, and to some degree, of the father as well. It is a proven fact that mothers who smoke or drink during pregnancy, give births to children with some health problems, which could be minor or major depending upon the degree to which the mothers smoked or drank. Areas, where waters are polluted, are also known to have children with some birth defects. If some nutrients are lacking in mothers during pregnancy, their children are likely to have some birth defects. In Western countries where they have advanced technology, doctors are able to discover defects in fetuses, and in many cases correct the problems. I have come to know some cases where doctors in Canada have performed operations on fetuses to fix some serious defects. Now, if Waheguru were to punish those individuals, He would not have allowed the operations to be successful. And if Waheguru did not want a person to have that problem, then why did the fetus have that problem to begin with? The point again is that the problem was man made.

It's not just the humans that suffer from birth defects, some animals living in unhealthy conditions also have the same problems. I'm sure all of you have known a buffalo or a cow suffering miscarriage. Scientists have discovered that animals living in polluted lakes give births to defective offsprings. **From all these examples, it becomes more and more clear that we create problems for ourselves, Waheguru simply delivers justice through His laws."** Bhai Sahib took a few sips of water.

"It's all very convincing that you've said so far, Bhai Sahib, and I do agree that the environment plays a major role in our well being, however, there's story about a leper in Deepal Pur who was forced to leave the village and live outside because of his obnoxious body odour. Guru Nanak Dev Ji visited this leper, and treated him. I don't know the whole holy Shabad, but Guru Nanak Sahib told him that when one forgets Waheguru, he suffers all sorts of health problems, and advised him to remember Waheguru all the time. I guess, my question is: you say that environment and body chemistry affect our health so much so that even Guru Har Krishan Sahib contracted small pox in Delhi when He was exposed to the bacteria, but, Guru Nanak Sahib attributed the leper's problem to his forgetting Waheguru, How do we reconcile the two? Bibi Raman Deep had a very valid question?

"You've a very important and a probing question, Bibi Ji, and there's no contradiction between Guru Nanak Sahib's eternal advice and the environmental conditions. First, let me recite that part of the holy Shabad that Guru Nanak Dev Ji delivered to the leper.

- ———— The body that forgets Waheguru's Naam becomes haven to a variety of diseases. Such a person indulges in sensual pleasures, and becomes host to diseases and suffers like a victim of tuberculosis. ———— **(Dhanasari M:1, 661)**

As is clear from the holy Shabad, a person who forgets Waheguru, also forgets his moral and ethical limits, and indulges in sensual pleasures. He eats unhealthy spicy foods and uses intoxicants, sleeps irregular hours and rarely exercises. Under these conditions, he is bound to be unhealthy. On the contrary, an individual who remembers Waheguru, will lead a very health and moral life. He will not violate laws of nature (Waheguru's Huqam), and will likely stay healthy.

As discussed earlier, environmental conditions affect everybody but there are two big differences. First, an ethical man is more likely to be healthy and strong with a lot of internal resistance, and is far less likely to be attacked by the poor environmental conditions than an unethical man who is more likely to be week with low internal resistance. Second, there is no doubt that Waheguru always shields His devotees from all trouble. When His devotees are affected by some hostile agent, He protects them. On the other hand, an individual who has forgotten Waheguru will not have that special protection. There are many examples in Sri Guru Granth Sahib where Waheguru protected His beloveds, and many holy shabads which attest to this. A few examples that come to mind quickly include holy child Har Gobind Ji's healthy survival from a severe attack of small pox and death of Sulhi Khan who was on his way to attack Guru Arjun Dev Ji. As a result, no harm was done to Guru Ji. Also, Kabir Sahib was not attacked by the elephant when the then king ordered Kabir Sahib to be trampled over by the beast. After that Kabir Sahib was shackled, hand-cuffed, tied and thrown into the river, Ganges, on the orders of the same king, but, Kabir Sahib again survived. Another example is of the freedom of Naam Dev Ji from the confinement of the king Muhammad Tughlak, who had put Naam Dev ji in prison and would not release him until he brought the king's dead cow back to life - which did happen. There are many more examples like this.

A few holy Shabads in this context are as follows:

- The undescribable Waheguru protected (child Har Gobind) from the attack of small pox through His kindness. Anyone who sings the praise of Waheguru in the company of holy men drinks the real Amrit (the liquid of immortality) and leads a real (spiritual) life. **(Gauri M:5, 200)**
- Waheguru was very kind, and all the diseases and discomforts in life were completely dispelled. Worship Waheguru all the twenty four hours, oh my mind, and all success will be yours! **(Sorith M:5, 619)**
- I took the medicine of Waheguru's Naam, and as a result, all my troubles were completely uprooted. I found complete comfort and bliss as my discomforts and worries were dispelled by Guru's Shabad. **(Assa M:5, 378)**

There are many, many more holy hymns on the subject,

but I think these are enough to get the idea. So, as we see, there's no contradiction at all between Guru Nanak Sahib's advice and the affect of the environment. I hope, I have addressed your concern, Bibi Ji." Bhai Sahib looked at Bibi Raman Deep and again took a short pause.

"Yes, you did, and did it very well. Thank you very much." Bibi Raman Deep seemed satisfied.

"I have a question too, Bhai Sahib, and it's related to the very first question by Bibi Surinder Kaur. Are the time and medium of our death predetermined by Waheguru? And if they indeed are, and we are killed by someone, should the killer get the blame or not?" Bhai Kanwar Jit Singh had another important question.

"I remember the first question, and I know I haven't answered that yet. That's a very important and pertinent question, Bhai Sahib, and perhaps most difficult to answer. So, before I attempt answering this, let us have some historical perspective on this important topic.

- All of you heard about Sajjan thug who had built a lodge for travellers where he apparently provided all comforts to the travellers, but killed and looted the rich who stayed there. Guru Nanak Sahib went to him to reform him, and to stop him from the heinous sin and crime. If Waheguru had planned all the deaths that way, Guru Nanak Sahib - who was the biggest champion of obeying Waheguru's Huqam - would have accepted Sajjan's killing and looting as Waheguru's Huqam (if it was His Huqam), and would not have gone to see and reform him.
- When Baabar attacked Emnabad and brutally killed hundreds (or even thousands) of innocent people, Guru Nanak Sahib, who was there at the time felt the agony of human suffering and was so moved

that He even complained to His dearest Lord - Waheguru - about the barbaric destruction brought by Baabar. The holy Shabad about the attack is recorded on page 360 of Sri Guru Granth Sahib (Assa M:1). If all those deaths were planned by Waheguru, Guru Sahib would not have complained.

- You also know Kauda, the cannibal, whose diet included human flesh. Again Guru Nanak Dev Ji educated him and put an end to his despicable practice. If Waheguru had planned all those deaths of humans, Guru Ji would not have gone to see Kauda and reform him.

There are many other happenings where Guru Sahib stopped the ill practices of human torture by other evil human beings. Some of the examples include the practice of human slavery in Ruhel Khand, the confinement and slavery of humans by Noor Shah - the hypnotist - and so on.

- Guru Nanak Sahib also strongly opposed the practice of Sati in the Country whereby the widows were forced to burn themselves alive at the pyre of their husbands. Guru Amar Das Ji launched a forceful campaign to put an end to this barbaric practice, and persuaded Emperor, Akbar to pass a law against this. If the deaths of the satis were predetermined by Waheguru, Gur Amar Das Ji would not have launched that campaign to end the ill practice.
- There is a holy Shabad by Guru Arjun Sahib against the practice of Sati:

  With the expectation of reuniting with the dead husband, the wife burns herself alive on the pyre of her husband, but she cannot be reunited with her loving husband like this. Following the examples of others, **widows force themselves to burn alive** on the pyre of their husbands, but they

> cannot get the company of their dead husbands. On the other hand, they are born again and again in different life forms. ——————— **(Gauri Guarary, M:5, 185)**

Now pay attention to the wording of this holy hymn where Guru Sahib says that widows force themselves to burn alive. It is perfectly clear that their burning alive was **NOT** predetermined by Waheguru. They were forced (or in a few cases chose) to burn alive. In other words, they have a choice to burn themselves or stay alive. So, Waheguru does not force them to die. Likewise there is a holy Shabad by **Guru Amar Das Ji** in which, describing the small authority of rajahs, He says that how many people can be killed on the orders of a rajah. What Guru Ji really means is that a small rajah controls the lives of a very few people. But the important implication of this holy Shabad is that a rajah, or some other official in authority, can kill some people.

The above examples of reformation, and Guru Arjun Sahib's Shabads make it perfectly clear **that not all deaths are caused by Waheguru, and are avoidable. So, yes. A murderer must be held accountable for his crimes. Their victims could have lived.**

If we look at the world statistics of births and deaths, we find that the infant mortality rate has gone down dramatically, and the life expectancy rate has gone up. As discussed earlier, some of the epidemical diseases have been eliminated. So, the statistics also support the conclusion that some deaths can be avoided. Historically, the Sidh yogis are known to have prolonged their lives, and live for a few hundred years. That is why Guru Nanak Sahib Ji wrote in **Jap Ji** that if someone is able to prolong his life to ten times the length of all the four yugas, and that person is also well known in all the nine regions of the earth, and everybody gladly accompanies him out of respect, it is still insignificant if he is not in the sight of Waheguru, and nobody even talks to him in the Court of Waheguru.

This again supports the conclusion that not all deaths are predetermined by Waheguru. But mind you, Guru Granth Sahib is full with holy shabads that the world is mortal and whoever is born must die even though we don't know when. Even nonliving things must come to an end eventually. **So, most deaths are predetermined by Waheguru. Which ones? We don't know.**

"Forgive me for interruption Bhai Sahib, but I am a little confused now. What you say is very logical, but religion is not always logical. I had believed all my life that all deaths are planned and caused by Waheguru, but, deaths by torture or by unnatural ways are given to evil people as punishment. Won't you expect people like Hitler, who killed and tortured millions of people, to get a prolonged and a painful death as punishment for his brutalities?" Bhai Dalip Singh had not finished his last sentence completely when an elderly man, Bhai Karnail Singh asked. He seemed very unhappy.

"I would like to concur with you, Bhai Sahib, but there are a few problems problem with that." Bhai Dalip Singh said smilingly. Some painful grimaces also appeared on his face. He asked for a glass of water.

"I have said this many times that Waheguru's ways are mysterious, and we will never, never be able to know them. **However, religion is NOT illogical**. But, let me first address your concern. If all deaths were predetermined by Waheguru and all painful deaths were reserved for evil people, then what can we say about the supreme and unparallel sacrifices of the four Princes of Guru Gobind Singh Ji - two of whom were walled with bricks at very young ages. What possible sins or crimes must have they committed? The exemplary martyrdoms of Guru Arjun Dev Ji and Guru Tegh Bahadur

Sahib will have no reverence if that is the way they were planned. The list can go on and on in our history". Bhai Sahib paused for a while. His voice seemed to be choking.

"Second, there is a slight contradiction in your question. On one hand you are saying that all deaths are caused by Waheguru, but on the other you are holding Hitler responsible for millions of deaths and torture. If all deaths are planned by waheguru, then Hitler was only an instrument, and should not be held responsible for his savage actions. That's where I quote guru Nanak Sahib that Waheguru's Huqam can never be described. It seems that most deaths are planned by Waheguru and their precise time is fixed, and that time will never pass no matter what. But, because human body is destructible, it can be destroyed by some other means too, some deaths could happen prematurely. As already discussed, Waheguru has made definite Laws to govern this universe. As long as those Laws are being followed, the outcome is natural. When we say that something has happened by Waheguru's Huqam, it simply means that Waheguru did not interfere to stop the happening. We have also discussed that normally, Waheguru does not interfere with the operation of the universe. He interferes inly when His top devotees need His help. At the risk of repeating myself to extreme boredom **I must go to my initial point of the Great Guru Nanak that nobody can describe the Huqam of Waheguru. So, the best thing for a Sikh to do is to try his best to maintain good health, stay away from trouble where possible, sing the praise of Waheguru, and accept His Will (Huqam) gladly to leave the world as the time comes."** Bhai Sahib said in conclusion to end the session.

Everybody thanked Bhai Sahib with an enthusiastic salutation of 'Waheguru Ji ka Khalsa, Waheguru Ji ki Fateh'. Bhai Sahib had given them a lot to ponder about (or may be nothing). Bhai Kashmir Singh also richly thanked Bhai Dalip

Singh, and reminded the congregation about the departure of Bhai Dalip Singh the next day. Everybody again felt very uneasy at the announcement. But, they knew they could not do anything about that. Lungar was served as usual.

18

Status of Women

Another beautiful afternoon was adorning the farmhouse of Bhai Kashmir Singh, and hundreds of people who had gathered to listen to the highly informative and thought- provoking lectures of Bhai Dalip Singh were enjoying the beauty of nature while waiting for Bhai Sahib to appear on the stage. The size of the congregation was the largest ever today at the Farmhouse because everybody had come to know that today was the last day for Bhai Dalip Singh. He was leaving tonight for some other destination. Everybody wanted to say him an affectionate goodbye.

"Waheguru Ji ka Khalsa, Waheguru Ji ki Fateh." Bhai Dalip Singh appeared on the stage soon and greeted the enthusiastic gathering with his usual big smile.

"Waheguru Ji ka Khalsa, Waheguru Ji ki Fateh." The audience responded to the greetings with a loud roar reflecting their great enthusiasm, and took their seats on the carpet.

"I'm noticing many more women in the audience today than normal, so let's talk about the status of women in society as preached and practiced by Guru Sahiban and their Sikhs. Does someone have preference for some other topic?" Bhai Sahib sought the concurrence of the audience on the choice of his topic.

"That's perfect. You've made a very appropriate choice. Please begin educating us." A large number of voices could be heard. There were more female voices than the males. The women seemed really excited.

"Thank you. Let me start by saying that as far as realization of Waheguru is concerned, the gender is not an issue at all. As illuminated by Guru Sahiban, males are by no means superior to the females in the eyes of Waheguru. The two genders are created simply for the perpetuation of the species, and all animals have males and females within their species. No species can multiply without one or the other gender. So, both the genders are equally important and should be treated with the same respect in the society. They may have different roles to play, but both deserve equal recognition. The realization of Waheguru depends upon the deeds of an individual - whether male or female. To, deemphasize the importance of one gender over the other, Guru Sahiban have given this verdict that there is only one male in this universe - Waheguru. All other human beings are females.

- There is only one male in this universe - Waheguru. Everybody else is female. **(Wadhans ki Vaar, Sloak M:3, 591)**

Guru Nanak Sahib has written many times that the same Waheguru is present in women as in men or in any other living being for that matter. So, how can women be any inferior to men in any respect in the eyes of Waheguru? Since any human is capable of realizing Waheguru, women are as likely to realize Him as men. Listen to the following holy Shabad.

- ———The ruler of the body-like city (Waheguru) is always new (shows His affection in many different and amazing ways), and like a child who is pure hearted, never shows any discrimination or enmity toward anyone. ———Although He is present in all men, women and animals alike, He is none of them in particular.———**(Maru M:1, Ashatpadian, 1010)**

In many shabads, Guru Sahiban have addressed mother when describing human weaknesses or while praying to Waheguru thereby highlighting the importance of mothers and hence of women. For example listen to the following holy Shabads:

- I am spiritually alive as long as I remember my Waheguru, and I am dead when I forget Him.——
——Waheguru is the only everlasting power, and so is His praise. Why should anyone ever forget Him, oh my **mother**? ————**(Assa M:1, 10)**
- I have spent my entire life in seeking sensual pleasures, and have not worshiped Waheguru. What should I do now, oh my **mother? (Maru M:9, 1008)**
- My life has been guided by the powerful feeling of attachment to worldly things and by the darkness of ignorance so far. How can I realize Waheguru now, oh my **mother**? ————**(Sorith M:9, 632)**
- This is the blessing from your **mother,** oh my son! May you never forget Waheguru even for a single second, and worship Him all the time. May you worship the limitless Waheguru all the time whose worshiping dispels not only your sins but those of your ancestors as well, ————**Gujri M:5, 496)**
- Your son has earned something very precious, oh my **mother**! It is Waheguru's Naam which I recite while walking, sitting, awake or while asleep. For me Waheguru's Naam is my wealth of all sorts including my food, my traditional idol worshiping, and disciplining my urges through hard physical torture.————**(Gujri M:5, 495-6)**
- Guru's feet are very sweet (comforting), oh my **mother**! Waheguru grants access to Guru's feet only to the lucky people who are then blessed

with millions of comforts when they 'see' the Guru.———**(Todi M:5, 717)**

There are many more holy shabads like these which have been addressed to mother highlighting the importance of the females. Not only that, in most of Their shabads about the union with Waheguru, Guru Sahiban have portrayed Themselves as females in relation to Waheguru, and have described the union of human beings with Waheguru as being similar to the union of a male and a female in matrimony. Guru Sahiban have advised us to acquire the good qualities of the female to realize Waheguru as the husband. This portrayal of all humans - males and females alike - further eliminates any disparity between the males and the females, and places no restriction of any kind on the females to realize Waheguru. Even though there are hundreds of holy shabads, I'll quote only a few to clarify my point.

- What are you conceited of, oh ignorant young woman! Why don't you enjoy the love of your Waheguru-husband in your heart? The husband is very close to you (in your heart), why are you looking for Him outside (in the forest or in the mountains)? ————**Tilung M:1, 722)**
- There may be many shortcomings and lapses in me, but I am still yours, oh my Waheguru-husband! The women who love and enjoy worldly things (maya) forgetting Waheguru, suffer and repent to moral death. ———**(Suhi M:5, 761)**
- My heart-bed has been decorated with bliss ever since I heard (realized) about Waheguru's arrival in my heart. ————By worshiping Waheguru, I have realized my cherished wish, and the auspicious time of my marriage (as a female) with Him has arrived.————**(Assa M:5, Chhant, 459)**
- Dedicate yourself to the feet of Guru Waheguru if

you want a true husband, oh young woman! You will have an everlasting husband because Waheguru is immortal and He will never leave you.————**Suhi M:3, Chhant, 771-2)**

- Let all of us female friends embrace one another and join in singing the praise of the all powerful Waheguru-husband. The True Master possesses all the virtues while we all human beings are full of vices.————**(Siri Raag M:1, 17-18)**

As is clear from the above holy Shabads and many more like these, Guru Sahiban have given all the importance to woman-like qualities for all human beings to realizing Waheguru. Not only that, Guru Nanak Sahib raised a powerful voice against any inequality for women, and condemned the discrimination against them through the following holy shabad.

- How can we treat women any inferior to men when everybody is born to women with the exception of Waheguru? Life starts inside the body of women and we are born out of women. We are engaged to women and we marry women. ———— Even emperors (or *bhagats*) are born to women. There is no discrimination in the Court of Waheguru based on gender. Only the faces of those lucky individuals glow (are honored) in the Court of Waheguru who have sung His praise with their tongue. **(Assa ki Vaar, Sloak M:1, 473)**

Whereas women were suffering an extremely low status in the male-dominated societies everywhere in the world, Guru Sahiban worked very hard to raise the status of women in all societies visited by them. In India, the woman was treated so badly that it had become an accepted norm to compare her to the shoe. She had no rights whatsoever, and she was treated like a piece of property. The husband could stake her at gambling, and she could be sold to somebody else. During the Moslem rule in India, the local ruler had the 'right' to call any newly-wed bride to spend the first night with him. Nobody dared to refuse their demand. In case of refusal, the bride was kidnaped by the army of the ruler, and the refusing relatives were 'taught' an exemplary lesson.

Among the Hindus the practice of 'sati' was followed strictly whereby a young widow had to self immolate at the lit-pyre of her husband - willingly or by force. Guru Sahiban raised very strong voice against this evil practice, and strived to improve the lot of women in every aspect of life. Women were appointed missionaries, and leaders in other fields. Widows were allowed to remarry and the practice of wearing veil by women was discontinued by Guru Amar Das Ji as a sign of equality with men. To further highlight the importance of women in marriage, Guru Amar Das considers a marriage between a man and a woman meaningful only if they have identity of views through mutual respect, and one partner simply does not impose his/her wishes on the other.

- A man and a woman cannot be considered a couple simply because of their marriage; they are a real couple only if they one soul even though there are two bodies. (They have identity of views through mutual respect). **(Suhi ki Vaar, Sloak M:3, 788)**

Kabir Sahib has expressed a similar view on the importance of women when disapproving the custom of circumcision among the Muslims.

- Where have the Hindus and the Turks come from? —

———If conversion into Islam requires circumcision, then what can be done about women as they cannot be circumcised? So, (because of this inability), it is better to stay as Hindu. I cannot part with my wife who is a fifty percent partner in life.

Historical Events

Starting with Guru Nanak Sahib, all Guru Sahiban accorded the same status to women as men in all fields of life. Let us not pretend and be realistic that there are some natural fundamental differences in males and females. Men are physically stronger than women and can relatively endure much harsher environmental conditions. Women are also vulnerable to sexual persecution, and cannot do certain tasks that men can. That's the way Waheguru has created the two categories. With the exception of those limitations, women were treated the same as men by Guru Sahiban and their Sikhs.

When Guru Nanak Sahib left Sultan Pur Lodi for His first odyssey, His sister, Bibi Nanaki, took over to arrange for, and to hold holy gatherings. She became a pillar of Sikhism in that area and came to be highly respected. Likewise, Bibi Sabhraee, also known as Satviraee (sister of seven brothers) was a leading Sikh of Guru Sahib in Khadoor. She had accepted the responsibility to look after the needs of all the visiting Sikhs whenever Guru Nanak Sahib was in Khadoor. She was well respected by all the Sikhs. She was an unofficial missionary of her time. And after Noor Shah (real name Parbati), an extremely powerful hypnotist, surrendered to Guru Nanak Sahib in the field of mental powers, and became a dedicated Sikh, Guru Sahib appointed her the first missionary to spread the word of Waheguru. She proved to be a very effective missionary.

The women could attend all the religious gatherings and participate in all activities taking leading roles in appropriate fields.

Bibi Sabhraee continued to command the respect of Sikhs, and a deep affection from Guru Angad Dev Ji, the Second Guru of the Sikhs. Guru Angad Sahib spent a few months at Bibi's house meditating in a closed room. The Bibi was expected not to disclose the whereabouts of Guru Angad Sahib. That indicates the trust of the Second Guru that the Bibi enjoyed. Mother Kheevee, the wife of Guru Angad Dev Ji, was the in-charge of the Lungar (common kitchen) at the time of Guru Angad Dev Ji.

Guru Amar Das Ji, the Third Guru, made it a condition that no woman wearing a veil could come to see Him because wearing a veil by women meant that they were the property of their husbands - a concept strongly disapproved by Guru Sahib. He also ordered the custom of 'sati' discontinued among His Sikhs, and made a strong recommendation to emperor Akbar to pass a law against the heinous practice. Guru Amar Das Ji appointed twenty three missionaries to preach Sikhism in far away places; **three of those missionaries were women.**

Guru Har Gobind Sahib, the Sixth Guru, traveled all the way from Amritsar to Kashmir to acknowledge the devotion and faith of 'Mother' Jassi in Guru Sahib, and to bless her.. Guru Tegh Bahadur Sahib had named the present town of Anand Pur Sahib, Chack Nanaki, in honour of His mother.

Women continued to enjoy more and more freedom and greater and greater rights with each succeeding Guru. At the time of preparation of 'Pahul' by Guru Gobind Singh Ji for the very first time, the honour of adding patasas (bubbly sugar cakes) to the 'Pahul' went to Mother Jeeto Ji, the wife of the Tenth Guru. Also, at the time of the Tenth Guru, Gobind Singh Ji, women began to train in weaponry and wear weapons for self defense. Not only that, they even began to take part in combat operations. Bibi Bhago is a well known example who fought bravely along with her Sikh brothers against the army of the Governor of Sirhand who had been on the attack to capture Guru Gobind Singh Ji.

After the death of Baba Banda Singh Bahadur, Punjab was fragmented into small regions, called Missels, ruled by

Sikh Chiefs. At least one of the missels, Kanhayya, was headed by a woman - Sardarni Sada Kaur - who later became the mother-in-law of Maharaja Ranjit Singh. There were many other Sikh women who fought in battles with great chivalry and taught the aggressors such lessons that they never forgot them. Bibi Harsharan Kaur was one of them. The fort at Jamraud at the border between Afghanistan and now Pakistan (then Punjab, India) was a highly strategic fort militarily purposes. It had been built by the Afghans and was used to launch attacks on Punjab. Its control was highly crucial to any party. The Fort had been conquered by Sardar Hari Singh Nalwa, the chief of Maharaja Ranjit Singh's army. Now it was being commandeered by Sardar Mahan Singh when the Afghans attacked and besieged the Fort. There were only a few soldiers left in the Fort. It was extremely important to inform Sardar Nalwa about the attack and to seek help to defeat the enemy. Sardar Nalwa was about 40 km away in another fort. It was extremely difficult to escape from the Fort of Jamraud to take the message to Sardar Nalwa because of the tight besiegement. With total disregard for her life, Bibi Harsharan Kaur undertook the responsibility to take the message to Sardar Nalwa, and did that successfully.

Rani Sahib Kaur, the sister of Sahib Singh, the teen-aged Maharaja of Patiala, is another example of the important role that the Sikh women played in all aspects of life. Having conquered much of India, the Marhattas, who had become a huge force, attacked the regime of Patiala in Punjab in 1793. Sahib Singh, who was not prepared for such a surprise attack, requested his sister, Rani Sahib Kaur to help him. Rani Sahib Kaur took part in the battle herself, and displayed such courage and organizational skills that despite the much smaller number of soldiers in the army under her command, she repulsed the attack by the Marhattas, and drove them out of her state. All this became possible only because of the way with which women began to be treated starting with Guru Nanak Dev Ji.

Guru Sahiban accorded great respect and dignity to women who thus acquired great self-esteem.

"Are there some questions?" Bhai Dalip Singh asked. No further question came forward.

Bhai Dalip Singh thanked everybody in general for their affection and respect they had shown for him. He also thanked and Bhai Kashmir Singh in particular for all his planning and for being a wonderful host. This was Bhai Sahib's last day here. Everybody thanked Bhai Dalip Singh for enriching their lives by sharing his knowledge in a very effective and pleasant fashion. Bhai Kashmir Singh thanked Bhai Dalip Singh profusely and honoured him with traditional siropa. Nobody wanted to leave but they had no choice. Bhai Dalip Singh promised to come back again. The congregation was adjourned with a loud slogan: "Bolle So Nihal, Sat Sri Akal" as a mark of an affectionate farewell for Bhai Sahib. Lungar was served. Private meetings with Bhai Sahib continued until late at night.

Glossary

BAANI (OR GURBANI): In common usage of the term, baani means language. But as used in Sri Guru Granth Sahib, Baani or Gurbani implies writings of Guru Sahiban or any other holy man as recorded in Sri Guru Granth Sahib.

BAIRAG: (a) Detachment from worldly attractions. (b) Feelings of unhappiness due to separation from the Guru or any one person you love.

BAIRAGI: An individual who has renounced the worldly desires.

BHAGAT: A staunch devotee of Waheguru. It also means a devotee who has realized Waheguru.

GURMAT: Teachings (or philosophy) of the Guru

HAUMEIN: Selfishness; Ego

HEAVN: A Hindu religious ceremony whereby they worship their gods. A fire is lighted and kept alive by pouring butter oil on it continually. The devotees sit around the fire and the priest utters some mantras (hymns).

JANEYOO: A cotton thread worn around the neck by the upper-class Hindus with the belief that it dispels all the sins and keeps the mind pure. A special ceremony is held when a young boy wears the thread for the very first time. Lower-class Hindus and women are not allowed to wear janeyoo.

MANTRAS: Holy hymns of the Hindus.

MAYA: Anything and everything in the world that attracts human mind. It includes everything from worldly possessions to passion. Maya also includes all sort of feelings like love, affection, kindness, hatred, rage, revenge, and so on.

PARANTHAS: Pan fried bread with or without stuffing. The stuffing may include potatoes, cauliflower, reddish or some other vegetable.

POORIES: Deep fried bread.

QAZI: A Muslim priest who also has some magisterial powers.

RAGAS: Different kinds of lyrics. For example a ballad or a sonnet. In addition to some other forms of lyrics, there are 31 main Ragas in which the holy compositions of Guru Granth Sahib have been written.

ROTI: A home made bread. It is normally round, and baked in a pan or in an oven.

SHABAD: Any holy composition in Guru Granth Sahib.

SHIVALING: A stone replica of god Shivas genitals.

YUGAS: The four major time eras - Sat yuga, Treta yuga, Duapar yuga, and Kalyuga. Sat yugs is the longest and Kal yuga is the shortest. Even Kal yuga has a length of 567000 years.

YAGGAS: A Hindu tradition of serving meals to the so considered holy men, and later to the poor as well. The idea was to please gods. Centuries ago, only rajahs used to have yaggas to please gods for some special favours. It is considered to be a virtuous deed to perform yaggas.

REFERENCES

1. White, H.E. (1972). Modern College Physics. New York: D. Van Nostrand Co.
2. World Book Encyclopedia (1999). Volume 15. Pages 541 - 42.

INDEX

❑❑❑